ESSAYS ON BORNEO SOCIETIES

UNIVERSITY OF HULL PUBLICATIONS

HULL MONOGRAPHS ON SOUTH-EAST ASIA

HULL MONOGRAPHS ON SOUTH-EAST ASIA NO 7

ESSAYS ON
BORNEO
SOCIETIES

edited by
VICTOR T. KING

Published for the UNIVERSITY OF HULL *by the*
OXFORD UNIVERSITY PRESS
1978

Oxford University Press, Walton Street, Oxford OX2 6DP

OXFORD LONDON GLASGOW
KUALA LUMPUR SINGAPORE JAKARTA HONG KONG TOKYO
DELHI BOMBAY CALCUTTA MADRAS KARACHI
NEW YORK TORONTO MELBOURNE WELLINGTON
IBADAN NAIROBI DAR ES SALAAM LUSAKA CAPE TOWN

British Library Cataloguing in Publication Data

Essays on Borneo societies.—(Hull monographs on south-east Asia; 7).
1. Ethnology—Borneo
I. King, Victor T   II. Series
301.29′598′3   GN635.B6   78–40317

ISBN 0–19–713434–3

*Printed in Great Britain by
Cox & Wyman Ltd., London, Fakenham and Reading*

To the
memory of
MERVYN JASPAN
(1926–1975)

PREFACE

THE present book has had something of a chequered history since its inception three years ago. Most of the papers were originally conceived in the context of a wider ranging venture; the remainder were added to meet changed circumstances. Initially the late Professor Mervyn Jaspan and myself perceived that there were a number of gaps in teaching materials on island South-East Asian ethnography and social anthropology. Along with most other South-East Asianists we had welcomed the publication of the two collections of ethnographic essays on Indonesia edited by Professor Koentjaraningrat—*Villages in Indonesia* (1967) and *Manusia dan Kebudajaan di Indonesia* (1971)—and, despite their shortcomings, the Human Relations Area Files volumes on *Ethnic Groups of Insular Southeast Asia* (1972a, 1975) edited and compiled by Frank M. LeBar. A noticeable gap, however, was a series of comparative studies of the upland (or alternatively hill, interior or upstream) peoples of island South-East Asia. We decided to initiate a series of five volumes presenting different aspects of the social anthropology of a number of 'upland' peoples. Scholars who had first-hand research experience of these societies would be invited to make contributions. Each volume for the series would broadly cover one of five main fields of interest—social systems, economics, politics, religion and problems of development. Later, to keep the project to manageable proportions, we restricted our main areas of concern to four large islands—Sumatra, Borneo, Sulawesi and Luzon.

At first the response was encouraging and it looked as if this rather ambitious endeavour might eventually reach fruition. Then certain problems arose which necessarily reduced the scope of the project. Some of the original contributors had to withdraw because of other commitments, and more seriously and sadly Mervyn Jaspan died suddenly in London. This meant not only that his papers on the Rejang of Sumatra would no longer be forthcoming, but that, in addition, the burden of editorship fell on my shoulders. His specialist knowledge of Sumatra and the Philippines and broad expertise on island South-East Asia were also lost to the series. After much deliberation I decided to change the format and initially concentrate on a single volume on Borneo societies. This meant that those contributors who had agreed to produce papers on other areas of South-East Asia were asked to withdraw. I wish to take this opportunity of thanking them all for their consideration in understanding my problem; particularly Professor P. E. de Josselin de Jong who had already written his paper on the Minangkabau of Sumatra when the series was suddenly terminated.

In the circumstances, there seemed to be a number of advantages in restricting the volume to Borneo. First, my own fieldwork experience and interest in the area enabled me to handle the various papers more competently. Secondly, the bulk of the papers already received or agreed upon for the first volume of the original series were concerned with Borneo. Thirdly, there are similarities in culture and society among Borneo peoples and this permits fairly close controlled comparison of certain socio-cultural aspects among some or all of the groupings studied. Finally, there is room for a volume of comparative ethnography on Borneo. This would meet the needs of those individuals involved in teaching courses on South-East Asian societies in general and Bornean peoples in particular. It would also assist those anthropologists who require relatively easy access to a body of illustrative data on cognatic or bilateral societies somewhat similar to *Social Structure in Southeast Asia* (1960) (edited by George P. Murdock). This would serve to complement, qualify and modify some of the general remarks made by Murdock in his introduction to that volume. What should also be borne in mind is that an ethnographic collection need not be, and generally is not totally devoid of analysis and theoretical import, and it is hoped both in the introduction and in the papers in this present volume that some light will be cast on certain analytical and conceptual problems.

With these considerations in mind, I decided to use some of those Borneo papers which were originally intended for the five-volume series. These included the articles by Appell, the Hudsons, Morris, Rousseau, Whittier and myself. Most kindly the authors agreed to this new format, but it should be remembered that the contributions were largely written within a rather different context. Nevertheless, at an early stage contributors had been asked where possible to write pieces which could, at least to some extent, stand independently of the other volumes. Therefore, five of the papers were easily incorporated into the Borneo project. The exception was that of the Hudsons. Originally this paper was intended to provide the broad background data of Paju Epat Ma'anyan social organization, the operation of which was illustrated by a case study. Various other aspects of the particular case were then to be developed in the course of the five-volume series. Despite this problem I thought that as the Hudsons' case material was new and interesting, and, as it made an important contribution to studies on the least known part of Borneo (i.e. Kalimantan), it should be included in the new collection. I also still entertain the hope that, in the spirit of the original project, complementary volumes (particularly on Bornean economics, politics and religion) will appear in the not-too-distant future, given the necessary finance, time and goodwill.

It remained to select additional contributors to bring this new collection to an acceptable length. There have been quite a number of anthropological studies of Bornean peoples completed in recent years. Yet because of certain financial constraints the present volume could not exceed some nine or ten papers. Eventually Sather, Schneider and Crain were invited to contribute; the choice of their papers and indeed the others was based on three main criteria.

First, I tried to give the three major political divisions of Borneo (Sarawak, Sabah, Kalimantan) about equal attention. By far the greatest number of field studies have been carried out in Sarawak and Sabah; on the other hand, Kalimantan, despite its size and the number of ethnic groupings found there, has been virtually neglected by anthropologists. Of course, some ethnic groupings, such as the Kenyah, Kayan, Selako, Lun Dayeh/Lun Bawang, Bidayuh Land Dayak and Iban are located on both sides of a political boundary, and thus to a certain extent there is less need to think in terms of artificial divisions in providing for a balanced coverage of Bornean peoples. But the political boundary which divides the northern, formerly British and now Malaysian area (Sarawak and Sabah) from the southern, formerly Dutch and now Indonesian region (Kalimantan) is significant in the sense that these two areas were subject to broadly different colonial administrations and therefore to rather different historical experiences. Furthermore, this boundary will continue to mark out somewhat different social, economic and political futures for the peoples on either side of it. The various field studies in this present collection comprise three undertaken in Sarawak by Morris, Rousseau and Schneider, three in Sabah by Appell, Crain and Sather, two in Kalimantan by the Hudsons and King, with Whittier's work divided between Kalimantan and Sarawak.

Secondly, I wished to cover, as far as possible, a significant number of the important indigenous groupings in Borneo which had been studied but which had not already been dealt with in easily available, full-length monographs. These included the Bajau Laut, Coastal Melanau, Kayan, Kenyah, Lun Dayeh (sometimes classified misleadingly as Murut), Ma'anyan, Maloh, Rungus (a Dusun group) and Selako. The Iban were omitted because of all Borneo societies they are the most well known, largely through Derek Freeman's excellent monograph *Report on the Iban* (1970). Other important peoples which have been studied such as the Punan, Penan, Bidayuh Land Dayak and Ngaju, could have equally well received attention. However, the limitations of space demanded selection, and I simply chose to ask for contributions from those anthropologists personally known to me and/or those whom I knew through their writings. My choice of contributions was also designed to provide examples of most of the major ecological types in Borneo. The Kayan and Kenyah are primarily swidden agriculturalists who farm interior hilly or upland areas; Maloh cultivate dry and swamp rice on the flat, fertile banks of slow-flowing rivers; some Lun Dayeh communities grow wet rice while others are primarily involved in dry rice agriculture; the Melanau coastal peoples rely mainly on sago production; and the Bajau Laut are fishermen.

Thirdly, I wanted to present, within the confines of a basic exposition of the main elements of social organization of the peoples considered, a variety of different emphases. The varying emphases presented are presumably determined not only by the nature of the empirical data confronted, but also by the individual fieldworker's analytical and ethnographical interests. Thus, for example, Rousseau stresses the importance of social stratification, noting that kinship has a 'residual role' to play as an organizational principle in Kayan society; Appell attempts a precise delimitation of Rungus social entities on the basis of certain observational procedures directed towards establishing the degree of corporateness of units in the economic, jural and ritual realms; Schneider addresses himself, among other issues, to the position and role of Selako village officials; Crain utilizes the notions of social exchange and reciprocity, highlighted particularly in his consideration of Lun Dayeh marriage transactions; Sather looks in detail at the structure and developmental cycle of the Bajau Laut village household and draws attention to the presence of extended or multiple families in a bilateral society; the Hudsons provide an illuminating case study to illustrate certain elements of Paju Epat Ma'anyan social organization; and finally, Whittier, Morris and myself take a rather more straightforward approach by outlining a range of features of Kenyah, Melanau and Maloh social organization respectively, based principally on the criteria of residence/locality, kinship/descent and rank. Perhaps a volume of comparative ethnography should have aimed for a greater degree of uniformity among the various papers, but in my opinion the restriction of the contributors to more or less the same kind of subject matter would have been unrealistic, given their different backgrounds, approaches, and interests, and the intrinsic differences in the social organization of the peoples studied.

Although I have edited the volume I am deeply indebted to all the contributors who have offered valuable criticism on the form and content of this book. However, I am entirely responsible for the introduction and no doubt not all my remarks would earn the support of all the contributors.

I would like to thank Mr. Lewis Hill for his reading of certain sections of the book, particularly the introduction, and for his valuable comments and suggestions, and Dr. David Bassett who commented on various matters of grammar and style. My sincere thanks also go to Mrs. Pat Wilkinson who typed the manuscript, and Mr. Derek Waite of the Brynmor Jones Library, University of Hull, for drawing the map. The inspiration for the book came from Mervyn Jaspan and it is dedicated to his memory.

V.T.K.

University of Hull
July 1976

CONTENTS

LIST OF ILLUSTRATIONS

MAP

FIGURES

TABLES

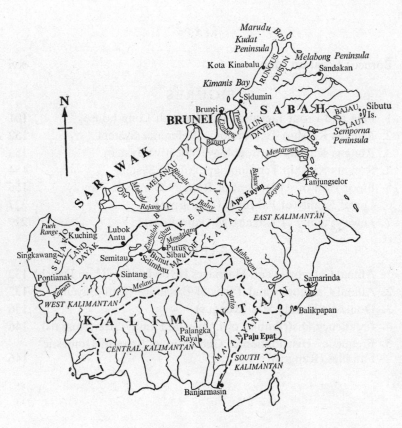

Borneo: Location Map

1

INTRODUCTION

Dayak and Malay*

THE societies described in this book can, with possibly two exceptions, be classified under the general rubric 'Dayak'. This is an imprecise but useful term normally employed to denote the indigenous non-Muslim (non-Malay) peoples of Borneo. Dutch and German scholars regularly used the word 'Dayak' to cover all non-Muslim indigenes, but English writers tended to restrict it to the so-called Land Dayak (Bidayuh), inland of Kuching, the Sarawak capital, and the numerous and widely spread Sea Dayak or Iban. According to one explanation 'Dayak' ('Dyak') or 'Daya' ('Dya') in some Borneo languages means 'interior' or 'interior/inland person', although it is often used in a derogatory fashion by such people as the coastal Malays to mean something akin to 'rustic' or 'yokel' (Hudson, 1967c:24–8).

The term 'Dayak' has the disadvantage that it obscures specific differences in origins, culture, social organization and economy between the various non-Muslim ethnic groupings in Borneo. On the other hand its use is not without foundation. It serves to draw attention to certain common features of these Bornean peoples which complement and, in some cases, underlie the seemingly marked divergences. All Dayaks have broadly the same physical characteristics; their languages can be categorized together as 'Malayo–Polynesian'; most peoples share some similarities in material culture such as in agricultural, domestic and other equipment and in longhouse domicile; finally there are some characteristic customary practices and associated beliefs, for example, the taking of omens from birds and animals, head-hunting and its rites, and the belief in a spirit-world. Furthermore, E. R. Leach in his pioneer study *Social Science Research in Sarawak* pointed to certain principles of Dayak social organization which are likely to define a 'Bornean type of pattern of organisation' (1950:57) (see below). It is also clear from historical and oral sources that there were significant population movements in Borneo in the past, and these were presumably accompanied by, on the one hand, a degree of fission and socio-cultural differentiation of originally similar ethnic groupings, and on

---

* Short passages of this section and the subsequent section on Ecology and Location are reprinted from a brief article entitled 'Dayak' in *Family of Man*, vol. 2, pt. 24, 648–52, by kind permission of Marshall Cavendish Publishers Ltd.

the other the fusion and interpenetration of different groupings (King, 1976c:87–105). Cultural exchange was also facilitated by fairly widespread trade.

The common features of these Bornean peoples and their history of socio-cultural fission and fusion mentioned above have meant that ethnic boundaries are not, in general, clearly defined, but, on the contrary, are blurred and in a state of flux (King, 1972:96). What is more to the point is that differences between groupings do not usually lead to sharp socio-cultural disjunctures. Instead individuals can move across boundaries with a considerable measure of ease, and may, at any one time, share elements from two or more different ethnic categories. These considerations have presented major difficulties for those scholars interested in the formulation of comprehensive and unambiguous classifications of Borneo peoples, although I would suggest they lend greater justification to the cover term 'Dayak'.[1] For the above reasons I have not attempted to locate the peoples described in this volume in an overall ethnic classification,[2] nor have I the space to consider details of the differences and similarities between them in the diverse spheres of ecology, culture, and historical and political experiences. Much of the relevant background data can be found in the introductions to each paper, while for interested readers wider ranging ethnographic material in English can be obtained from such books as *Critical Survey of Studies on the Languages of Borneo* (1958) by A. A. Cense and E. M. Uhlenbeck, *The Pagan Tribes of Borneo* (2 vols.) (1966, reprint) by Charles Hose and William McDougall, *The Natives of Sarawak and British North Borneo* (2 vols.) (1968, reprint) by H. Ling Roth and *The Peoples of Central Borneo* (1974) edited by Jérôme Rousseau. There is also a useful section on Bornean ethnography in the reference works edited and compiled by Frank M. LeBar entitled *Ethnic Groups of Insular South-east Asia, Vol. I* (1972a:147–97), and *Vol. II* (1975:1–13).

Perhaps a word should also be said about the term 'Malay' by way of clarification. In normal usage the category 'Dayak' is contrasted with that of 'Malay', which refers to the Muslim, predominantly coastal fishing and trading people of Borneo. For ease of comparison Malay peoples are not considered in the present volume, nor are such immigrant groupings as the Chinese or Indians. Like the category 'Dayak', the label 'Malay' covers a range of peoples. Present-day Malays in Borneo originate from a mixture of peoples including converted Dayaks, Malays proper from such places as Sumatra and the Malayan Peninsula, Bugis, Banjarese and Javanese. They are all defined basically by their sharing of the Muslim faith.

Islam was probably introduced into western Borneo in the late fifteenth or early sixteenth century (Veth, 1854:193; Hall, 1970:207), although one authority has claimed tentatively that the advent of Islam occurred in the late fourteenth or early fifteenth century (Harrisson, 1968:180–4). The spread of Islam and hence Malay culture was not the result of a large influx of Muslim peoples, rather it was more the consequence of indigenous pagan peoples converting to Islam and 'becoming Malay' (*masok Melayu*). This process has obviously resulted in marginal or transitional ethnic groupings. For example, sources on West Kalimantan mention the *orang-pengaki* (Enthoven, 1903:168–9) or Pekaki Malays who were Dayaks recently converted to Islam. These were nominal Muslims who continued to live in the characteristic Dayak long-house, and to follow Dayak customs such as drinking rice wine and eating pork. Similarly peoples such as the Coastal Melanau of Sarawak, and the Bajau Laut fishermen of Sabah, described in this volume, were formerly pagan, but over time significant numbers have embraced Islam. Again many of these converts are probably only nominal Muslims. Difficulties in the classification of these transitional peoples led Leach to coin the novel term 'Para-Malay' for those like the pagan Melanau 'who . . . adopt a Malay style of living in the general form of their community organisation and whose members show a general tendency to enter Islam . . .' (1950:33). However, to my knowledge Melanau and Bajau Laut do not call themselves Malay.

Ecology and Location (see map)

Borneo consists of an interior upland core of ancient rocks, deeply incised by numerous rivers radiating outwards like the spokes of a wheel. Most rivers are navigable and provide the most important means of communication so that there is a concentration of human habitation along them. The coastal belt largely comprises a swampy and intractable terrain; the soil is peaty with large areas covered by nipah palm, mangrove and low grade forest. These areas are irregularly interspersed with stretches of beach and rocky promontories. The majority of Malay fishing villages are found in the coastal region, as well as peoples such as the sago-producing Melanau who inhabit the delta regions of the Rejang river through to Bintulu and the Bajau Laut fishermen scattered along the eastern and north-western coasts of Sabah. Proximity to the coast has presumably been an important factor in the Melanau and Bajau Laut conversion to Islam. While some peripheral communities of the Rungus Dusun of Sabah, and the Selako Dayak of Sarawak and West Kalimantan are also found relatively near the coast, they have not become Muslim to any marked degree, nor have they turned to a coastal way of life. Instead, they generally cultivate dry rice and other products by swidden agricultural methods in upland or hilly areas, like many other interior Dayaks. Some Selako also farm swamp rice in lower areas.

Inland there are, in general, areas of low undulating hills, inter-penetrated and surrounded by alluvial flood-plains. These lowland areas are very extensive in western and southern Kalimantan. Along the forest-lined rivers Malay culture has spread into regions originally opened up by swidden-cultivating Dayaks. Here some Malay and Dayak communities are in close proximity to one another. They are linked principally by trade, but in the past a number of Dayak villages were nominally under the political domination of the various Malay states in Borneo. The Dayaks generally cultivate dry rice on a shifting, slash-and-burn basis, and where possible some plant swamp rice. They also hunt wild animals and gather forest products for subsistence and exchange. One of their most important cash crops is rubber. Large tracts of virgin forest have already been cleared in these 'middle' regions and signs of soil exhaustion and erosion are evident in places. The Maloh in West Kalimantan and the Ma'anyan of Paju Epat in south-eastern Kalimantan occupy this kind of terrain, while in south-western Sabah Lun Dayeh settlement extends from lowland areas where rice is grown in rain-flooded fields, to interior, higher regions where hill rice is the primary crop. Lun Dayeh villages are also found largely away from the coast in Sarawak, Kalimantan and Brunei.

Finally in the interior zone of uplands covered by extensive areas of thick rain forest are such societies as the Kayan and Kenyah. These peoples rely almost exclusively on swidden agriculture, hunting animals such as wild pig, deer, monkey and bear, fishing and gathering various jungle products. The Kayan and Kenyah are found in central Borneo on both the Sarawak and Kalimantan sides of the border. Some of their villages are also in close contact, mainly for purposes of trade, with nomadic hunting and gathering populations such as the Punan and Penan. These nomads are, however, increasingly adopting a more settled way of life.

Borneo Societies

For the remaining part of this introduction I propose to address myself to a few general, and in some cases tentative remarks on Bornean social organization or social systems,[3] since the collection of papers is largely concerned with this topic. This will enable the reader to link some of the aspects of the various papers together in a more comprehensible manner.[4]

Bornean societies are, for better or worse (cf. Leach, 1961:1–27), generally classified as 'cognatic' or 'bilateral'.[5] Following Murdock, the general term 'cognatic' refers to a kinship system in which, in ideal terms, the ascription of statuses is based on kinship ties traced equally through both the maternal and paternal sides, or which allows for a choice to be made in affiliation between the mother's and father's kin (1960:2–6; see also Peranio, 1961:95).

There is obviously a danger of misplaced emphasis in categorizing total societies according to their kinship systems (Appell, 1976c: vi–vii, 3). This is particularly so for societies like those in Borneo in which kinship may not necessarily be, and frequently is not the all-important organizational principle (see below). On the other hand, in the absence of acceptable alternatives I prefer to follow generally agreed upon usage and refer to whole societies as 'cognatic' and/or 'bilateral'.

Edmund Leach's discussion (1950) of the societies of Sarawak provides us with a convenient comparative framework for considering all the Borneo societies described in this volume. He isolated certain general principles of social organization 'which appear to apply to all the indigenous peoples of Sarawak', and he also ventured to add that 'it is likely that these [principles] are valid for the whole of Borneo' (p. 57). This 'Bornean type of pattern of organisation' which Leach posited is 'particularly noticeable in the field of kinship' (p. 57) and its main defining criteria are as follows (pp. 57–63):

— the presence of a 'personal kindred' which, despite some ambiguities (see below), was nominally defined by Leach as 'the whole body of an individual's [recognized] relatives' (pp. 61–2).
— a common pattern of kinship terminology which classifies kin by generation and which distinguishes the 'immediate family group' of a given individual from collateral relatives on both the maternal and paternal sides (pp. 57–60).
— ambilateral (ambilineal) descent, whereby inheritance and political succession 'at any point [are] as likely to pass to a female (or through a female) as to a male' (p. 62). Leach was referring here to a type of descent reckoning and not to the formation of 'corporate groups' on the basis of descent.[6] He also noted that the 'kinship structure' of the long-house communities which he observed was 'either one of several homologous segments, or else of several stratified classes' (p. 60). In each case the units were non-exogamous and comprised close kin, but Leach was undecided about whether to label these 'ambilateral descent groups' (see below). However, he was definite that, in his survey, there was no 'semblance of a unilateral exogamous descent group of the ordinary clan-lineage type' (p. 60).
— the existence of a politically influential 'house owning group' defined as 'a small group of closely related families the members of which had a more direct descent linkage with the ancestral founders of the house (or village) than other members of the community (p. 61)'. This group is found both in societies with marked 'class distinctions' and in those which are organized along more egalitarian lines.
— long-house domicile, although Leach indicated that some indigenous communities, especially those in proximity to Malays had begun to

build separate family dwellings. A further point was that, in some cases, the long-house was equivalent to the village, while in others, a village comprised more than one long-house (pp. 62–3).

George P. Murdock, in his comparative study of cognatic kinship has also pointed to the kindred, and in addition, 'the small family' or 'small domestic unit' as the main defining characteristics of bilateral societies such as those found in Borneo (1960:2–7, 14). The prominence of these two features for Murdock is also related to the fact that in these bilateral societies 'extended families' are 'invariably absent' and so-called 'ambilineal ramages' [descent groups], are 'usually absent' (p. 14).[7]

This present introduction examines Leach's observations and assesses the utility of part of Murdock's work in the light of subsequent research, and also points to possible future lines of enquiry in the examination of the societies of Borneo. My main point stemming partly from both Leach's and Murdock's pioneer and wide-ranging endeavours is that it can be fruitful to compare different Bornean societies selectively in terms of such features as household (or family) organization, descent and its concomitants, kinship terminology, and long-house and village organization. On the other hand some of Leach's defining criteria and those of Murdock require qualification and elaboration. More particularly the work of both these authors tends to place too much emphasis on kinship as an organizational principle in bilateral societies.

Bilateral Kinship and the Kindred

Following specifically on Leach's recommendations in his general survey of Sarawak, three studies of important indigenous societies there were undertaken by H. S. Morris on the Melanau (1953), W. R. Geddes (1954a) on Bidayuh Land Dayak and J. D. (Derek) Freeman on the Iban (1955a/1970, 1955b). Of these it was probably Derek Freeman's meticulous and stimulating monographs and some of his subsequent papers (1958, 1960, 1961) which first drew wide anthropological attention to some of the organizational principles and social units in societies of this kind. There is very little work on bilateral organization in South-East Asia which does not refer to Freeman's study of the Iban of the Baleh region, and this present collection of essays is no exception. He has provided the base-line for comparison and most Bornean scholars have assessed at least some of their findings in relation to Freeman's observations on such features of Iban society as the *bilek-family* (or household), the kindred and the long-house.

George P. Murdock's influential *Social Structure in Southeast Asia* (1960) consolidated the importance of Freeman's work by using the latter's Iban material as a Bornean example when putting forward some broad guide-lines concerning the types and organizational variations of cognatic societies. It cannot be denied that Murdock, in particular, was working in the shadow of models and concepts which had been applied and developed in relation to unilineal descent systems. In his introduction to the book he bemoaned the fact that for cognatic social systems there was among anthropologists 'no solid consensus regarding organizational principles, typology, or terminology comparable to that achieved for unilineal social systems' (p. 2). Murdock consciously attempted to impose order on societies which, in general, lacked the relatively clearly defined corporate descent groups of unilineal systems. This attempt at precision may have served to confuse as much as to clarify the features of bilateral systems in particular.

For Murdock, one of the main characteristics of bilateral societies is the kindred. Leach too stated that it is a characteristic kinship grouping in Bornean societies. Furthermore, one of Freeman's most influential analytical contributions has been his study of the kindred in which he emphasized the importance of consanguineal kin in the formulation of the concept of the kindred (1960:71). After Freeman's careful and detailed article (1961) on this concept it would seem that there was little need for dispute. The kindred was here to stay, and certainly it was the saviour of some students of bilateral societies, myself included, who now had a concept, rooted in kinship, with which they could organize their empirical data. Consequently, most, if not all monographs on a bilateral society devote at least some attention to the kindred. However, several problems have been confronted in applying Freeman's and Murdock's original Ego-focused, consanguineal-based construct to fieldwork material.[8]

Thus, attempts have been made at reformulating the concept of the kindred and apparently marked variations in the characteristics of kindreds reported from different societies have emerged. Some kindreds are said to be Ego-focused, others seem to be mainly focused on a conjugal pair and/or nuclear family, still others vary between Ego and a married couple according to situation. Kindreds also vary in their range and composition—some ideally include only a small circle of closely related kinsmen, others cover a large number of distant relatives as well; some comprise purely consanguineal kin, others in addition recognize spouses of blood relatives, still others apparently include these two categories of kinsmen plus a spouse's kinsmen. Kindreds perform a number of functions in some societies, and are much less important in others. Certain social systems seem to manage quite satisfactorily without a kindred, or more exactly in them the concept of the kindred in Freeman's sense appears to have no indigenous equivalent and is therefore difficult to apply.

These differences seem to me to demonstrate two basic problems in the analysis of bilateral kinship. First, in the general absence of corporate descent groups the anthropologist is quite naturally drawn to kinship relations focused on a given individual and/or conjugal pair. This is a logical outcome of the need to ask informants about the kinsmen they recognize and the linguistic categories used to locate these relatives in an indigenous model of the kinship system. Second, variation in types of kindreds, or their presence or absence in certain societies, may sometimes be a result of differences in emphasis and perception on the part of different anthropologists, rather than the consequence of fundamental structural differences between particular bilateral social systems. In other words, anthropologists may differ in their stress on various orders of data, for example, indigenous statements about ideal relations between kinsmen and certain semantic distinctions in kinship terminology, observations by the anthropologist of actual activities and events, and both his and his subjects' interpretation of this phenomenal order. In attempting to convey understanding the anthropologist may emphasize certain aspects of indigenous thought and/or action at the expense of others, according to his and/or their perception of its significance and the particular data he happens to have on record. He is also often influenced by models and concepts used by his colleagues and has to decide on their appropriateness for his own material. In the analysis of bilateral kinship these difficulties are complicated by the fact that kinship terms are often flexibly and variably applied, obligations attached to kinship are generally not supported by strong jural sanctions and are frequently situationally determined, and diverse relations are usually comprehended in a consanguineal kinship idiom. In this situation the personal judgement of the anthropologist may intrude quite forcefully, though few anthropologists make the point as explicit in their writing as did Appell in rejecting the utility of the term kindred in the analysis of Rungus Dusun society. He stated:

But even if a society recognizes that a range of cognates shares a similar social characteristic, and if this social category is then given a name, should we term this a kindred? *Here we enter the realm of personal opinion*, but I would not refer to such a social isolate as a kindred. I would prefer to reserve the term kindred for that type of social isolate which has reached a higher level of hypostatization in the society in question (1967:204, my emphasis).

Freeman also took up this point in his comment on Geddes' description of the Bidayuh Land Dayak kindred when he wrote:

Geddes' 'personal kindred group' *would . . . appear to be a special construct of his own*, bearing little resemblance to the kindreds reported from other Dayak societies (1961:201, my emphasis).

Clearly there is an implication in both quotations that another field-worker using different criteria might possibly recognize rather different social units within these societies.

There seem to be two main alternatives after acknowledging the difficulties involved. Either we can simply abandon the concept of the kindred as unmanageable and imprecise, or recognize that, despite its problems for the analysis of bilateral kinship in general, in some cases it remains a useful analytical tool. I suggest that we continue to use the term in our examination of kinship networks focused on an individual and/or conjugal pair, in certain societies, and following Mitchell (1963), this mode of analysis would also seem to have relevance for some lineal societies.[9]

With these observations in mind, we return to the consideration of the kindred as a defining characteristic of bilateral societies in general and Bornean societies in particular. I suggest that the apparent variation in types of kindred and the attendant difficulties of determining the bases of these differences, the possible analytical utility of the concept in lineal societies, and the fact of its presence or absence in certain bilateral societies is not really a basis for comparison. If we take some of the papers in this present volume, we are left with an impression of the indeterminacy of the concept in comparative terms and its unsuitability as a defining feature of certain types of society. In their paper the Hudsons see the Paju Epat kindred as significant within the context of membership in a bilineal descent group (*bumuh*), and employ a number of operational definitions of the kindred to analyse Ego- and conjugal pair-focused kinship relations. Crain uses the term in Freeman's sense, but he also notes that there are no 'kindred-based action groups' in Lun Dayeh society. Appell suggests that 'the Rungus social system does not include the concept of the kindred' and Rousseau maintains that there is no Kayan word which can be translated as 'kindred' (again in Freeman's sense) since their term for 'cognate' is also extended to include affines.[10] On the other hand Whittier states that although the Kenyah do not have a term which can be translated as 'kindred', principles generally associated with the concept of the kindred are important organizational features within Kenyah society. After my use of a flexible notion of the kindred[11] in earlier papers on the Maloh (1974:210–13, 1976b:140–2) I have since decided against this imprecise usage for the description and analysis of Ego- and conjugal pair-focused kinship ties. I now believe it obscures rather than clarifies the nature of Maloh kinship and its degree of importance in their social organization. Finally, Morris, Sather and perhaps Schneider do recognize the utility of Freeman's concept in its original form in the context of Coastal Melanau, Bajau Laut and Selako society respectively.

The difficulties involved in granting the kindred a positive status as a bilateral kinship entity also find their parallel in Murdock's perception of cognatic societies in general as constituting a positively defined 'type' or 'category' with certain recognizable and comparable features stemming largely from the principle of cognation. In contrast to his view I tend partly to agree with Needham's statement that

it is probably not useful to assume that cognatic societies must characteristically have some special forms or principles of social organisation in common. It is at least arguable that cognatic societies are classed together primarily because of what they *lack* ... In other words, cognatic societies constitute a negatively defined class, and are thus recalcitrant to any comparative investigation into what positively typifies them (1966:28).

Furthermore

The cognatic recognition of relatives is common to all societies and characteristic of none. It is not that there are two opposed and mutually exclusive modes of organisation—lineal descent and cognation—for lineal descent systems also recognise cognation (p. 29).

In contrast to Murdock, and indeed Leach, I suggest that it may not be particularly fruitful to put as much emphasis as they do on cognatic/bilateral kinship, and this includes the concept of the kindred, in the delineation of a positively defined type of society.[12] It would seem to be more appropriate to recognize that cognation/ bilaterality is a defining characteristic of Bornean societies by default, and that other organizational principles such as residence, and in some cases rank, may take on much greater significance in comparative analysis. However, my disagreement with Murdock in particular is more one of emphasis and degree, since kinship will always remain an object of investigation as will its role in relation to other principles of social organization.

Quite naturally in small-scale village communities certain obligations and codes of behaviour stem from relations between kinsmen. There are, for example, rules governing sexual access between various categories of kin and certain relatives may often depend on each other for the supply of goods and services especially in the activities surrounding birth, marriage and death.[13] It is therefore important to establish the various categories of kin recognized. All the present papers (some more than others) devote at least a degree of attention to kinship and give details of kinship terminologies which, as Leach indicated, are usually founded in Borneo on two common principles. The first is categorization by genealogical level, which is expressed in behavioural terms in the respect due to seniors by their juniors. Marriage and sexual relations between closely related kinsmen from different genealogical levels is also usually disapproved of in a number of Bornean societies (e.g. Maloh, Melanau, Paju Epat

Ma'anyan). Secondly, there is commonly a terminological differentiation of a given individual's immediate family members (parents,
siblings, children) with whom sexual activity is strictly forbidden
from maternal and paternal collaterals with whom, in a number of
cases, it may be allowed.

Leach noted that there are exceptions to the general terminological
type above such as the Murut-Kelabit (1950:59–60). This present
volume also specifies Lun Dayeh and Rungus Dusun as peoples
among whom genealogical level is ignored in the affinal terms *iban*
and *ivanon* respectively. In addition, in certain societies, in the actual
use of kinship terms there is frequently no distinction between
siblings and cousins, or between one's own children and siblings'
children (e.g. Kayan, Kenyah, Lun Dayeh). Given these exceptions,
can kinship terminology be used as a defining characteristic of a
Bornean pattern of organization, as Leach suggested? It would then
seem that this is possible, but only in a somewhat limited sense. As
Needham has pointed out, these terminological systems are not so
much jural classifications as 'means to the genealogical recognition of
an individual's kindred' (1966:29) and, as I have already stated, in
practice, terms are often flexibly applied, and obligations stemming
from kinship are frequently contingent and situational. However,
the comparative investigation of Bornean kinship terminologies
and the reasons for the variations between them has not progressed
very far. One significant point which does emerge is that when we
compare societies where rank rather than kinship is the more important organizational principle, we find rank generally associated
with fewer kinship terms and a less marked distinction between consanguines and affines.

That kinship is not the most important principle for the formation
of social groupings in some of the societies of Borneo can be illustrated by reference to various papers in this present collection. For
example, Rousseau argues for the Kayan that the role of kinship is
'residual' since it is not the basis for the existence of a village or the
location of farm areas, nor is it a basis of membership in agricultural
work teams (see also King on the Maloh and Whittier on the Kenyah)
or in a farm-house. In the papers on the Maloh, Melanau and Rungus,
it is specifically stated that the granting of village or long-house
membership is not dependent on kinship links with other inhabitants
but on the permission of the village leader(s), sometimes in consultation with other villagers. Morris, in his discussion of the mobilization
by Melanau aristocrats of specific task groups, also points out that
although the core may be composed of close kindred, the leader was
unlikely to regard the members of this grouping as kinsmen; instead
he saw them as neighbours, clients and slaves. In this connection,
one would expect that, in the stratified societies of Borneo where the

system of ranks is still in operation, the principle of stratum ascription would reduce the structural significance of kinship (see Rousseau on the Kayan). But even in the non-stratified societies (see Appell on the Rungus), as for that matter in those with ranks, group formation seems to be significantly determined by residential propinquity (for apparent exceptions see, in particular, Schneider on the Selako). Finally bilateral societies, lacking an all-embracing and well-defined system of corporate descent groups, may be expected to permit greater emphasis on choice in cooperating with kinsmen and generally lay less constraint on kinship relations. Both Crain's paper on the Lun Dayeh and Sather's on the Bajau Laut point to the significance of choice in the affiliation to social groupings in bilateral societies.

The Household

Murdock's second main characteristic of bilateral societies was that the 'small domestic unit' is 'invariably prominent'. This observation deserves some comment. First, Smart (1971:81–85) has already drawn attention to the fact that Murdock merged the three concepts of 'family', 'household' and 'domestic unit' and that these terms are not necessarily synonyms. The first usually refers to a kinship unit, the second to common residence and the last to the sharing of certain tasks, such as the supply and preparation of food and the care of children (see below). Second, despite the fact that in bilateral societies the statistically most common or the culturally ideal type of domestic unit may be the 'nuclear family' or a 'stem family' (p. 2), Murdock's characterization was essentially static and did not consider variations arising from the developmental cycle of these units (Smart, 1971:77–81). Third, Murdock stated that 'the small domestic unit is fundamentally a bilateral kin group and . . . must . . . be defined in such a way as to exclude any lineal principle' (p. 3). This in turn led him to the implied position that the 'extended family' is in some way incompatible with bilateral social systems (pp. 3–4). The problem here is that he was not totally consistent in his use of the term 'extended family'. In his earlier book, *Social Structure*, it is commonly applied to a unit comprising parents and two or more married children (1949:2, 23–4, 33–5). In his later work this type of unit becomes a 'lineal family' and the term 'extended family' is reserved for units including two or more married siblings in the senior generation. I would point out not only that extended families are normally thought of in Murdock's original sense, but also that using either definition they have been reported in various bilateral societies and should not be thought of as inconsistent with this type of social organization.

In the present volume those social units which I choose to call 'households' receive a good deal of attention since they are generally one of the most important social, economic and ritual groups in Bornean societies (see especially Appell on the Rungus). Obviously, the presence of households is not a positive defining characteristic of bilateral social organization or of a Bornean type of society exclusively, since most societies have them; but in the absence of an overall descent group structure the hallmark of studies on Bornean peoples has been the detailed analysis of the composition, characteristics, functions and developmental cycle of these units. This social group is principally defined by the occupation of an apartment in a long-house, or a separate dwelling in a village. Again, the terminology designating these units varies according to different anthropologists' differing emphasis on their kinship, residential or functional characteristics. Among Maloh, for example, as among others such as the Kenyah, Melanau, Bajau Laut, Selako and Kayan, the individuals inhabiting a long-house apartment or a separate house constitute a household and are normally referred to as a whole by the indigenous term used to designate the residential structure in which they live. However, some authors draw attention to the domestic activities of household members and prefer to use the term 'domestic families' (see Appell and Crain).

In general, Bornean peoples are monogamous, although polygyny occurred on occasion among such societies as the Melanau and Kayan. At any given point in time the largest percentage of households in most Bornean societies can, in terms of kinship composition, be categorized as nuclear or stem families and this supports Murdock's observations. But in some societies there is also a significant percentage of extended family households. The most marked is in Sather's Bajau Laut sample where they comprise 60 per cent of village households while in Whittier's Kenyah sample they constitute 22·85 per cent of households in Long Nawang and 19·35 per cent in Long Moh (referred to there as 'joint families'). In these cases the number of household members is also greater (e.g. an average of 12·2 among Bajau Laut, 7·8 among Long Nawang Kenyah and 9·2 among Long Moh Kenyah) when compared with societies such as the Rungus (average household size 4·52) in which nuclear and stem families are the norm. Extended family households have also been reported less significantly among such peoples as the Melanau, and it would seem that, particularly in the stratified societies of Borneo, they were much more common in the past (e.g. Maloh). With the exception of the Bajau Laut, this phenomenon appears to be partly related to the type of long-house and the degree of permanency of settlement.[14] Traditionally, peoples such as the Melanau, Maloh and Kenyah built solid houses high off the ground. This presented problems for married children wishing to secede from their natal household since it was difficult to accumulate enough resources to build a separate apartment with its massive support posts at the end of the long-house. They often had to wait long periods until the house was rebuilt, and Morris notes for the Melanau that 'apartments were very crowded'. In the case of the Bajau Laut, although there were generally conflicts of interest between the component units of an extended family, the absence of a household estate to quarrel over and the periodic dispersal of 'conjugal families' during fishing voyages help to relieve tensions and delay the break-up of the larger multiple households. Thus the above cases reveal that an extended family structure can be a significant feature of bilateral societies.

In general outline the developmental cycles of households in Bornean societies differ very little from each other. There is a desire on the part of married couples to achieve independence during their lifetime, and apart from one child who is usually charged with the care of ageing parents, most married children set up independent residence and establish a separate household. But within this overall process of 'partition', as Freeman called it, there are considerable variations in its frequency, timing and form both between different societies and between households within the same society. For example, among the Rungus a married child usually leaves the natal household fairly soon after marriage and establishes a separate household and domestic unit. Among Maloh, the process usually takes longer, so that a married child may live with his/her parents for a number of years within the village, while farming separately. The child and his/her family thus form an independent household and domestic unit for part of the year, but after the harvest they return to the parental household and co-operate together with the parents in household tasks and share some of the food supplies. Eventually, when sufficient resources have been accumulated, the junior branch secedes. At any one time two married couples may reside together, but, unlike in the past, this is a very temporary phenomenon. Almost the same situation is described for the Kenyah among whom each married couple living within the same long-house apartment (*lamin*) is expected to cultivate its own fields. Nevertheless, the married couple (*tudo* family) which is a separate productive unit for cultivation, comes together in the village household at the end of the agricultural year to pool food and cook in common with other members. This practice differs slightly from Maloh where only part of the food is pooled while, if possible, the junior branch retains some resources to finance its eventual separation. Extended family households are also more common among Kenyah who, unlike Maloh, have generally retained their long-house domicile.

A greater degree of separation is found among Kayan because, Rousseau notes, although two married couples may temporarily reside in the same long-house apartment, they may constitute a separate 'economic' unit. Furthermore, Morris points out that, among the Melanau, a household may have contained the several separate families (*tagen*) of married children and that tagen were considered as distinguishable units if they catered separately (i.e. domestic units). But he notes that 'in practice the line between tagen was often hard to draw precisely'. This splitting up of larger household units into smaller ones centred on constituent conjugal pairs is also found among the Bajau Laut. Production there is largely in the hands of smaller units, which Sather terms 'conjugal families' (*dabalutu*). On the other hand, as with Kenyah, and to a certain extent Maloh, there is a system of communal consumption and shared access to material assets and labour within a larger village household.

I have left the Paju Epat case until last since it is somewhat different from the societies mentioned above. The Paju Epat village mainly comprises extended family households (*lewu'* families); these own the separate village houses and heirloom property and, among other things, they regulate primary use rights to swidden lands. The Hudsons note that the size of these lewu' families is declining, but the important point is that they ideally comprise separate units termed *dangau* families, which come together to reside in a village house. The dangau family is a smaller unit, focused on a conjugal pair, which occupies a swidden field house (dangau) away from the village; it is this and not the lewu' family which is the primary social, economic and ritual unit of Paju Epat society. In terms of actual composition the extended families of the Bajau Laut village household and the Kenyah lamin are similar to the Paju Epat lewu' family, and furthermore the Bajau Laut 'conjugal family' and Kenyah tudo family resemble the Paju Epat dangau family. The important difference is that the Paju Epat dangau family is the key social unit and retains its autonomy in the village household, whereas both the Bajau Laut conjugal family and Kenyah tudo family pool resources within the more important village households.

There is thus a variety of permutations of units based on a conjugal pair in Bornean social organization. Within the same society they can be understood largely in the context of the household developmental cycle, but among societies as a whole differences in the timing of partition, and the degree of autonomy in production, consumption and so on seem to be related to an amalgam of factors, not least of which are the permanency of settlement, stratification and the associated structure of the long-house. Nevertheless, the desire for ultimate independence on the part of the married couples and their wish to reduce conflicts between each other generated within the confined space of a long-house apartment or village house usually lead to partition. Furthermore, units of production are usually small in that often a nuclear family engages in rice cultivation by and for itself. In the case of the Bajau Laut, the importance of the 'conjugal family boat crew' seems to be partly related to certain techniques and conditions of production, particularly since fishing grounds are scattered and require frequent mobility. Swidden agriculture, with its extensive use of resources, may also be associated with smaller, dispersed productive units. But this observation demands considerable qualification, and it can hardly be a complete or satisfactory explanation for a particular aspect of social organization.

Despite an extensive form of exploitation, small units tend to come together characteristically to construct smaller versions of long-houses near the rice fields. However, this practice is by no means universal in Borneo, nor is it a necessary technical requirement of swidden agriculture. In the head-hunting past the construction of farm-houses or field houses may have been partly related to the need for security and protection while distant from the main village. Whittier also notes that among the Kenyah the coming together of small families to form a common field house may point to potential lines of fission within the village. The institution of co-operative work groups and labour exchange between small units based on strict reciprocity is also a common feature of Bornean social organization. This co-operation seems to stem, in part, from a social desire to work with others in that in arduous and often tedious work it is more pleasant to have companions to lighten the burden (Geddes, 1954a: 70–3). In purely technical terms work sharing is not always necessary nor may it increase productive efficiency. Geddes reported for the Bidayuh Land Dayak that the labour exchange system 'results in fields being worked for comparatively few days; it does not provide any incentive for increased pace of work; it penalises those who are deficient in foresight; and it produces large working groups whose output per man is lower than that of individuals or of smaller groups' (p. 72). Crain too notes that co-operation may be uneconomic for some Lun Dayeh domestic families. On the other hand, Rousseau has indicated that Kayan are more active when they work together in groups (1974a:126). Nevertheless, I would argue that overall groupings formed in the context of swidden agriculture arise from social rather than technical considerations.

Another important point in any discussion of the household in Borneo is its degree of continuity. Freeman's earlier analysis of the Iban bilek-family revealed that it is a unit which has continuity through time. One married child remains within its parents' household and 'from one generation to the next, one elementary family grows out of, and succeeds another, in an unbroken sequence' (1970: 13). This is the case in some other Bornean societies in which one child remains with his/her parents and inherits property and/or rights in it, especially rights over land, directly from them (e.g. Kenyah, Maloh, Selako). In contrast, households in certain other societies do not persist from one generation to another in this way. For example, Sather points out that among the Bajau Laut the original parental household eventually dissolves—Bajau Laut parents bestow their possessions on their children as they secede from the household. One child usually remains with the parents but the only items left are a share of the parental property plus, occasionally, the house, although this structure is soon dismantled and replaced. Sather suggests that this lack of actual continuity, as opposed to structural continuity, and the desire for independence from parents is related to the fact that Bajau Laut recognize no corporate estate in which interests and rights can be maintained and passed on. This in turn might be related to a fishing economy which does not make the establishment of lasting rights in property such as land possible.

On the other hand, some agricultural societies in Borneo do not establish permanent rights even in tracts of land. Appell states that after the first clearing of primary jungle a Rungus domestic family only has rights to use it, and after secondary jungle has re-established itself anyone is entitled to farm that area in subsequent years. There are no shared rights in land to transfer to junior generations, and movable property such as brassware and ceramics, is divided between the children. However, as in other Bornean societies, one married child is usually charged with the care of ageing parents. At first sight this fact would seem to indicate actual household continuity, but Appell states that 'it does signal the termination of the parental domestic family. For, at that point, the retained earnings of the natal family of the child are no longer viewed as the property of that family. Instead they are usually devolved on the child, becoming his/her individual property.'

The situation is complicated when we turn to the Kayan, who also do not establish permanent rights over land, yet acknowledge the continuity of the household. In form, Kayan property inheritance appears to be little different from that of the Rungus, but Kayan perceive that although heirloom property is divided and some children no longer remain in the natal household, they still retain 'kinship' links with it; one child also remains with his/her parents. The difference between Kayan and Rungus seems to be one of indigenous perception, rather than depending upon such criteria as the location of specific jural rights in, for example, property. This difference in 'ideal' might also explain why the Lun Dayeh domestic family 'dissolves' after a period of time, and yet why, unlike Rungus, there appears to have been in the past a continuity of rights in land from one generation to another. Finally, there is the Ma'anyan case. The

Hudsons point out that a dangau family 'dies with the focal couple or with the absorption of a surviving spouse . . . into the dangau family of a married child'. Yet, unlike the dangau family, the larger lewu' family does seem to persist, since permanent use rights are established in swidden land and the lewu' family regulates these.

Descent and House Owning Groups

Leach noted that bilateral kinship groupings 'appear to be inconsistent with the co-existence of any large-scale unilateral *exogamous* descent groups . . .' (1950:58). Instead he drew attention to the common principle of ambilateral (ambilineal) descent among Sarawak, and by extension Bornean societies, whereby property and office can pass to or through either a female or a male. This form of descent would indeed seem to be characteristic of Bornean peoples although in some societies descent in the male line may be preferred, e.g. Melanau, Kenyah, Lun Dayeh. But the issue of whether this descent principle can also give rise to corporate descent groups has engendered a degree of controversy in Bornean studies.

Differences of opinion about whether a particular bilateral society possesses descent groups very often revolve around the different conceptions of what constitutes such groups. Therefore, before proceeding further it is necessary to set down what are considered to be the main defining criteria of a corporate descent group in bilateral societies.[15] Nominally it is a unit[16] which in ideal terms exists in perpetuity, and is formed, at least partly, on the basis of a principle of descent, since it comprises those descendants of a given ancestor traced through both male and female lines. However, most anthropologists require that there be further conditions of corporateness, and these are frequently closely interrelated. Those generally agreed upon are: identity usually indicated by a name or term; certain closure rules such as genealogical depth, residence and so on, which along with descent differentiate members from non-members; operation in relation to a specific resource or resources such as land, and/or a specific activity or activities such as ritual, so that there is a fairly regular coming together of members (or at least their representatives), a recognition of common aims and interests, and usually the presence of a common authority and a degree of organizational autonomy.

Despite the existence of descent units in Borneo which are named and/or acknowledged in indigenous terminology and which share rights in certain resources, their members or representatives may not generally recognize common aims or identity, they may not participate in particular activities together, nor may they possess an independent authority. Where this sense of unity or corporateness is less marked I prefer to call these entities 'descent categories', although in practice the line between descent groups and categories may be difficult to draw precisely.

Let us now turn to some of the Bornean societies in which units based on descent have been reported. Geddes' study of Bidayuh Land Dayak land tenure revealed in a relatively detailed way the operation of descent in the transmission of rights in land; this gave rise to named *turun* or what he termed 'descent groups' (1954a, 1954b). The system operated in such a way that a person who established rights to land by the clearing of primary jungle, then passed these on un-divided to all his male and female descendants. Contrary to Geddes, I would hesitate to call these combined descendants 'descent groups' since this conjures up an image of corporate units.[17] As Geddes him-self indicated

[turun] are groups of people linked together by sharing rights in particular areas and they have no reality apart from those areas. This very fact makes them of little value as a basis for the organisation of other social relation-ships of a more permanent order, for the particular set of persons with whom any man is associated differ according to the particular piece of and in which he is interested at any moment (1954a:59).

Morris, in his present paper, has in mind the same problem when he points to the fact that where there are what he calls 'cognatic descent groupings' any given individual may belong simultaneously to a number of these units, since he can theoretically inherit use rights from all his ancestors who happen to have cleared primary jungle. This commonly results in conflicts of interest and thus Morris notes that 'it is almost impossible for such groups to develop strong corporate characteristics' and that, among the Land Dayak, descent groupings are 'very lightly corporate in nature'. Allen in his com-parative analysis of Iban and Land Dayak social structure stated more positively that turun 'do not in any sense constitute either a corporate group or a jural entity, they do nevertheless exist as a collectivity or category' (1970:193).

In this present volume there are two societies which have descent units designated by indigenous terms; these units are similar in some respects to those of the Bidayuh Land Dayak. The Hudsons have reported them for the Paju Epat Ma'anyan and call them 'bilineal descent groups' (bumuh). I have described them for Maloh and call them 'property-based descent categories' (*kapulungan*). In both cases membership in these entails the sharing of rights originally established by a given ancestor or ancestors not only in land, but also in other items of property, such as fruit trees, heirlooms, houses (Paju Epat only) and long-house support posts (Maloh only). In every generation there is also a custodian who looks after the estate. It is this person who resides in the parental household after marriage and is in the line of descent from the founding ancestor. Any individual has membership in a number of these units and therefore a choice of which links he wishes to emphasize; and there is a continual sloughing off of members as individuals stress certain links at the expense of others or move away and allow their rights to lapse or simply forget about them. Rights are graded in such a way that those individuals living in close physical proximity to the custodian have priority in use rights as against their relatives who live elsewhere.

In my terms the Paju Epat bumuh and the Maloh kapulungan seem to be more corporate than the Bidayuh turun, since in the former two cases rights are shared in a range of property and there is a custodian or a common authority who presides over the estate and is empowered to act on behalf of the members. Although the Hudsons with some justification call the bumuh a 'descent group', I have hesitated to use this term in the Maloh case, because the kapulungan shares some features with the Bidayuh turun, and individuals or households are usually alone responsible for informally activating rights in land and fruit trees, and deciding whether to join with other members in a dispute against outsiders concerning their land. In other words, there is not, in general, the recognition of common interests and a regular coming together of kapulungan members or their representatives. Only where a plot of land is claimed by two members of the same kapulungan is the custodian called in to resolve the dispute. This situation may be partly the result of the fact that up until recently there has not been great pressure on Maloh land resources. The custodian is, however, important in any decisions affecting the use of heirloom property by members. As we shall see below, in certain cases these Maloh descent units may take on much more corporate characteristics.

Similar principles of inheritance involving at least shared rights in land also seem to be present among the Kenyah, Lun Dayeh and Selako (and formerly among the Melanau [Morris, 1953:12]). Crain mentions the use of pedigrees among Lun Dayeh in establishing rights to use areas of land, although these appear to be diminishing in importance, and they do not appear to give rise to recognizable descent units. Whittier does not refer to the existence of descent units among the Kenyah but indicates that rights to land (and heirloom property) are located within households, and that individuals who marry out retain their use rights in the land. Permission to activate these rights and to use heirlooms must then be obtained from the household head who acts as the custodian of the estate. Finally, Schneider provides an interesting line of argument for the Selako which is relevant to the degree of corporateness of descent units in Bornean societies. He draws attention to the fact that in the long-house communities which he studied there was clearly discernible what Leach chose to call 'a house owning group'. This was a small group of closely related families which was more directly linked to the ancestral founders of the long-house and/or village than other villagers; political authority was also in its hands. Leach described this group as generally 'a limited extended family having a common ancestor two to three generations back' (1950:61).

As Leach has already indicated such a house owning group is a characteristic feature of Bornean village social organization. In the more stratified societies (e.g. Kayan, Kenyah, Maloh, Melanau) it is given formal recognition as the hereditary and privileged aristocratic element from which the village political élite is drawn: it even occurs in such 'non-stratified' or more egalitarian societies as the Iban, Lun Dayeh and Selako. There is, however, less definitive information on this point for the Bajau Laut, Paju Epat and Rungus Dusun.

Schneider calls these dominant groupings of families in Selako society 'corporate descent groups'. They are defined by descent and residence: they share common interests usually directed towards the establishment of political control; they co-operate closely in economic affairs; they have someone to represent them; and they maintain a joint estate which 'consists of a fund of prestige and rights in land inherited from their common ancestor'. It seems justifiable to label these house owning groups as 'descent groups'.

In societies such as the Maloh (and possibly the Kenyah?) in which groupings of aristocrats, in particular, dwelling in the same village share a common interest in maintaining an estate (i.e. belong to the same kapulungan), have a monopoly of political and ritual power, expressed in the figure of the aristocratic headman, and meet together regularly, then these units would seem to take on the characteristics of localized corporate descent groups. However, the kapulungan of other villagers and even those of some groupings of aristocrats which have recently declined in economic, political and ritual power, do not seem to warrant the designation 'descent group'. Furthermore, there are individuals, particularly those of slave descent who do not belong to kapulungan and who do not maintain a joint estate, but simply divide up any property which they might acquire. Finally, it would seem that in the Maloh ideational world these kapulungan are not particularly important when compared with such social features as the household, the village and ranks. In other words, an individual Maloh does not primarily orient himself and his behaviour with reference to the ideology of descent and descent units.

We are also faced with societies in which house owning groups of closely related households do not maintain a common estate and in these cases the appellation 'descent group' is entirely inappropriate. The Melanau have a hereditary aristocracy but property is divided on death, and there is no evidence of corporate descent groups. Individuals of the same rank do share rights to use certain symbolic property (indicative of their rank) especially at weddings, and this, according to Morris, is 'the only sense in which the members of the grouping could be said to be corporate'. The Kayan also possess a marked aristocratic stratum but no permanent rights are established in land, and here too other property is subsequently divided. Again there would seem to be no chance for the emergence of any descent units based on a shared estate.

Apart from land, there are other items of a relatively permanent nature which may provide the focus for particular descent units. Besides the bumuh, the Paju Epat Ma'anyan have a *tambak* group which the Hudsons also classify as a descent group. It is a named, discrete, mutually exclusive group focused on a 'carved ironwood box into which the ash residue of its members' remains is placed at the conclusion of the *ijambe* cremation ceremony'. It also owns some heirloom property, and it has a custodian. On the other hand, Appell hesitated to call these tambak groups 'descent groups' and preferred the term 'cognatic-structured kin groups', since he stated that 'actual membership in them is dependent on choice of residence and includes affines as well' (1969:52).

Despite the fact that Rungus do not recognize permanent use rights in land, they have descent units associated with cultivated and non-cultivated trees. Rights over trees may be divided among offspring on inheritance and this method is apparently becoming more common. But there is a practice among Rungus whereby trees 'may be devolved upon all heirs, both male and female without division'. Appell concludes that these tree-focused descent units are not 'cognatic descent groups', although some anthropologists might suggest that they are. Instead he suggests that in his terminology they can be termed a 'descent collectivity'. They are amorphous, their boundaries are ill-defined in terms of actual co-activity, membership can lapse and be forgotten; they are not named nor is there a special term for them; an individual has membership in a number of them; all members do not enjoy the harvest equally; and even in the case of cultivated trees in which one person has the responsibility for caring for the trees and acts as the representative of other right holders he has 'no sanctions to control deviant behaviour within the social isolate separate from those available to all in the larger jural system'.

A number of features pointed to by Appell in the case above are shared by other types of descent unit in Borneo, and it is my tentative suggestion that only in certain contexts when individuals tracing descent from a common ancestor share rights in an estate, acknowledge a representative, recognize other common interests (e.g. political, economic) and come together fairly regularly, can we speak of descent groups proper. I realize there is bound to be continued dispute on this issue, but I hope this discussion will stimulate much more detailed investigation into the problems touched on above.

One further question remains in this regard—why have some Bornean societies developed shared rights in land in particular, while others have not done so? Allen, in his comparison of the Iban of the Baleh and Bidayuh Land Dayak social structure already mentioned, suggested that differences between them can be related to differences in the availability and utilization of land. Among Iban each bilek family is recognized as having rights in its own areas of jungle; it does not share rights with others, except temporarily after the 'partition' of a bilek family; and it does not hold rights over jungle in perpetuity; when it moves from the long-house then its rights in the jungle in that territory lapse. But in Bidayuh Land Dayak society all the descendants of an ancestor theoretically share rights in his land in perpetuity. Allen stated that this difference in land tenure is due to the fact that the Baleh Iban studied by Freeman 'are still pioneers with plenty of virgin land awaiting exploitation' (1970:194). They can easily use land once or twice, then move on to more productive virgin jungle. His conclusion was that among Iban

No descent units, whether groups or categories, can possibly develop around land rights for the simple reason that land is in such abundant supply that each plot is only used a few times. Problems of inheritance of land rights are therefore of little concern (p. 196).

On the other hand the Bidayuh do not have an abundance of primary jungle and much of their land is covered by secondary forest; a significant percentage of land is also suitable for swamp rice which allows rather more permanent cultivation. These factors plus one might add the confinement of the Bidayuh Land Dayak on all sides by neighbouring peoples led Allen to suggest that

Like the Iban, they [the Land Dayak] start with the basic proposition that the felling of primary jungle establishes full presumptive rights. But because this same plot will have to be used again and again over many generations, the criterion of descent from the original cultivator has come to be recognized as a title to future usage (pp. 196–7).

Allen was rightly reluctant to assert the causal primacy of environment but his personal opinion was that 'most of the sociocultural differences between Iban and Land Dayak ... are consequences rather than determinants of the kind of environment that the people live in' (p. 198). For these two societies this observation seems to hold. Furthermore, if we take other Bornean peoples then they too could fall within this schema. Both Maloh and Paju Epat Ma'anyan have descent units with permanent rights over land and both inhabit regions which have been fairly continuously exploited for a long period of time. Maloh, like Bidayuh, cultivate significant areas of swamp rice as well. The Selako who live in a similar environment to the Land Dayak also have descent units. However, we are confronted with certain difficulties when we consider the Kayan and Rungus Dusun. The Baluy area is sparsely populated by Kayan and as among the Baleh Iban, each village consists typically of a single long-house. In general, and despite the relative permanency of Kayan settlement when compared with that of the Iban, there is no scarcity of land among the Baluy Kayan and they establish no permanent rights over it (Rousseau, 1974a:118–19). Despite the apparent similarity in land availability Iban have rights in land while resident in a particular village, whereas Kayan do not. We could, of course, argue plausibly that Kayan (some or all?) have even more land available than Iban, and therefore there is no need to establish presumptive rights over land after clearing primary jungle. On the other hand we must also allow for the possibility that within the same environmental context and given the same technology there may be variation in response. Either way, in the absence of detailed ecological data, Allen's conclusions drawn from two societies can only be taken as a broad correlation, suggesting general tendencies, and marking the limits within which there are certain possibilities. Environment and technology interact and change with socio-cultural variables in often complex and various ways.

Allen's explanation meets with some difficulties in the case of the Rungus Dusun. We find that Rungus villages usually consist of more than one long-house and on the confined Kudat and Melabong peninsulas in Sabah land has been farmed relatively continuously. Yet, although they live in a rather different environmental situation from the Kayan, the Rungus have the same principle of land tenure, in that they do not establish permanent rights over land. In fact, arguing in completely contrary fashion to Allen, who proposed that relative scarcity of land is related to the formation of descent units,[18] Dixon has suggested that scarcity of resources might result in an absence of permanent rights in land, since land can then be more equitably distributed (1974:14).[19]

Clearly we need to have more detailed information on carrying capacities of land in relation to particular *perceptions* of the environment and various kinds and combinations of techniques of production. We need, in turn, to take account of the influences of values and social organization, particularly productive relations, on the exploitation of the environment. We have to acknowledge the possible effects of such factors as inter-ethnic relations expressed in, for example, warfare, migration, and trade on settlement patterns, population density and productive activities. These last factors are not readily nor necessarily directly related to techno-environmental variables. Finally, data permitting, we have to provide a historical perspective since both social forms and techno-environmental conditions vary in time. To my mind simple correlations between social organization and environment/technology are really only a starting point in the comparative analysis of Bornean societies, and they should lead us to the collection of more specific ecological material.

Long-house, Village and River-Based Grouping

In the context of the discussion of environmental conditions there is one social unit which deserves some mention and that is the village, usually defined as a territorial unit rather than a grouping based on kinship. The unity of the village is also frequently manifest in certain communal rituals such as cleansing the village of sickness or misfortune, and in political matters expressed in the office of the village headman or chief and/or the village elders. In most of the societies described in this volume the village holds rights in the land within a defined territory, in the sense that all village members have equal rights of access to that land. Appell terms these 'residual rights'. The interesting point is that in certain societies, particularly those which have large areas of primary forest available, the village normally comprises one long-house (e.g. Iban and Kayan), whereas in others there may be two or more long-houses per village (e.g. Kenyah, Lun Dayeh, Melanau, Maloh, Rungus, Selako). In a number of cases long-houses are gradually giving way to single-family dwellings, particularly in those societies which used to build large, fortress-like long-houses (e.g. Maloh). The Melanau no longer have any of their traditional houses remaining. On the other hand, Paju Epat Ma'anyan have apparently never known long-houses; neither have the Bajau Laut fishing communities. Instead both have villages of large, separate households occupied generally by extended or multiple families. Thus while Leach's suggestion, based on Sarawak data, that long-house domicile is another characteristic of a Bornean type of society, it is by no means a universal form of residence in Borneo.

In those villages consisting of more than one long-house there is considerable variation in the degree of autonomy of the individual long-houses, and in the political and religious functions they perform. Among Maloh, for example, each long-house retains a significant degree of autonomy, expressed in part in the possession of its own aristocratic long-house headman; and among Melanau, in the past, long-houses within the same village may even have differed from one another in dialect and custom. In contrast, in such societies as the Rungus the long-house, which has no recognized headman, is a less important unit when compared with the domestic family and the village.

The type of settlement pattern has also been influenced by a variety of factors. Long-houses or villages often divided as a result of such things as increasing pressure on resources in a given area or of internal conflicts. On the other hand, amalgamation of communities may have resulted from, for example, the decimation of the population by epidemics or the need for defence against superior enemies. However, overall there seems to be a relationship between the presence of long-house clusters and a more permanently settled society, although the Kayan appear to be an exception here. Such peoples as the Lun Dayeh, Maloh, Rungus and Selako live in relatively confined areas and also cultivate swamp and/or wet rice.[20] The Melanau are also semi-sedentary sago cultivators. On the other hand, the generally extensive and mobile farming methods of the Iban are associated with a more scattered settlement pattern. One can suggest, for example, that availability of land suitable for relatively sedentary swamp rice cultivation and the production of adequate supplies of dry rice allows a clustering of long-houses in a limited area. But this does not really explain why, for example, the Kenyah have large multi-long-house villages in an environment which is very similar to that of the mobile Iban. Again we have to consider other factors as well in a historical framework if we are to arrive at possible explanations for these differences. In the head-hunting past, there was the need for defence and therefore concentrated settlement, and this was a priority for certain peoples. Another factor may have been the existence of a strong aristocracy which prevented frequent turn-over in the village population by imposing fines on those households which wanted to move (e.g. Maloh, Kayan, Kenyah). Also, the confinement of certain peoples by their more aggressive neighbours may have necessitated the development of a comparatively intensive agriculture and a clustering of long-houses; and, in certain instances, population numbers may have been stable, allowing more permanent settlement.

Perhaps it is worth noting at this juncture, that the influence of the environment in Borneo does give rise more or less directly to a social unit which is characteristic of indigenous societies. This is the grouping which comprises those villages situated within the same river system or along the same river. Freeman chose to call this unit a 'tribe' in his study of the Iban (1970:73–4), but I refer to it as a 'river-based grouping' among the Maloh (see also the Kayan and Kenyah). Since the main lines of communication in Borneo follow the rivers it is not surprising that villages on the same watercourse tend to have more frequent contacts, are linked more closely by friendship and kinship, and may exhibit certain cultural traits which distinguish them from settlements along other rivers. In some cases it was also the largest unit in the past within which individuals did not take one another's heads (e.g. Freeman, 1970:126; King, 1974: 220-1).

Rank

Although rank is not a characteristic feature of Bornean societies Leach made a basic division between those peoples who possess hereditary ranks and those who do not. Morris also points to the existence of a collection of peoples such as the Kayan, Kenyah, Kajang and Melanau who 'all belong to similar stratified societies which stretch from the Coastal Melanau in a broad band across the centre of Borneo'. This category would also include the Maloh. He also states that these peoples differ significantly from such egalitarian societies as the Iban, Bidayuh Land Dayak, Dusun and Murut. To the latter group one could add the Bajau Laut, the present day Lun Dayeh (sometimes confusingly classified as 'Murut'), the Rungus (Dusun) and Selako.

Though an important division there is a danger of making too sharp a distinction between these two types of society. Leach noted that even among the egalitarian Iban certain communities had a noticeable 'class structure' (1950:27).[21] More recently Pringle (1970: 28, 36-7) has suggested that Freeman perhaps overemphasized the 'democratic' aspect of Iban society as a whole and that among the more settled Saribas Iban there is 'a very much greater sense of class' (p. 36). It must be remembered that in the past Iban had an institution of slavery and that even today 'a definite stigma still attaches to slave ancestry' (p. 28; Leach, p. 71).

If we look at other supposedly egalitarian Bornean societies we also see that in the past they presented a rather different picture. For example, Crain indicates that about 60 years ago the Lun Dayeh had a 'class' system consisting of aristocrats (*lun do*), commoners and slaves (*lun demulun*); this has since all but disappeared. Today the term lun do means 'successful' or 'meritorious' people rather than referring to aristocrats. The Hudsons also describe a formal 'class' system among the Ma'anyan comprising 'nobles' (*bangsawan*), 'warriors' (*panglima*) and 'clients' (*walah*). This formal division apparently declined after the Dutch officially abolished slavery in 1892, and now 'plays a minor role in mediating social relationships'. Appell indicates that the Rungus are basically egalitarian since there was no hereditary 'class' system; but 'a permeable class system' exists consisting of three grades—a wealthy, middle and poor class— in the past the last probably included a subcategory of 'slaves'. Finally, Schneider points to the existence of status and wealth distinctions among Selako, although there are no named hereditary ranks.

Even the more recognizably stratified societies which have a

hereditary aristocracy may become increasingly like the present
day egalitarian peoples above because their ranking systems are now
in decline. For example, the Melanau in 1950 continued to recognize
those who were slaves by origin, but the institution of slavery and
bond service had been in decay well before then under administrative
pressure, and was formally abolished in Sarawak in 1928. The ending
of warfare and head-hunting, the growth of an international sago
flour market and the decrease in aristocratic control over sago production and distribution also led to a relative decline in the power of
Melanau aristocrats, although Morris notes that 'their prestige
lingered on and was still an important aspect of the political system
in 1950'. The Maloh ranking system, particularly in the Embaloh
and Leboyan rivers, is also rapidly disappearing. The position of
Maloh aristocrats has been eroded by the abolition of slavery and
more recently by government policies designed to democratize village
political life. Other factors have been the introduction of education,
which has opened new channels for social mobility and provided the
basis for an alternative ranking system, and Christian influence,
which has undermined the ritual and symbolic foundation of aristocratic leadership. All these factors have in turn led to a reformulation
of graded customary fines and bridewealth in the Embaloh area in
favour of a more equitable system. Finally, the introduction of money
as a medium of exchange and the availability of new consumer items
have led to a decline in interest in the traditional heirloom property
which used to be an important symbol of rank differences. Like that
of the Maloh, the ranking system of the Kenyah has undergone some
changes with the abolition of slavery, the advent of Christianity and
the emergence of the syncretic religion called *Adat Bungan* (see
Whittier's paper below).

One society in which the traditional stratification system is still
more or less operative and readily observable is that of the relatively
isolated Baluy Kayan. Although slavery was declining in importance,
and had disappeared altogether in a number of villages, this was a
fairly recent phenomenon, and Rousseau reports that Kayan aristocrats still retain a significant degree of power. They are, for example,
still entitled to labour services and are free to participate in profitable
trading ventures and to perform important political functions.

In general, the stratified societies of Borneo can be distinguished
from those which exhibit more egalitarian tendencies by the fact
that the former have fairly clearly defined and named hereditary
ranks. Despite internal gradations within ranks, some social mobility,
and the sometimes uncertain position of individuals (and their offspring) who marry into other ranks (e.g. see Maloh, Kenyah and
Kayan) there were in the past three broad strata viz. aristocrats,
commoners and slaves. The aristocrats were to a large extent free of

agricultural work, since they had slaves to work for them, and they could expect corvées from their villagers. They could therefore organize and participate in profitable trading expeditions and thereby increase their wealth; they were usually important as leaders in warfare and raids; they performed a vital political function in that they normally monopolized the position of village chief or headman and acted as the main intermediaries with other communities.[22] They were also, in general, the custodians of the customary law. The commoners can be described as free agriculturalists. Apart from corvées and some goods due to the aristocrats, they lived in independent households and they had control over their own production and, to a large extent, the product of their labour. On the other hand, a number of slaves were generally owned by aristocrats and had little or no control over their work. There was also usually a subclass of slaves, whom Morris calls 'field slaves', who lived separately from their masters and who were more independent than those who were members of their master's households.

In addition to their economic and political superiority aristocrats were distinguished in a number of other ways. They usually played a key role in ritual (particularly agricultural rituals) and/or were entitled to perform different rites with different ritual paraphernalia from other villagers. They had a sacred status associated with their closer connection with the ancestral founders of the village. There were often other aristocratic entitlements such as the right to wear and/or use certain tattoos, items of ceremonial clothing and other decorations. Strata were also maintained by a tendency towards rank endogamy and this was reinforced by differential bridewealth payments according to rank; these payments differed not only in quantity but also often in kind. Aristocratic households usually had more members and these were naturally housed in larger apartments.

It is really only since the establishment of European government in Borneo in the nineteenth century that various changes, particularly the abolition of slavery, have led to an increasing egalitarianism among both the stratified and non-stratified societies. This is not to say that new stratification systems based on other criteria may not arise in Borneo, but what little evidence from historical and oral sources we have suggests that before these changes were set in train the two types of social system in Borneo once established were apparently relatively stable.[23] However, it is difficult to pin-point the reasons for the existence of on the one hand a hereditary, more formal ranking system among those societies generally located in central Borneo, and on the other hand surrounding peoples who, although recognizing wealth and prestige differentials, have more egalitarian tendencies.

Morris attempts to offer a functional explanation for the Melanau ranking system in particular, and suggests that in their inhospitable environment trade for essential commodities was made easier because a section of the population (i.e. the aristocrats) was freed from subsistence labour to go on trading expeditions and organize protection for productive activities. But he admits that this suggestion is 'far from conclusive' since non-stratified peoples such as the Iban and Bidayuh Land Dayak achieved the same ends without ranks.

A further attempt at explanation was put forward by Leach, but his suggestions relate to a period when some societies already possessed a ranking system. For example, he drew attention to the possibility of culture contact with stratified peoples such as the Kayan to explain the more marked stratification of Iban communities in certain areas (1950:27). He also stated for the Iban that 'kindred endogamy coupled with the absence of brideprice probably accounts for the marked lack of class stratification' (1950:70). Yet the absence of brideprice is just as likely to be a result of the lack of stratification as a reason for it, and in stratified societies individuals also often intermarry with close kinsmen, since it is one way of maintaining rank boundaries.

Pringle has commented on the difference between Iban unstructured society and their 'anarchic way of life' and Kayan stratified society (1970:35-6). He suggested that Iban egalitarian political institutions may be related to their mobile life-style which may in turn be associated with cultivation of less fertile soils and overpopulation in their homeland and the easy availability of vast areas of surrounding virgin jungle. But he readily noted that a problem exists here because

'. . . conditions similar to those experienced by the Ibans did not necessarily result in other Iban-type cultures. The Kayans were also expanding in the early and middle years of the nineteenth century. Yet Kayan society certainly did not develop along Iban lines' (p. 36).

An important qualification is necessary. Pringle did not make it sufficiently clear that Kayan stratification was a pre-nineteenth century phenomenon and that despite Kayan mobility the migrations were led and presumably controlled by aristocrats. Furthermore, Kayan were not continuously nor frequently on the move. On the other hand the more mobile egalitarian Iban studied by Freeman were true pioneers who had only recently moved to the Baleh. Indeed, as Pringle himself noted, the more permanently settled and longer established Saribas Iban were more stratified and had a greater sense of rank than their pioneering cousins.

If we take into account a fairly long period of historical development, there might well be a broad relationship between the formation of a ranked social system and relatively permanent settlement, perhaps facilitated initially by low population, by available land for swamp rice and/or by more fertile soils, favourable terrain and suitable climate for the production of a surplus of dry rice. It goes without saying that strong leadership can more easily develop where there is a relatively settled population and, in addition, where there is an available food surplus to support an aristocracy which can then indulge in political and ritual activities, and profitable trading ventures. On the other hand, in certain cases, ability to control the flow of trade goods may itself have generated rank differentials.

Friedman (1975:161–202) has recently put forward a plausible model to explain the generation and decline of stratification among the Kachin of Highland Burma. His argument put very simply is that the formation of ranks is the result initially of the production of a surplus by a particular group of people (in this case a Kachin lineage); this surplus is redistributed to other villagers and can be translated into prestige, 'social value' and political and ritual power by means of feasts held on behalf of the whole community before the spirits of fertility and prosperity. A similar process might well have been operative in some Bornean societies. Certainly if we look at Bornean aristocrats today and in the recent past, their main functions are and were political and religious. There is also evidence to suggest that Maloh aristocrats (and possibly those of the Kenyah), for example, were responsible for the redistribution of some surplus produce gained through agriculture and trade and the presentation of offerings in agricultural and other festivals[24] performed in honour of the deities and spirits. These rites have gradually disappeared, but there was among Maloh (King, 1976a:137) and Kenyah (Whittier, 1973:74–6) a prestige system, to some extent outside the more rigid system of inherited rank, which was based on an individual's ability to hold and/or participate in a graded scale of feasts. These festivals may have originally provided the means to convert the possession of surplus products into political and ritual power.

Nevertheless, the data from other stratified societies such as the Melanau and Kayan is less definitive. Among the Kayan aristocrats were released from productive activity by the system of slavery and compulsory labour services, but Rousseau points out that there is no inequality on the basis of landownership since land is a free good, and the village chief has no redistributive role (1974a:374–6). Instead it appears that Kayan stratification exists because some individuals have been able to develop a key political role especially in inter-village relations (pp. 406, 413, 441). This, in turn, arises mainly from the fact that Baluy Kayan villages are for various reasons—ethnic, social and ecological—isolated from each other with little mobility and contact between them. Thus inter-community linkages can only really be created by aristocrats, who normally marry outside their own village to maintain the rule of rank endogamy.[25] They also have time to participate in extra-village activities, being free from subsistence production. This kind of situation would not seem to apply to such an extent to the Maloh and Kenyah whose long-houses and villages, in the past (as well as today) were not so isolated one from another. In fact, among the Maloh, contacts and communication between villages, at least those in the same river system, were frequent and relatively intense.

However, in the case of the Kayan and Maloh, and indeed the Kenyah and Melanau, communities as a whole were and are today comparatively immobile, and this settled population base seems to be one factor in the development of systems of stratification. The existence of an aristocracy also reinforces permanency of settlement, since strong leaders can usually maintain control over their subjects, and in the case of the Maloh, Kayan and Kenyah, for example, village aristocrats could restrict the movement of and impose fines on those villagers wishing to leave to reside elsewhere.

If we now turn to the more egalitarian Iban, then a plausible case may be made out here for a possible link between continuous movement of individuals and groups over a fairly long period of time, and the lack of a marked ranking system. Local overpopulation, demographic instability, an unfavourable environment for the continued provision of subsistence, prodigal agricultural practices, the availability of large areas of virgin jungle nearby, and also perhaps the search for heads, may have stimulated continuous Iban movement. The lack of permanency of a pioneer population would have made it difficult for Iban leaders, even if they secured a political following, to consolidate and legitimate their power. This factor of instability may also have relevance in the case of the relatively unstratified, yet mobile Bajau Laut fishermen. On the other hand it is always problematical to suggest which factor or factors may be responsible for variations in social forms, particularly in the absence of detailed historical data.[26] For example, the Bidayuh Land Dayak, Rungus Dusun and Selako have remained relatively unstratified despite an apparently fairly settled overall population, though there appears to have been a significant movement of households between long-houses and villages in these societies. They are therefore exceptions to the general principle outlined above, and one can only guess at the reasons for this. In the distant past they may have been more stratified than at present, or alternatively they may have indeed been much more mobile. They may not have possessed the mechanisms (e.g. feasting) to convert surpluses into prestige and social position, or closer contact and movement between villages in these cases may not have required a political élite to maintain inter-village contacts. These suggestions need to be pursued with reference to more detailed data.

Conclusions

I have attempted by way of introduction to bring together rather diverse material from various Bornean societies using the common principles which Leach isolated in his general survey of Sarawak. Overall I have some doubts about the comparative utility of the personal kindred in Leach's (and indeed Murdock's) schema, and I am doubtful about the tendency to emphasize kinship as a general organizational principle in Bornean societies. Nevertheless, I follow Leach in recognizing the validity of the heuristic device which posits a Bornean type of society, since this allows the selective comparison of certain social forms generated by particular organizational principles as variations on a single theme. It seems to me that some of the most fruitful lines of enquiry lie in the comparative analysis in Borneo of, for example, household structure, descent units and rights in property, village organization and the house owning group and social stratification.

In this introduction I have simply posed a number of problems and advanced some very tentative suggestions for explaining them, but offered few, if any solutions. This is for the unexceptionable reason that it is impossible to proceed without taking into account the nature of the historical development of the societies discussed. Unfortunately most scholars of Borneo peoples, myself included, have not addressed themselves as much as they might have done to the collection of historical data, and it is a painful fact that knowledge of contemporary or recent situations alone will never be enough fully to explain variations and differences in social organization within and between particular societies.

NOTES

1. For an informative discussion of the problems of ethnic classification in Borneo see Leach (1950:46–56), Harrisson (1950:271–80) and Hudson (1967a, 1970:301–18). For an interesting examination of ethnic identity in one part of central Borneo, and an explanation of the complex categorization of the peoples there see Rousseau (1975:32–49).

2. The nine peoples in this volume would appear to be at least partially distinguishable ethnic groupings, but I know of no generally agreed upon classificatory framework which could accommodate them all. Later in this introduction I divide the peoples considered into two broad sociological categories based on the presence or absence of formal and hereditary rank distinctions (see also Leach, 1950:60–1). Those with clearly marked ranks are the Coastal Melanau, who have historical and cultural links with interior peoples usually labelled 'Kajang', and the central Bornean peoples—Kayan, Kenyah and Maloh. Those without hereditary ranks, at least at the present time, are the Selako, Lun Dayeh, Rungus Dusun, Bajau Laut and Paju Epat Ma'anyan.

3. In the Preface and Introduction I use the term 'social systems' and 'social organization' synonymously to refer very broadly to social statuses and institutions, and the relationship between them. These are all based primarily on the principles of kinship/descent, locality/residence and rank. I am fully aware that there are various conceptions of what constitutes 'social organization' or 'a social system', but I have kept my definition deliberately general to allow contributors to pursue their own ethnographical and analytical interests while at the same time ensuring that there is reasonably full treatment of such social features as the household (or domestic family), the long-house, village, kinship terminology, descent units, work groups, social stratification and village leadership.

4. For a relatively comprehensive and interesting discussion of the state of anthropological and ethnographical research in Borneo, and the development of analytical orientations in the study of the social organization of Bornean societies see G. N. Appell's editorial Preface and Introduction to *The Societies of Borneo: Explorations in the Theory of Cognatic Social Structure* (1976c:v–viii, 1–15) and his Introduction and Chapter One in *Studies in Borneo Societies: Social Process and Anthropological Explanation* (1976d:1–26).

5. The terms 'cognatic' and 'bilateral' are sometimes used interchangeably. In this introduction I retain the term 'cognatic' to refer to all 'non-unilineal' societies and I use the term 'bilateral' to cover a subtype which includes those societies characteristic of Borneo. The term 'bilateral' is generally applied to societies without 'descent groups' (see below) (Murdock 1960:1–14 and Peranio, 1961:93–113). In a previous paper I avoided using the term 'cognatic' since it has the meaning of 'akin by birth', and this has introduced, to my mind, bias in favour of consanguineal kin as against affines in the study and analysis of these types of system (see King, 1976b:121–45). Nevertheless, it is a generally accepted term in the literature and to avoid unnecessary semantic quibbling I continue to use it here.

6. On the other hand, Murdock (1960:9–14) used the term 'ambilineal' to refer to a subtype of cognatic societies like certain of those found in Formosa and Polynesia which have a number of defining characteristics or 'structural criteria' particularly the usual presence of 'extended families' and 'ambilineal descent groups' (or 'ramages'). The discussion of the existence or non-existence of 'descent groups' in Bornean societies will be taken up in detail later in the introduction. Murdock's other two cognatic subtypes are 'bilateral', exemplified by South-East Asian lowland peoples such as the Javanese, Cambodians and Tagalog and certain interior peoples of the Philippines and Borneo (p. 6), and 'quasi-unilineal' societies such as the Sinhalese (p. 7).

7. Murdock also referred to a more or less common pattern of kinship terminology, and marriage and residence prescriptions or preferences in bilateral societies.

8. For a full discussion of the difficulties inherent in the concept of the kindred as defined by Freeman, and also Murdock, see Mitchell (1963, 1965), Hudson (1967:270–4, 287–90), Smart (1971:70–107) and King (1976b).

9. Also see Murdock who recorded the presence of kindreds in some lineal societies (1949:56–7, 60–2).

10. It is worth noting that the general Iban term *kaban* which Freeman translated at one point as 'kindred' is also extended to affines.

11. See also Leach (1950:61–2) who stressed that the kindred is a relative concept, and, at least initially, appeared to follow Nadel in using it to embrace not only consanguineal but also affinal categories of kin.

12. This consideration highlights the general problems involved in typologizing and comparative analysis some of which Leach has drawn attention to under the general label 'butterfly-collecting' (1961:1–27). However, despite the difficulties posed by these activities, I feel that given more detailed data, particularly of a historical kind, certain features of Bornean societies can be fruitfully compared and generalizations drawn from them. Indeed this would seem to me to be one of the ways foward for anthropologists concerned with Borneo.

13. See the various papers for details on marriage rules and preferences, post-marital residence, incest prohibitions, adoption, the recognition of various categories of kinship, forms of address, teknonymy and so on.

14. Among Bajau Laut no long-houses exist. It should also be remembered that in the case of societies such as the Kenyah, Maloh and Melanau long-house type and permanency of settlement are themselves related to social stratification.

15. See, in particular, the papers by Peranio (1961:93–113) and Firth (1963: 22–37) for a detailed discussion of the problems involved in defining what constitutes a 'descent group' in cognatic/bilateral societies. In this introduction I follow Firth's line of argument that the term 'descent' need not, and indeed should not be confined to *unilineal* corporate kin groups', nor should the definition of membership in a descent group be restricted to recruitment on the basis of descent alone (pp. 35–6).

16. My use of the terms 'unit' or 'entity' in this introduction is to refer to any social grouping whether it be a corporate group or otherwise.

17. Peranio (1961:97–9, 107) has cast doubt on the corporateness of Bidayuh turun. He saw the Land Dayak descent system as similar to that of the Bisaya of Sarawak who have what he termed 'aggregates' or 'cognatic descent categories' (1972:165). Similarly Peranio was of the opinion that by his definition the 'bilateral descent groups' of the Sagada Igorot of Luzon, reported by Eggan (1960:29–30), are simply 'categories based on descent lines' (pp. 98–9, 107).

18. In this context there is a problem posed by the Rungus 'tree-focused' descent units. Appell says that trees are not a scarce good in the Rungus economy, yet descent units form around them.

19. The possible reasons for the non-establishment of permanent rights in land among the Rungus in particular have also been debated at length by Appell (1971b:17–21), Dixon (1974:5–15) and King (1975b:12–16).

20. This does not take account of the fact that a village comprising one large long-house may be more populous than one consisting of two or three small long-houses. But, in general, long-house clusters tend to be more heavily populated than single long-house villages.

21. He suggested that the Iban of the Baleh region had a class structure 'more marked . . . than in other parts of the Iban country' and this may have been due to contact with the stratified Kayan (1950:27). On the other hand, Freeman's work on the same region revealed that Iban society was 'classless and egalitarian' (1970:129).

22. In the case of the Melanau there was no recognizable headman or chief, rather political control was in the hands of a small grouping of aristocratic elders. These elders might appoint someone to represent them for a specific purpose.

23. This apparent stability must not be taken for granted, and given more detailed historical data it may well be the case that the situation in Borneo is similar to that which Leach reported for the amorphous collection of peoples in Highland

Burma labelled 'Kachin' (1964). Leach described a process of 'oscillation' among 'Kachin' communities between two ideal political types, that is, 'egalitarian'/ 'democratic' and 'hierarchical'/'autocratic'. On the other hand, if it turns out that in general 'Kachin' have been more unstable than Bornean societies, then this difference may be related in some way to the differences in their respective social orders. The 'Kachin' are organized in agnatic lineages and practise matrilateral cross-cousin marriage, whereas in Borneo, societies are bilateral. The comparative investigation of Highland Burma communities and those in Borneo, particularly the examination of the generation and decline of ranking systems, may turn out to be a fruitful one.

24. Although Lun Dayeh no longer have an aristocratic stratum Crain notes the continued existence of 'elaborate agricultural feasts' sponsored by 'core families'.

25. There are usually very few aristocratic households in a given village, and therefore to maintain the ideal rule of rank endogamy, and, at the same time avoid an incestuous union, aristocrats normally have to find partners outside their own village. In contrast, commoners, who are more numerous, can find a spouse within their own village and often prefer to do so (e.g. Melanau and Kayan).

26. See my papers for a brief sketch on the contrast between Maloh hierarchy and Iban egalitarianism and their associated sociol-cultural features (1976d: 306–27, 1976e:85–114).

2

THE COASTAL MELANAU*

H. S. MORRIS

THE Melanau of Sarawak are a diverse set of peoples who speak related dialects, not all of which are mutually comprehensible. In 1960 just over 44,000 people were counted as Melanau, of whom about 10,000 were still pagan. The rest were Muslim, except for a small number of Roman Catholic Christians (Census 1960).

The Melanau population inhabits the coastal area stretching from the delta districts of the Rejang river north-eastwards to Bintulu. These people have cultural, linguistic and social links with the Kajang groups living in the middle Rejang and Baluy river areas, as well as with other groups along the coast to the Baram river and in the interior hilly districts (Clayre, 1972a:482–562; 1972b). Although it is probably legitimate to speak of a Melanau culture and type of social structure, it is doubtful how far any one group can thereby be distinguished from related peoples in the interior, whether of the Kajang groups, who claim close historical connexions with the Coastal Melanau, or of other groups who make no such claims. One group almost imperceptibly merges into the next until it ultimately becomes very difficult to decide what connexion the last has with the first. Ethnographers and the people themselves do, however, agree, in spite of difficult borderline cases, that the Kayan and Kenyah peoples differ significantly from the Kajang and Melanau groups in language and culture, though all belong to similar stratified societies which stretch from the Coastal Melanau in a broad band across the centre of Borneo. These stratified societies differ markedly from the more egalitarian groups, such as the Iban and Land Dayak, in south and south-western Borneo, and from those in the north, such as the Murut and Dusun.

* The fieldwork on which this article is based was made possible by grants from the Colonial Social Science Research Council and the Sarawak Government in 1948–1950, from the London School of Economics and Political Science in 1963–4, from the Social Science Research Council, London and the London-Cornell Project in 1970–1. My thanks are also due to several Curators of the Sarawak Museum and their staff. I owe a special debt of gratitude to Mr. Tuton Kaboy and Dr. Iain Clayre who worked with me in the field and to Melanau friends in the Oya and Mukah rivers, too many to mention by name. I am also deeply in debt to Professor E. R. Leach and my wife, Barbara E. Ward, and many academic colleagues who over the years have guided, commented on, and criticized my work on the Melanau.

The coastal district of Sarawak inhabited by the Melanau is a low-lying swampy plain, often below sea level, made up of poor, peaty soil covered by dense tropical forest. In places the swamp extends inland as far as 20 miles before the land rises to undulating hills. The swampy soil does not easily allow the inhabitants to grow hill rice by swidden cultivation, the characteristic mode of farming of people in the interior districts. The Melanau coastal area is traversed by meandering rivers, all flowing roughly north-west into the South China Sea. These rivers are tidal for considerable distances upstream, and during the north-east monsoon, from November to March, they are likely to overflow their banks and flood the surrounding land. Swamp rice (*padai paya*[1]), a strain of dry rice that tolerates wet soil, but not flooding, can be grown on the river banks, which are slightly raised and drier than the adjacent land. But rice grown in such conditions is an uncertain crop and is frequently ruined before it can be harvested. It cannot, therefore, be relied on as a staple food for the people inhabiting the area. The only food plant which flourishes in this environment is the sago palm (*metroxylon sagu*); and for many centuries the people living in these swamp forests, even those outside the Melanau district, have cultivated the sago palm. From it they produce a starch flour for subsistence and export.

In this swamp environment, which lacks certain essential commodities such as salt, iron, copper and stone, the Melanau could not be self-sufficient; and they were obliged to find produce for export, such as sago or forest products like rattan, gums and resins, beeswax, camphor, or timber. The exchange of these products for manufactured goods from Brunei, Pontianak, Malaya, Indonesia, Indo-China or China itself was a characteristic feature of the economies of the Melanau people and of many inland swidden cultivators as well. For the Melanau, this export and import trade was indispensible, whereas the swidden cultivators of the interior could, if necessary, have been self-sufficient. The trade was possible for them, as it was for the Melanau, only because their economies were based almost as much on hunting, gathering and river fishing as on cultivation. This dependence on hunting and gathering both for subsistence and exchange, distinguishes both the Melanau and the swidden cultivators from sedentary farmers, such as the wet rice farmers of Sabah, Java, and the mainland of South-East Asia, whose subsistence hardly depended on forest products, and whose habits of work and land use consequently differed significantly. The Melanau economy is in a very real sense halfway between those of sedentary farmers and of swidden cultivators, a fact that is reflected in certain aspects of their social system.

This study of the Coastal Melanau is mainly based on fieldwork undertaken in villages on the Oya and Mukah rivers. The observations and conclusions apply in particular to the village of Medong on the Oya river where most time was spent; they also apply rather more generally to the other villages of that river and the Mukah, and to some extent to the whole Melanau coastal district. No claim is made for the validity of the details of social and cultural behaviour outside the Oya river, but it does seem that a limited number of principles of social and cultural organization are valid over a wider area than the Oya river, though the manner in which the principles manifest themselves in the social system of any particular society may differ considerably, as was noted above, from one area to another. Even so, it is possible to speak with reasonable confidence of a typical Melanau culture and social structure which has affinities with the cognate cultures and structures of the other stratified societies of central Borneo.

Melanau History

The Melanau-speaking inhabitants of the coastal district have lived in the area for a long time; and the name Melanau, which they say was given to them by the people of Brunei, is correctly placed on some of the earliest maps made by the first European explorers of the region in the sixteenth century.[2] The Melanau refer to themselves as *a-Likou*, meaning the people of the river. For at least four centuries the inhabitants of the coastal district have been under the nominal jurisdiction of the Muslim sultans of Brunei, who placed their representatives at the mouths of the more important sago-producing rivers, especially the Oya and Mukah, to control the revenue from the sago trade, which was, until the district was conquered by the Rajah of Sarawak, an important element in the economy of Brunei.

The sultan's representatives, because they were settled in villages at the mouths of the rivers, were in some measure able to control the sago trade; but their political control over the villages upstream was minimal. Nor were they until the late nineteenth century particularly concerned to convert the pagans to Islam. The establishment of Singapore as an international market early in the nineteenth century introduced fundamental changes into the trade of the whole region of the Indonesian archipelago and in particular to the sago trade of the Melanau coastal district. Until then most sago had been exported as a food in the form of baked biscuit; but the demand through Singapore from the expanding textile industries of Europe and America was for cheap industrial starch, not food.

At least a decade, if not two, before James Brooke became Rajah of Sarawak in 1841, Malay shipping merchants from Kuching had begun to compete for sago in the coastal district with the established merchants of Brunei in supplying the new flour market in Singapore. In the years following 1841, Brooke expanded the territory of Sarawak at the expense of Brunei; and by the late 1850s found himself acutely short of money and at war with local Malay rulers who owed nominal allegiance to the Sultan of Brunei. Eventually, to secure the revenue of the coastal district by diverting the export of flour to Singapore through Kuching and to protect his Sarawak merchants, the Rajah in 1861 compelled the Sultan of Brunei to hand over to him the sago-producing area from the Rejang river to Bintulu.

The Malay merchants from Sarawak, whose interests Brooke set out to secure, were shippers and carriers. In competition with established local merchants and those from Brunei, they often found it difficult to buy flour. Some of them had therefore settled agents in the upriver villages to buy flour direct from the villagers. But neither these agents nor the shipping merchants themselves refined the crude flour bought in the villages into a product acceptable to the Singapore market. This was done in factories, mostly owned by Chinese merchants or the British Borneo Company at Kuching. As the coastal district settled down after the conquest, these merchants found it more convenient to move their factories to the sago rivers; and they and their agents gradually displaced the earlier Malay traders, both in the sago export business and in the new retail trade. With the opening up of the area and the expansion of a cash economy, the demand for new types of consumer goods from Singapore increased every year. The export of flour went up annually until about 1890, after which the tonnage exported remained roughly constant until the conquest of Sarawak by the Japanese in 1941. During the last three decades of the nineteenth century the financial stability of Sarawak rested largely on the sago industry.

Melanau Social Structure

Traditional Melanau society made use of three overlapping criteria in organizing social life. The first was that of local grouping; the second was that of kinship; and the third was that of hereditary rank. A Melanau thought of himself in each of these social dimensions. He was closely identified with a particular locality, especially with one long-house in a village whose inhabitants were thought to be, and often were, different from those of other villages, or even other long-houses in the same village, in matters of dialect and custom. As an individual, a man or woman was the focal point of a kindred with whose members he shared a wide range of social and economic interests regulated by principles of bilateral kinship. Lastly, he had by virtue of birth a rank status. The behaviour of one individual towards another in any context was largely determined by being a man or woman of a particular age and the fact that the two people were neighbours or strangers, kinsmen or not, of equal or different rank. Within the social order behaviour was regulated by the *adet*;

within the symbolic order ritual behaviour was governed by principles also called the adet, a term best translated as a principle of order rather than customary law, as is the common practice (Morris, 1967:189–216).

(i) *Local grouping*

Traditionally a Melanau village consisted of two or three long-houses. These houses (*lebu*) were massive wooden fortresses built on stilts, often 30 feet above ground level; and they were usually situated at the confluence of a strategically important tributary stream and the main river. Each village was politically independent within its own territory, and was frequently on terms of active hostility with its Melanau neighbours and the inhabitants of the hills upstream, most of whom from the beginning of the nineteenth century were Iban who had begun to invade the area.

The political control of a village was in the hands of a small group of aristocratic elders (*a-nyat*) whose families ideally owned the centrally placed apartments of the long-house, and who were said to be the descendants of the village founders. On each side of this core were apartments owned by freemen (*a-bumi*); and at each end of the house were the apartments of slaves (*a-dipen*). Most slaves were owned by the aristocrats (*a-menteri*). The investment of labour and capital in a Melanau long-house was so great that they were seldom moved or completely rebuilt. When peaceful conditions were established under Brooke rule, the houses were gradually abandoned, and their inhabitants built separate dwellings along the banks of the river.

Although physically one structure, a long-house was made up of separately built apartments, each owned and inhabited by a married couple and perhaps one married child, often but not invariably, the youngest. Much of the village life and ceremonial took place on the long verandah in front of these apartments, and when the small detached houses were built a great deal of the culture, especially the performance of large communal ceremonies, fell into disuse because no new central meeting houses replaced the verandah.

Surrounding each village was its territory. This extended up and down both banks of the river to named points, usually tributary streams, and away from the main river (*likou*) to the low watersheds dividing it from the adjacent rivers. A man's proper place was in the village in this territory, which he was prepared to defend against other human beings, but which, excluding the village itself, he shared with a variety of non-human beings. The village territory fell into three main divisions: the village settlement, likou; the cultivated area (*uma*); and the forest (*guun*). The cultivated area was, as it were, only half domesticated, and was not a wholly human domain.

Spirits and animals, and in some respects even the vegetation, had rights there; care was needed in working in it, for any creature that left its proper place in the world or trespassed on the rights of another disturbed the order of the adet and brought about trouble. The forest, though claimed by the members of a village as belonging to them, and not to neighbouring humans, was shared equally with other creatures who could be offended if they were ignored, and who could bring misfortunes on people who neglected or injured their interests.

Most members of a Melanau village were in fact related to one another by kinship, but membership of the village was with the consent of the ruling aristocrats and not by virtue of a kinship link.[3] Total strangers could and did join the village by marriage or invitation, but the people of the village did not think of it, either *de jure* or *de facto*, as a kinship group. It was a territorial group, corporate in as far as it owned a defined and defended territory and possessed a common adet which in details differed from one village to another. This adet was the principal unifying symbol of the village and was the collective responsibility of the aristocratic elders, among whom one was sometimes designated to act for specific purposes on behalf of the village (Appell, 1971a). In some villages unity was also expressed by guardian spirits, untypically invited to live there. In every village a ritual, the *kaul*, was performed each year to cleanse it of spirits who had illegitimately trespassed and taken up residence in a purely human domain.

The long-houses were abandoned in most Coastal Melanau villages during the late nineteenth century. When they moved from these houses people preferred to build their new separate dwellings beside those who had been their neighbours in the long-house. The result was a ribbon development along the river banks. Each new village was called a *kapong*, a word for a new form of settlement borrowed from the Malay. It was divided into a number of sub-villages (also called kapong) most of which were derived from the separate long-houses that had formerly made up the village. These sub-villages maintained many of the cultural differences and some of the institutional ones of separate leadership of the former long-houses. Moreover, they were also like the long-houses in being composed of clusters of neighbours (*a-sega*), who were in fact often close kinsmen (a-sega) as well. These small local groupings of neighbours were in theory, and often in practice, made up of people of the same rank. Within a village the cultural differences that distinguished the sub-villages, especially those differences of speech, were seen as important, though in relation to other villages they were ignored, and outsiders alleged that they could not perceive them. The Melanau explicitly used language to differentiate social groups; and every village took a pride in its own distinctive accent and dialect words.

The physical plan of these new villages differed from that of the long-house villages; but the principles behind them were the same. In the long-houses field slaves had been allowed to maintain separate households, which were supposed, though not always in practice, to be at each end of the long-house, said to be the more dangerous situation in the case of an attack. In the new kapong, slaves were often settled in separate sub-villages usually downstream on a ritually less desirable site, where they were placed between the main settlement and newcomers, such as the Malay traders who came as agents for merchants in Sarawak. Eventually these Malay traders intermarried with the Melanau; and Muslim sub-villages developed by a process of natural increase and conversion. At a later date when Chinese traders settled in the villages they, too, built their houses downriver as a rule from the new Muslim sub-villages.

These new settlements, composed of sub-villages each with its own characteristics and in some respects independent, varied in size between 300 or 400 and 1,000 people. The linking of sub-villages and the addition of new ones as the population grew, made it easy for separate villages to coalesce physically, though not structurally. This process was particularly noticeable on the Tillian river, a tributary of the Mukah, where formerly long-house villages had clustered rather closer to one another than the normal three or four miles between settlements. By 1950 the Tillian river villages had become a continuous ribbon of houses, extending three or four miles on each bank of the stream with a population of some 8,000 persons.

(ii) *Kinship*

The Melanau system of kinship reckoning is a bilateral or cognatic one in which the connexion with relatives on both the father's and the mother's sides of the family are more or less equally stressed in regulating social relations. The categories used by a Melanau for classifying his relatives are based on two main principles; the one a principle of classifying by generation, and the other, one of classifying by collateral remoteness from an individual. These categories are reflected in the kinship terminology which provides, as it were, an outline map to guide an individual in his expectations from and behaviour to different classes of relatives.[4]

The Principle of Generation

The classification of relatives by generation has the virtue, in the eyes of a Melanau, of ensuring that he does not offend against the adet in matters of respectful behaviour and sexual relations, and so incur social and supernatural penalties. All members of a senior generation are elders, a-nyat: disrespect (*tulah*), (which includes improper sexual relations), towards elders can vary in its consequences with the nature of the act. Any disrespectful action is *palei*, that is to say ritually improper; and as such disturbs the principle of order in the world that is embodied in the adet regulating the actions of all beings, human and non-human alike. Whom an individual may not marry is therefore prescribed in the classification of kinsmen.

Sexual relations, and consequently marriage, with any relative (except a second cousin) whom an individual considers to be close (a-sega), and to whom he applies kin terms, are disrespectful, and therefore ritually improper. Copulation with individuals in the individual family is so seriously improper and supernaturally dangerous that it is placed in a separate category, *subang*. The term for this type of incest is also used for sexual relations with the parents' siblings, but the danger of palei actions of this kind is less serious than it is within the immediate family. Similarly, improper sexual relations with other more distant kin, though palei, do not attract penalties under the adet administered by the aristocratic elders. Nevertheless, supernaturally caused misfortune is expected to follow, even if the individuals concerned have attempted to evade the impropriety by reclassifying themselves in the kinship system, so that they are either members of the same generation or distant relations to whom kinship terms are not applied, and with whom sexual relations are permitted.

The genealogical network which links an individual with his relatives constitutes his *susun*. This network is made up of a great many possible lines that lead back to particular ancestors. Such lines are called *laian*. Two related individuals, for instance, belong not merely to a kinship category such as cousin, but also to a laian that leads to their common forbear. The degree to which an individual segments his susun depends on the social context, which is usually one in which the symbols of rank are in question. For most purposes the major segments of paternal and maternal lines are sufficient.

The Principle of Collateral Distance

The principle of respect is also combined by a Melanau with that of collateral distance from an individual, as it was with that of generation, in grouping the relatives in his kindred into categories that impose obligations and expectations on him. With himself at the centre of all the people whom he calls relative, a Melanau groups them into three named classes in which no distinctions are made between generations and paternal or maternal lines of descent. Closest to him is his individual family (*tagen*). Next are those whom he calls close relatives (a-sega) comprising relatives up to and including third cousins: these are the people to whom kinship terms are applied. And finally, there is the category of distant relatives (*a-suku* or *a-senei*). Many people are not certain how far this category extends, though most agree that fifth cousins, often said to be 'half-strangers, though still of the blood', fall into it. The term a-senei, according to certain informants, covers all those people, on both the father's and mother's lines of descent, who will suffer from bleeding of the gums if the unwarranted killing of the individual who links them is not avenged. Sixth and even more distant cousins do not normally count as relatives, but it is often said that though they are strangers (*a-ki*) or villagers (*a-kapong*) they are connected and should not be treated as complete strangers. The Melanau do not have a word equivalent to the English word connexion for such people, nor indeed do they have a word for relative or kindred.

These collateral categories, with the exception of the individual family, are not organized as corporate groups, and exist only in reference to an individual. The members are not the same for any two people, unless they happen to be full siblings. It therefore follows that any kinship groups recruited by an individual from the categories which make up his kindred can in the nature of things not be held together beyond his lifetime; and even in that time they are unlikely to develop strongly corporate characteristics. Such an Ego-centred kinship grouping is not a satisfactory vehicle for handling and preserving an undivided estate over a long period; and the problems of transmitting joint property held by such a group from one generation to the next are almost insuperable. In other words, Ego-centred kinship groups tend to be *ad hoc* groups for particular tasks, and when the task is done the group is likely to disperse.

An individual Melanau could without much difficulty raise a kinship group for a work-party, a wedding, or a burial, all tasks with a limited term; but he could not so easily raise one for the management of property over years or for permanently backing a political position. An aristocrat could expect to mobilize a group of villagers for a war-party or for a trading expedition, and the core of the group might well be a selection of relatives from his kindred; but he was unlikely to regard the group as kinsmen, even if in fact they were. He was more likely to think of them as neighbours, clients, or slaves. Moreover, when the task was completed, he would not be able to hold the group together, though he might expect a kind of loyalty and readiness to join him in future groups from a small core or clique of people in exchange for protection and possibly for sago palms to work on a shared basis.

The Principle of Descent

The principle of descent for recruiting long-enduring corporate kinship groups suffers from serious disadvantages in a bilateral kinship system not found in a unilineal kinship system. Where kinship is reckoned bilaterally, men and women normally have equal rights in holding property. They can very often hold it individually, and men and women alike can be full and equal members of property-owning corporations. Consequently, if an individual who first acquired an estate passes it on his death to be held in some form of joint tenure by all his descendants, then the descent group will be made up equally of men and women with equal rights in the property. Moreover, an individual may belong to a considerable number of such descent groups, the membership of which is partly shared by other similar groups. In a situation of this kind, conflicts of interest are likely to be very common; and it is almost impossible for such groups to develop strong corporate characteristics, unlike the lineages of unilineal systems where an individual may in general belong to only one lineage. It is not surprising, therefore, that cognatic descent groupings, even though their membership is as clearly defined by descent as it is a lineage, are relatively uncommon.[5]

The Melanau made little use of the principle of descent in managing or in transmitting property from one generation to the next, except in the ascription of rank and the right to use its symbols. Every individual was a member of one of three categories known as *basa*. In its widest connotation this word means a species, a kind, a race; but in this context it means an individual's rank. A system of rank categories that is superficially not unlike the ranks of aristocracy, middle classes, workers and slaves of other societies cuts across the system of kinship categories, and like it, is not a system of corporate groups. In theory rank only passes down the male line.[6] An ancestor who first acquired certain symbols of rank for use on ceremonial occasions, notably weddings, could, strictly speaking, pass the right to use those symbols on his death only to his sons; but in practice he passed it to all his descendants, through both sons and daughters. It was not long before these descendants were unable even to guess who else could claim the right to use the symbols, or what lines of descent might be used to reach the first or an intermediate ancestor whose right to use them was undisputed. The only sense in which the members of the grouping could be said to be corporate was that all shared a right to use certain specified symbolic property and could object if a stranger claimed it. The members never met to safeguard or forward the purposes of the group as such; individuals were personally responsible for asserting and defending their rights. No representative was ever appointed to act on behalf of the whole membership, except that at a wedding the bride's father invited aristocratic elders to accept the bridewealth on his behalf and, in collaboration with the elders bringing it from the bridegroom's family, to make sure that all claims were valid.

Similar groupings, derived from descent but not overtly linked with the system of rank, also existed in connexion with items of food that were forbidden to all descendants of the individual who originally came under a prohibition against eating the particular food. These items of food (*barang palei*), ritually improper things, were associated with myths accounting for the prohibition; and, though not regarded as such, were in some degree indicators of rank. The ideal of rank endogamy implied that all the descendants of a man or woman belonged to the same rank; but these descendants, though bound together by a common prohibition, scarcely constituted a group, except that all were obliged to observe the same prohibition on pain of death or serious illness after eating the forbidden food. Like the members of the descent grouping claiming common symbols of rank, the members of a prohibited food group usually did not know one another, and never on any occasion met as a group. Moreover, it was possible to become free of the prohibition.

No other categories or groupings in Melanau society were mustered on the principle of descent, except some members of a family household. In the handling of property, whether tangible or intangible, the only groups with any marked corporate characteristics were the family household and the village itself. The latter, as we have already seen, was not considered to be a kinship group.

The household, which in the long-house was given the same name as the apartment (*suked*) and as the separate dwelling (*kubou*) in the new villages, was not a highly corporate group. An individual family (*tagen*), of which the legal owner of the apartment was a member, constituted the core of the household, which might also include the separate tagen of married children, lodgers, and, in some households, slaves. A married couple was usually treated as a separate tagen when it catered separately, though in practice the line between tagen was often hard to draw precisely. The household held no joint property on behalf of all its members; and though their welfare was in a sense a joint responsibility, its legal and political rights were the sum total of its members, in as far as they chose to exercise the rights for the benefit of all. The one partial exception related to property rights acquired by a man and woman during their marriage. Such property was held jointly by husband and wife for the duration of the marriage, and until the death of one spouse was no concern of other members of the tagen or the wider household. Because long-houses were seldom rebuilt, the apartments were very crowded, and even though they formed the most enduring element of the household group, an apartment was owned individually, usually by only one person, as inherited property, unless the apartment, having been built during a marriage, was marital property.

The stability of the household group did not wholly depend on the stability of the marriage of the owner of the apartment; for even if a divorce took place (which could happen at the suit of either the husband or the wife) the group was normally sufficiently large to allow it to continue to function as a group. A first marriage was arranged by the parents of the bride and groom. Negotiations, with the help of a go-between, were begun by a young man's parents, who approached the parents of a suitable bride, preferably a second cousin of the same rank and generation as the groom, and normally of the same village and economic standing. On the death of a parent the marital property (*serian*) was equally divided between the surviving spouse and the children, each child taking an equal share, regardless of sex or religion. All property which had come to the deceased parent by inheritance (*pesaka*), or which had been acquired before marriage, was divided equally only among the children. This fragmentation of property in every generation therefore meant that marriages had to be carefully arranged, especially among the upper ranks, to preserve an estate sufficient to maintain a proper position. Among the aristocrats, in particular, although a marriage was more often than not arranged to accumulate an adequate estate for the young couple in the village of their birth, nevertheless, considerations of a political alliance with other villages might override the preference for village endogamy. In 1950, three-quarters of the married people living in Medong, a village on the river Oya had been born and married in that village. In a sample of 161 out of a total of 255 current marriages in the village, 56 per cent were household matrilocal, 32 per cent patrilocal in residence and 12 per cent were resident in houses belonging to sons, grandsons, affines, or strangers. Most marriages were monogamous, though under the adet a man could, with the consent of his first wife, take a second wife into the household. Normally the request led to the first wife's divorcing her husband, who left the household if she were the owner. In 1950 only two men in Medong were married to more than one woman; in both cases there were only two wives. A survey of 217 marriages in the village showed that 64 per cent of the pagans and 67 per cent of the Muslims had married only once; 24 per cent and 23 per cent twice; and 12 per cent and 10 per cent more than twice (Morris, 1953: 53–81).

(iii) *Rank*

When a Melanau child is born it belongs to a rank (basa) which may be that of an aristocrat (menteri), a freeman (bumi) or a slave (dipen). These categories, like those of kinship, are not corporate groups; and, because a child is automatically ascribed the rank of its father, rank and kinship are intricately connected with one another. An individual's genealogical network (susun) and the lines of descent (laian) which make it up are closely connected with a particular rank, namely that of the ancestor to whom, however directly or indirectly, the laian ascends. In theory marriage ought never to occur between members of different ranks; and, if the preferred marriage with a second cousin were always observed, not only would the rank categories remain unmixed, but neither would it greatly matter that the theory of ascribing rank, or, more exactly, of using symbols that have come down from an ancestor only through the male line, was not always observed. A preferred marriage ought also to ensure that the rule of strict endogamy within the theoretically caste-like ranks is observed, and to make certain that the lines of descent, the laian, are, as the Melanau say 'joined again'.

In practice rank endogamy appears never to have been more than an ideal and a tendency; for there always seem to have existed formalized methods of crossing the rank barriers. The three ranks were sub-divided, and in both the Oya and the Mukah rivers there were in fact five basa, each distinguished by 1950 by name and the right to use certain symbols at weddings, and rather less importantly at birth and death ceremonies and on other minor occasions. A man acquired wealth and position by claiming high rank; but members of different ranks were not distinguishable by specific sub-cultures. In 1950 all the Melanau were peasants with very minor variations in life-styles.

The aristocratic category was divided into *basa pengiren*, limited to individuals descended from the Muslim Brunei aristocratic families that had settled at the mouths of the rivers, and *basa menteri*, comprising the highest rank of pagans and those of their number who had been converted to Islam. In 1950 in Medong there were no representatives of basa pengiren but the members of basa menteri formed 9 per cent of the total population of the village.

The rank of freeman was also sub-divided into two sub-categories: *basa bumi*, sometimes known as *basa bumi ateng* or the true *bumi*; and *basa bumi giga'*, the freemen who may be summoned, *giga'* (in contrast to the true freemen who have to be invited, *megam*), to work or to help aristocrats or other freemen in agricultural or other tasks. Most of the bumi giga' were in fact freed slaves. In Medong 43 per cent of the population were true freemen and 36 per cent freed slaves, the total category amounting to 79 per cent of the people of the village.

Although slavery and all forms of bond service were formally abolished by the Rajah of Sarawak in 1928, the institution had been in decay among the Coastal Melanau, under pressure from the Rajah's administrative officers, for several decades before then. Nevertheless in 1950 those who were slaves by origin were still known and numbered 7 per cent of the total population of Medong.[7] In other villages the number of slaves was higher and on average amounted to about 10 per cent of the Melanau of the Oya river. Slaves were either people born into slavery or those who were captured in war, or who had been forced into slavery by debt or by being left orphans without kinsmen or other guardians. Slaves were of two kinds: house-slaves (*dipen dagen lebu'*), who lived in the household of their owner; and field or outside slaves (*dipen ga'luer*) who owed services of various kinds, but who were permitted to live separately in their own house-holds and apartments.

Although a slave was in a certain sense a chattel, in that he or she could formerly be passed from one household to another as an item of bridewealth or could be sacrificed at the final interment of the owner, nevertheless he could own property in his own right and could also buy his own freedom.[8] The redemption or ransom of the rank of a slave (*terbuyh basa*) was by set stages, each step (*tirih*) marked by a fixed weight of brassware, which was also the bride-wealth that the owner, acting in *loco parentis*, could claim on the marriage of a female slave.[9] This public demonstration of a slave's exact status brought it into line with the other ranks, in which an individual's status was also publicly shown at the marriage of a daughter in the bridewealth, also measured by the weight of brass-ware, which the father could claim.

Moreover, as with slaves, anybody could redeem his rank and raise his status by giving extra brassware as bridewealth. A freed slave about to marry a true freewoman could 'redeem his rank' and become bumi ateng by giving brassware, known as 'the nine steps' (*ulan betirih*) before handing over the bridewealth at his wedding. Similarly a true freeman could raise his rank at his wedding by giving 'the fifteen steps' (*limah belah betirih*) thus becoming menteri, though of a second-class kind not able, strictly speaking, to claim the use of the aristocratic sword at his daugher's wedding.[10]

The ideal formulation made by the Melanau of their ranking system would have led to social consequences that were not in fact found. If the theory were strictly followed, the rank categories would be endogamous groups, and it would not be unreasonable to expect to find that the systems of status based on kinship, economic, ritual and political power tended to coincide with the system of rank status. By 1950, whatever may have been the situation a hundred years earlier, this did not occur; and, in spite of the high value put on the minutiae of the rank system, no Melanau deceived himself in believ-ing that it worked as described. It is sufficient, informants said 'for the pronunciation of the adet to be observed'. Moreover, although a man might say, 'We, the basa menteri, do this or that', he was not referring to a group of individuals with a corporate existence who met together to forward their own interests. Rather, he was referring to a hierarchy of values, or what might perhaps be called a blueprint of proper behaviour that might or might not be realized in practice.

The question therefore arises, what is the use in a small-scale society of such an elaborate ranking system? One answer may be found in the way the various institutions worked in conjunction with one another to allow the people to exploit an inhospitable environment. Traditionally, the Melanau economic and ranking systems, together with the organized groups and leaders provided by the political and kinship systems, facilitated trade by setting a section of the population relatively free from the tasks of farming and hunting and gathering in order to organize protection and large trading expeditions for essential commodities. But such an answer is far from conclusive; for the same ends were achieved by other people in Sarawak, as, for example, the Iban or the Land Dayak whose societies made use of many of the same structural principles as were used by the Melanau, but without that of ranking.

The Political System

Before the Brooke conquest of the coastal district in 1861 and the subsequent pacification of the area, the Melanau formulation of their rank system appears to have been closer to what in fact took place than happens today. Once peace was established and it was safe to work alone in the forest, a man could by sheer industriousness become rich. He could then, if he wished, by selecting suitable lines of descent, and with the assent of carefully chosen aristocratic friends, lay claim to a high-ranking status for himself; and so become one of the ruling elders of the village. Social climbing of this sort was not, of course, an innovation. The administration of the adet, and therefore the political control of the village, always had been in the hands of a group of aristocratic elders. No single elder was superior to the others, though he might have special knowledge that fitted him for particular tasks. A man with unusual skill in war was put in charge of raids and the defence of a long-house in an attack. There are many well-known cases of men of low rank who were called on to lead the village when there was no aristocrat of equal ability.[11] But leadership of this or any other kind was not formalized as a permanent office, and there were no single political chiefs who ruled villages as of personal right.[12] Occasionally a leader of outstanding influence arose who was able to persuade the elders of his own village, and even others, usually on the same river, to follow him; so that during his life he acted as a great political leader. But his power rested on alliances that invariably dissolved at his death.

This problem of, so to speak, *ad hoc* leadership is closely related to the kinship system in which relationships are organized bilaterally. An individual may possibly be able to mobilize a group of kinsmen, with himself as the rallying point, for a continuing task; but his successor, with a different kindred, will have to raise a band of different people, whose only real interest in the task, apart from the conventions and reciprocal bonds of kinship, may be in what the leader can offer them. In the conditions of the Melanau economic system the development of any corporate interests and the continuity of such groups become difficult. A Melanau aristocrat could expect to raise a group, based perhaps on a core of kinsmen, for a war party, making a sago garden, or for a trading expedition; but he could not rely on holding the group together for any length of time. In Brunei and other Malay sultanates, where the rank and kinship systems did not differ in essentials from that of the Melanau, aristocrats were able to hold a permanent following of retainers by offers of continuing economic advantages; but, as with the Melanau, the division of an estate at a death among all the children presented leaders in every generation with the problem of finding the means of keeping a following together. In Melanau society no single leader was ever able to consolidate a large enough economic basis to allow him to outstrip his peers and ensure a continuity of dominance for his children.

Before the Brooke administration put an end to raiding and warfare, the political and economic power of the aristocrats was probably greater than it was subsequently. Although any villager had the right to fell virgin forest and make a sago plantation, usually it was only an aristocrat who could recruit the guards needed for any prolonged work away from the village. In 1861 most sago plantations seem to have been owned by aristocrats, though in theory there was nothing to prevent anybody from owning land. In 1950 the aristocrats of one village in the river Oya owned 75 per cent of the cultivated land, whereas in another village, which, in contrast with the first, had specialized for the past sixty years in growing sago for the cash market, the commoners had gone into the forest and cut out plantations, and the aristocrats owned only 23 per cent of the cultivated land against 71 per cent held by other ranks. On the other hand the average holding of an aristocrat in the latter village was almost 16 acres per head against an acreage of less than 5 per head for the other ranks (Morris, 1953:80–2).

Although sago and not rice was traditionally the staple crop of the Coastal Melanau, the annual cultivation of rice was nevertheless an important feature of economic life, and was controlled by the aristocratic elders. In all Melanau villages two or three large areas on raised river banks were cleared of trees and set aside for rice farming on a two or three year cycle. These fields were large enough for each household in the village to have a strip for growing a year's supply of rice.

The clearing of the land, its division into strips, the organization of labour and protection from enemies while working it, and the rituals to mark the opening of the season's work and the commencement of the harvest were under the direct supervision of the elders. Each separate household (even those of field slaves permitted to live in their own households) had a right to be allotted a strip for one year to cultivate and harvest for its own use. On the other hand no household had the right to any particular piece of land in the current or any subsequent rotation. There was nothing to prevent the members of a household from clearing unclaimed ground elsewhere in the village's territory for a rice farm; but a single individual, even an aristocrat and elder, was unlikely to be able to raise sufficient protection from enemies to contract safely out of the traditional scheme of communal cultivation. With the disappearance of dangerous enemies after 1880 the situation changed, and, as single individuals were able to go alone in safety into the forest and build a fortune by their own efforts, the control of the aristocrats diminished. Added to the loss of their role as organizers of the export trade, their effective power declined, though their prestige lingered on and was still an important aspect of the political system in 1950. To be politically effective any powerful man in a village eventually took steps to establish aristocratic status for himself.

The accounts of trading expeditions in the late eighteenth and early nineteenth centuries, organized by their grandfathers and great-grandfathers, were still remembered by old men and women in 1950. On these expeditions sago, in the form of baked biscuit, together with jungle products, was carried in sailing boats to Brunei, Pontianak, Johore, Singapore and Sumatra. It is in this context that the institution of slavery becomes important. The fact that the sago palm is harvested all the year round meant that the men in an ordinary household could be set free only for short periods, which were, it is true, sufficient for short trading trips up and down the river to collect salt and dried fish and timber, but which were not long enough to allow the men to go on voyages that sometimes extended to several months. It is significant that in the villages of the Melanau and the other stratified societies of Borneo for which information exists, normally the aristocrats and slaves formed about 10 per cent of the total population.[13] The establishment of Singapore at the beginning of the nineteenth century as an international market for sago flour, rather than baked sago biscuit, set afoot changes that ultimately undermined the ranking system of the Coastal Melanau, and led to the conquest of the district by James Brooke.

Until the conquest, the Sultan's representatives from Brunei had controlled most of the sago trade because they controlled the mouths of the rivers; but with the growth of the market in Singapore, Malay shipowners and carriers from Kuching and Singapore began to call more frequently at the Melanau coastal ports for sago flour. As they were not infrequently hindered in obtaining cargoes, they began, well before 1840, to settle agents, usually Muslim Malays from Kuching, in the villages upriver in order to buy flour directly at the source. The Brunei merchants had never bothered to do this, and the competition of merchants from Kuching had already produced bad feeling before James Brooke even arrived in Sarawak. The new Muslim settlers in the Melanau villages married local pagan women and continued the process of conversion which had made rather little progress in the three to four centuries during which the Brunei settlers had been living in the small towns at the mouths of the rivers.[14] The Malay merchants living in the upriver villages also took away the function of the pagan aristocrats as the organizers of overseas trade. By 1950 there was no memory in the villages of the Oya river of any large aristocratically-organized trading expedition later than about 1830.

After Brooke's conquest of the coastal district, the export of sago flour was almost wholly routed through Kuching. But the flour bought from the Melanau villages was poor in quality and needed further refinement before being sold in Singapore. The Malay merchants from Kuching were mainly carriers and did not refine the flour bought on the coast. Chinese merchants and one European firm, the Borneo Company, bought it from them and refined it in factories in Kuching or even in Singapore. When these merchants moved their factories to the sago-growing areas they took with them Chinese agents and traders who rapidly displaced their Malay predecessors, who had pioneered the business of buying produce from the Melanau and setting up retail shops for selling the many new types of consumer goods that were beginning to be imported from Singapore.

From about 1820 until just after World War II, the general structure of the Melanau sago trade was shaped by the need of the Singapore market for cheap industrial starch and did not alter in essentials, although different people took over the refining and export of the crude flour produced in the Melanau villages. The power of the Muslim families from Brunei was undermined when they lost the revenue from the sago trade; but the loss was compensated for in part by the new administrative arrangements made by the Government of Sarawak. The Rajah's principal concern with the Melanau villages was to preserve law and order so that a regular revenue could be drawn from the sago trade. He therefore interfered with traditional political and social arrangements as little as possible. He placed European officers in charge at the mouths of the Oya and Mukah rivers; and because Sarawak, under the original grant from the Sultan of Brunei, was officially a Muslim state, he drew most of his assistant Native Administrative Officers from the Brunei families whose members had previously controlled the sago trade. For administrative convenience too, the Rajah soon appointed headmen, with the Malay title *tua kampong*, to all the Melanau villages. In the early days these headmen were normally selected by the Native Officers, sometimes in consultation with the aristocratic elders. They usually chose a Muslim trader settled in the village to be headman. In the course of time one of the aristocratic elders was more often chosen, but even today a headman's powers are thought by the villagers to rest solely on the administration and police force, and to have little to do with the traditional adet which he normally administers. In practice he does so in consultation with the other elders and performs most of his other official duties with their advice and co-operation.

The Rajah's only direct intervention in the sago industry was to make a few regulations to improve the quality of crude flour produced in the villages, by stipulating the use of straining cloths and of standard weights and measures. With the arrival of Chinese buyers and retail traders additional regulations were made to control some of their trade practices and to prevent them from acquiring Melanau sago land; for conflict between the immigrant Chinese and the Melanau soon became quite serious. In an attempt to control the situation all Chinese traders were forbidden to live in the villages, and were directed to settle in a few designated bazaars that were in effect new Chinese villages. Although these regulations made it difficult for the Chinese to live in the long-houses or the new-style Melanau villages that were growing up, they did not succeed in keeping the traders, the shops, and the factories out of the villages. In the final count the Melanau themselves wanted their services. Moreover, as time went on they gave up a large part of their traditional subsistence economy in favour of expanding the acreage of sago plantations and producing flour for cash. By the end of the century they had become peasants, dependent on an international market in starch for obtaining the cash with which they bought most of the necessities of life. By 1890 the annual export of sago flour from the coastal district reached a level that remained roughly constant until the Japanese conquest in 1941. From 1861 until the end of the century the financial stability of Sarawak had been founded and developed on the revenues obtained from the Melanau sago trade.

The growth of Singapore as a market for sago flour, and not as a market for the sago biscuit that had traditionally been exported by the Melanau, set in motion forces of change that eventually undermined the traditional structure of Melanau society. But these forces worked slowly, and in 1950 it was still possible for the elders of the villages to say 'We do not throw away our adet.' By this they meant that, although there had been changes in the form of their villages, and that traditional clothing and economic exchanges were different, nevertheless the formal structure of their society remained what it had been a hundred years earlier. In the main the elders were right in their assertion. The structural principles underlying the economic, the political, the kinship, and the ranking systems, though subjected for over a century to new pressures, had not as yet shifted sufficiently to produce a new structural balance. In the years following 1950 a few technical innovations in the sago industry tipped the balance, so to speak; and today the traditional structure of Melanau society is rapidly vanishing. The most important of these innovations was the introduction by Chinese factory owners of simple and cheap machinery which made it possible to process sago flour entirely in factories, so that the role of the Melanau was reduced to that of growing the palms and selling them to merchants. Many were forced to sell their land and emigrate as landless peasants, or seek temporary work elsewhere in Sarawak. The new structure of Melanau society that is emerging in the coastal district is in many respects very different from the traditional one that survived until 1950, though, of course, a great number of the structural variables are still the same, but with a different importance.

NOTES

1. *Padi paya* in Sarawak Malay. Unless specifically noted all indigenous terms in this article are in the Malay dialect of the Oya Melanau language.

2. See, for example, map in possession of Sarawak Museum with the following: 'Insulae Indiae Orientalis Praecipuae in quibas Molluccae celeberrime sunt.' Note on this map reads 'This map must have been compiled subsequently to 1541 for the meridian of Corvo has evidently been taken as the first meridian . . . Published about 1595. Date of map about 1569.'

3. In point of fact a Melanau belonged to his village, as a rule by birth; but in contrast with the Iban a stranger coming into the village even without kinship links did become a member. The situation was more like that in a Land Dayak village where any outsider with the consent of the villagers could settle in it. In effect both the Iban and Land Dayak systems encouraged incomers; for with traditional swidden cultivators there is usually a greater shortage of manpower than of land. In the Melanau system the greater constraint in the welcome of strangers reflects, as it were, the halfway situation between swidden and sedentary agriculture where capitalized land rather than labour is of prime importance. Cp. Freeman (1970) and Geddes (1954a).

4. The system of kinship terminology of the Melanau is similar to that used by many other peoples of Borneo.
(i) Kin are classified by generation, and, omitting the individual family and affines, kinship terms are limited to five in number: grandparents and collaterals of their generation (*tipou*); parents, siblings and all collaterals of their generation (*tua*); cousins (*jipou*); children of siblings and cousins (*naken*); own grandchildren and all children of naken (*sou*).
(ii) The terminology is of the type called 'lineal' but has classifying features. The speaker's individual family is set apart by special terms: father (*tama*); mother (*tina*); sibling (*janak*); child (*anak*).

(iii) Collateral relatives of all generations are merged into categories, the boundaries of which are not always strictly defined. The individual is at the centre of all these people whom he acknowledges as relatives, who therefore constitute a kindred (Freeman, 1961). In the Melanau language, this category of relatives, the kindred, has no special name, but is negatively defined by names for people who are not kindred, not relatives, but who are strangers (*a-ki*), or villagers (*a-kapong*).

(iv) Affinal relatives are set apart terminologically from blood relatives, but the terms are limited to four: parent-in-law and, if necessary, their siblings (*metua*); sibling-in-law (*ma'it*); child-in-law (*benatou*); spouse (*sawa*). The relationships summarized in these terms, except those with the spouse, tend to be formal, and are often considered difficult. Although affinal terms may be extended to the spouse's relatives, wherever possible such persons are placed in a category of blood relative. In the small, largely endogamous community of a Melanau village, most individuals are in fact blood relatives, and if the preferred marriage with any second cousin is regularly followed, then the reasons for keeping the number of acknowledged affinal relationships to a minimum can readily be appreciated.

(v) Terms of address are few and reflect the principles of generation and respect: grandfather and males of his generation (*ipum*); grandmother and females of her generation (*ine'*); father (*apa', pa'*), or formerly (*amam*); mother (*ma'*) or formerly (*ina'*); parent's siblings (*wa*); child, and, on occasion, any member of a younger generation (*ido'*). Today most of these terms of address, except ma' and pa' are obsolescent, and personal names are used. The names of parents-in-law must never be used and as a rule a member of a senior generation is not addressed by name, for it might be disrespectful to do so.

5. Cp. Appell (1971a). See also Geddes (1954a, 1954b) where cognatic descent groupings among the Land Dayak are described. It is worth observing that Land Dayak descent groupings are very lightly corporate in nature, and that their functions are limited to allocating the use of jointly held land (and to *one* member for growing hill rice over a period of one year after it has been left to lie fallow for 10 to 12 years). The groups have no other function, and the members do not elect officers or even necessarily know the full extent of the membership. Each member is required to validate his claim to cultivate the land if he makes a claim to use it.

6. The word *laian* (see p. 44) is based on the root *lai* ('male') though in practice a particular laian may pass through women, as for example, in tracing connexion with a matrilateral cross cousin (*jipou laian tina*).

7. The total population of Medong in 1950 was 904 persons. The 5 per cent of the population not included in the percentages quoted in the text was made up of foreigners or those who for a variety of reasons could not be classified.

8. From 1870 onwards there were many cases in the district courts at Mukah and Oya in which the right of a slave under traditional adet to his own sago plantations was successfully affirmed against aristocrats; and even more cases on disputes about the price already paid and still owing for the redemption of a slave (see *Sarawak Gazette* 1872 onwards).

9. The Malay word *tebus* is cognate with the Melanau *tebuyh*, and means 'to redeem or ransom, especially of getting things out of pawn and acquiring debt-slaves [by handing over the amount of the debt to the creditor]' (Wilkinson, 1959: 1181).

10. For a detailed account of the connexion between the formal and the actual rank and kinship systems see Morris (1953:51–107).

11. Cp. Boyle (1865:284–5). 'The Kennowit chieftain, Joke, . . . was born a slave, and remains so, I believe, to this moment; nevertheless, he has been elected to

preside over a considerable clan, and is followed in the field by a hundred free warriors . . . Hereditary rank is very little regarded among them in comparison with actual superiority . . . the unworthy scion of ten generations will be readily ousted in favour of a low-born hero.'

12. Cp. Rousseau (1974a). The Kayan and the Kenyah peoples of the interior districts differed from the Coastal Melanau in having highly institutionalized offices of village chiefs, selected from a group of aristocrats, whose powers, though limited in certain respects and by the threat of deposition, were very considerable.

13. Cp. Rousseau (1974a). A long-established and economically important exchange of forest products for goods manufactured in coastal Malay cities or by people overseas existed in the interior groups; and in the societies in which ranking systems were found, the trade was largely monopolized by the aristocrats, who, like the Melanau aristocrats, were partly set free by a system of slavery and labour contributed by ordinary villagers.

14. So little had the Brunei settlers been concerned to convert local pagans that in 1900 over one-third of the population of the village of Oya at the mouth of the river were still unconverted. By 1950 there were no pagans at all left in the village. The Rajah was so anxious to maintain peace and productivity in the Melanau sago district that he prevented Christian missionaries from establishing any stations in the area until 1900, when he permitted the Roman Catholics to open a mission in Mukah.

3

THE SELAKO DAYAK*

WILLIAM M. SCHNEIDER

THE Selako Dayak are an ethnic group numbering approximately 10,000 persons. Many of them live in long-houses. They still practise their indigenous religion and subsist on the cultivation of hill and swamp rice as well as other garden crops. Selako are divided more or less evenly between the Malaysian state of Sarawak and the Indonesian province of Kalimantan Barat. However, those in Sarawak are all either immigrants or descendants of immigrants who have moved over the Pueh Range from Kalimantan during the past 150 years (Kaboy and Sandin, 1968). Hudson on the basis of a linguistic survey describes the Selako as 'ranging from southern Sambas in Kalimantan Barat to Lundu District in Sarawak's First Division' (1970:301). Those of western Lundu District are the only Selako in Sarawak.

There is reason to believe that the Selako are the northernmost of a number of very closely related ethnic groups stretching a considerable distance into Kalimantan Barat. Word lists (Hudson, 1970) for several groups from this province are virtually identical to Selako, and Selako informants indicate that there are only slight differences in pronunciation between the languages of some of these groups (e.g. Selako and Banana'). Differences in custom law are described as equally small.

The Selako language is also closely related to Malay and Iban although this does not extend quite to mutual intelligibility. Hudson (1970) proposes that Selako be included in a group of languages for which he suggests the term 'Malayic Dayak' to indicate those languages descended from 'proto-Malayic', but spoken by non-Muslim peoples of Borneo.

Like most of the non-Muslim groups of Borneo, the Selako are an inland rather than a coastal people. Many villages both in Sarawak and Kalimantan include expanses of low-lying swampy plain on which the villagers cultivate swamp rice in permanent plots. This

* The research on which this paper is based was carried out between October 1969 and July 1971 under the sponsorship of the Sarawak Museum and the University of North Carolina at Chapel Hill. It was funded by a National Science Foundation Graduate Fellowship and a National Science Foundation Dissertation Research Grant.

is always in addition to swidden cultivation of rice and other crops on upland slopes. Much of the area, particularly above 1,000 feet, is covered in dense forest on which Selako rely for a great deal of their food and other resources.

Rice cultivation is the dominant economic activity of Selako, and its demands order the yearly calendar of individual and group effort. Much of Selako religious practice is based on a rice cult concerned with the successful planting, growth, harvest and storage of the rice crop. Selako cultivate many other crops as well. Cucumbers, radishes, pumpkins and other gourds are grown in the swiddens, and cassava, raised in small gardens, is an important rice substitute. Maize is grown primarily as a cash crop.

Trees of various species such as rambutan, banana, illipe nut, citrus, coconut, areca and other palms produce fruits, oils, sap, leaves and bark for food and manufacturing. The illipe nut harvest provides a large cash inflow on an irregular basis every few years. Rubber and pepper are the most important cash crops and both have been cultivated for many decades.

Gathering and hunting are also important. Women spend much of their time gathering wild vegetable foods, particularly leaves and berries. Dyes, ropes, rattan, bamboo, leaves for packaging and roofs, wood for fuel, building material and tools are all-important forest products. Wild pig is the most important game, but other animals, such as anteaters, tortoises, pythons, lizards, monkeys and gibbons are occasionally taken. Pigs, gibbons and monkeys are frequently killed while raiding crops. Most men hunt sporadically, and a few spend hundreds of hours a year in the forest. The men also gather honey.

Until very recently the only domesticated food animals were pigs and chickens. These are consumed only in a ritual context (unlike wild animals). Dogs and cats are also kept. Selako have no draft animals.

The data on which this paper is based were gathered during field research carried out primarily in two neighbouring Sangkuku' Selako villages in Sarawak (see below). However, brief visits to other Selako villages in Sarawak and conversations with informants indicate that the social system described here is or has been shared by all the Sarawak Selako as well as some or all of the Kalimantan Selako.

The two villages studied are unique in at least two respects. Their lands include a strip of coastline several miles long on their northern border. This results in the inclusion of beach and mangrove terrain which is not present in other Sarawak Selako villages. The coastal environment, however, appears to have had little effect on their social system in spite of a hundred-year residence in the area. Less than half-a-dozen families own even small boats; and little use is made of maritime resources except for occasional beach gathering.

The second distinctive characteristic of these villages, and the primary reason for their selection as a research site, is the continuing high percentage of their residents dwelling in long-houses. This is likely the result of their relative isolation as compared to the other Sarawak Selako villages, all of which have easy access to the Lundu-Sematan highway.

Social Organization

Kinship, locality and office are the principal strands intertwined in the system of Selako social organization. These combine to produce the significant groups and categories of Selako. Although we separate these different strands in analysis of the system, it is important to be aware of the degree to which they are bound together. Kinship is a determining factor in residence decisions, so that the members of a long-house or hamlet tend to be near relatives, and there is always a higher degree of interrelatedness among the members of a village than there is across village boundaries. Residence decisions determine rights in corporate descent groups. A man achieves office with the help of his kinsmen and legitimates his claim to office by descent from a recent office-holder. A village achieves its status as village through possession of the requisite offices. Descent groups come into being, in part, from competition for office and are expressed through their localization in long-houses and hamlets. Kinship, locality and office are analytically separable, but in action become a single phenomenon.

Rank, in the sense of a stratified social order of difference in primary economic activity, does not exist in Selako society. Every able-bodied adult of the same sex performs similar daily subsistence tasks. But there are distinctions of relative status and wealth in Selako society. There are rich and poor, and Selako rank individuals relative to one another by reason of birth alone, albeit not in named classes. Relative status becomes important in terms of political action and eligibility for office. Its relevance should become more apparent in the discussion of office and descent groups.

There are four types of Selako groups that are localized, associated with specific territories. These are, from most inclusive to least inclusive: the *adat* group, the village, the *tumpuk* (long-house or hamlet), and the *biik*-family household. The adat group is a loose association of villages bound by ties of descent from common mother villages and a body of common ritual practice, lore and custom. A village is made up of a number of biik-families, some of which are grouped into tumpuk.

The village, the tumpuk and the biik-family are involved in a dynamic system of political interaction which is revealed only by examination of a village or group of villages over a time depth of several generations. At any one time most of the biik-families in a village are clustered together in several tumpuk. Tumpuk of any appreciable size (more than half-a-dozen biik-families) tend to be political factions in competition for village offices. They wax and wane in size with the political fortunes of the kin groups which form their nuclei. Thus, there are usually only one or two large, politically dominant tumpuk in a village at one time, and there are always a few isolated biik-houses or small tumpuk of two or three biik-families. These may in the past have been associated with larger tumpuk, but for the time being are not closely allied with any faction. Village fission occurs where one tumpuk comes to dominate village affairs, forcing others, unwilling to accept the situation, to follow their own officers.

The Biik-family: Household and Corporate Group

The Selako biik-family is the fundamental social unit of Selako society.[1] It is a corporate, property-owning group which persists through the generations. It is the primary unit of production and consumption, bears the responsibility for the socialization of children, and relates the individual to the wider Selako society.

The biik-family holds rights to land. It also owns the stock of rice stored from the previous harvest as well as items such as large Chinese jars, gongs, woven mats and heirloom jewellery. Along with these, the dwelling house itself, also termed biik (Schneider, 1975), and in some cases several other buildings, constitute the principal properties of the biik-family.

There is a body of special household ritual (*rukun*) which is specific to the biik-family and provides a charter for its existence as a social and spiritual entity. Special rice strains and paraphernalia related to the storage and handling of rice are identified with this household ritual, and these are all in the custodianship of the women of the household.

Biik-family structure and continuity are determined by the practice of the biik retaining some of its children after marriage and incorporating their new spouses. All Selako newly-wed couples reside after marriage in the biik-family of one of the partners to the marriage. But only one partner may remain permanently to inherit the biik with his or her spouse. This pattern of post-marital residence results in household structures and dynamics of family fission similar in broad outline to that described for the Iban by Freeman (1958).

The biik-family is the most enduring Selako social institution. Individual biik-families maintain their identity through the generations independently of particular villages or tumpuk. This continuity is conceived in terms of the passage of rice and associated household ritual and paraphernalia between women of succeeding generations. Most Selako reside after marriage with the family of the wife. Even for those who do not follow this ideal pattern, it is said that rice and ritual pass between women, husband's mother and son's wife. The younger woman adopts the household ritual of her mother-in-law. Thus, while it frequently happens that a son and his wife inherit the biik-family, in Selako minds the matrilineal continuity of the biik remains.

The leadership of the biik-family is always ritually vested in a single senior couple. The man is referred to as *tuha biik* ('biik elder'), although a widow may also be so labelled. The senior couple (or individual) gives up its post of authority when its contribution to the household declines noticeably relative to the younger generation.

There is a sharp division of labour in certain biik-family tasks. Men hunt and women gather. Women sow rice and weed while men clear fields and dibble. Women do tightly woven basketwork, but men do openwork with rattan. Thus, some baskets are the joint product of a man and woman. Men kill and butcher animals. They always serve as the family priest. They also represent the family's interests in political councils and legal disputes, although women sometimes participate in these, and the covert influence of women is occasionally made quite apparent even in village politics.

The pattern of post-marital residence in which one married child remains permanently to inherit the biik-family gives rise to a geographic cluster of related biik-families. These are the biik-families of siblings who have resided after marriage in their parents' biik-family. These form the core of long-houses and hamlets.

The Tumpuk: Long-house and Hamlet

Selako biik-families usually occur in localized clusters called tumpuk, each made up of from two to thirty or more families. Traditionally, a tumpuk comprised biik-families arranged linear-fashion in a long-house. Since the time of the Japanese Occupation, long-houses have gradually given way to hamlets of biik-families arranged in clumps associated with particular localities. These too are tumpuk. Their underlying principles of organization are essentially the same as those of long-houses, but relations between the component biik-families may be less frequent and intense.

The tumpuk is a political and ritual unit as well as a residential aggregate. It also has some economic functions and constitutes the key social environment in which most of the significant public events occur among Selako.

Ritual activity, although almost entirely sponsored by biik-families, draws on tumpuk resources and may involve all tumpuk members. These may contribute food and labour, act as officiants in ritual, serve as audience, and join in a communal meal. In certain types of ritual activity such as succession to office or the compromise of disputes by sacrifice and/or payment of fines, participation ratifies important legal, political or economic transactions.

Tumpuk also provide a labour pool from which task groups of various kinds are drawn. The most important of these, readily identifiable with the tumpuk, are the traditional co-operative labour groups formed during different stages of rice cultivation. These and other similar groups associated with modern government-assisted agricultural co-operatives are often explicitly identified with specific tumpuk. Other task groups, for example, in hunting or ritual, tend to be drawn from the tumpuk. This co-operation is partially a function of the localization of a large number of close relatives in the tumpuk, but it can be demonstrated that locality alone is an important variable here (Schneider, 1974b).

Each tumpuk is ideally headed by a *tuha rumah* (lit: 'house elder') who serves as a rather unobtrusive leader in community projects and the settlement of disputes. He represents the tumpuk interests in village councils and, in the absence of important village officers resident in the tumpuk, the house elder is its most important personage. His actual degree of authority in any circumstance is very low.

The importance of tumpuk as an institution and the identity of particular tumpuk are explicitly marked in Selako ritual. Every time a domestic pig is killed, the house elder, or a substitute, from each tumpuk represented at the ritual, is presented with a gift of cooked pork and rice. The identity of specific tumpuk is marked by the scheduling of important festivals. Festivals involving the sacrifice of pigs are scheduled by a village officer even though these festivals are sponsored by biik-families. This officer co-ordinates festive activities by restricting festivals to one tumpuk in the village on a given day. This allows visiting at important festivals by residents of the entire village.

The tumpuk as an institution is central to the structure of the society, but particular tumpuk are ephemeral. Against the backdrop of continuity inherent in the village and the biik-family, the tumpuk is most clearly seen as a temporary grouping of biik-families linked by ties of affinity and consanguinity through a time span of one or two generations. Tumpuk are not corporate groups, although they are residential manifestations of Selako corporate descent groups. Long-houses and hamlets coalesce around a group of closely related biik-families in the process of acquiring political power and office. Most of these families are related by descent from a recent common ancestor and thus share a common descent line (*katurunan*). Their joint estate consists of a fund of prestige and rights in land inherited from their common ancestor.

There is some evidence that this type of relationship between descent groups and long-house communities may be widespread in Borneo. Leach seems to indicate this situation in his *Social Science Research in Sarawak:*

In all the long-house communities which I was able to observe in any detail it was noticeable that political authority rested with a small group of closely related families the members of which had a more direct descent linkage with the ancestral founders of the house (or village) than other members of the community. . . . This *house owning group* is in general a limited extended family having a common ancestor two to three generations back [1950:61].

Although he explicitly avoids labelling the 'house owning group' as a descent group, this term seems valid for the dominant group of families in Selako tumpuk.

The residential alignment of a group of closely related biik-families in a tumpuk is to a great extent a function of post-marital residence practices. In the first few years after marriage the couple always resides with the natal biik of one of the spouses; but only one married child from a sibling set may remain permanently in the biik. Thus, in all biik where more than one sibling has taken up post-marital residence, this situation is only temporary. All but one married sibling must eventually establish their own independent biik-families. They quite commonly build their new residences beside their natal biik. In the past this would usually have been a new apartment in a long-house, but today a frequent practice is to build a separate house a few yards away in hamlet-fashion.

Small units of two or three biik related in this way are sprinkled throughout every Selako village, some forming tumpuk of their own, others embedded in larger groups. A unit of this kind co-operates very closely in economic affairs, sometimes even to the point of maintaining a joint estate in land, yet the component biik-families retain their independence.

A very few of these small groups of related biik manage to maintain their residential linkage into the third generation so that some biik in the group are related only by first cousin ties resulting from descent from a common set of grandparents. These units may maintain their residential linkages over several generations, sometimes amassing sufficient numbers to emerge as the core of a good size long-house or hamlet and become a political force in the village. Once established as a tumpuk of half-a-dozen or more biik, it may begin to attract other, more distantly related families that are not already involved in similar co-residential arrangements of their own. In this way large tumpuk, occasionally of two dozen or more biik, are formed as centres of political power that compete for office and authority within the village.

The key factor in the formation of a strong residential kin group of this kind is the activation of the descent line into a corporate descent group held together by a common interest (cf. Peranio, 1961). All Selako obviously possess numerous descent lines, but only a few ancestors are frequently selected for attention in this manner. A particular descent line may be cited to legitimate claims to high social status or to account for physical or personality attributes. Likewise descent from an ancestor who first cleared a plot of land may be noted to establish a claim to use that land.

Activation of a descent line into a corporate descent group occurs where an apical ancestor creates a fund of property composed of land and prestige that is preserved and increased by his descendants. An individual who clears, and thereby establishes title to quantities of land beyond the needs of his own biik-family increases his relative social standing and that of his biik and lays the foundations of a potential corporate descent group. Excess land may be loaned to others; it may also result in the biik-family's retention of a greater proportion of children after marriage than other biik-families, thus expanding the size of its tumpuk or coming to dominate its tumpuk. If, after the death of the couple who first cultivated the land, their children and other descendants do not divide the land but continue to hold it jointly while residing in different biik-families, then a corporate descent group including individuals in a number of biik-families is established. It should be observed that while all descendants of the apical ancestor inherit rights in his land, ordinarily these rights are exercised only by those descendants who reside after marriage with their natal biik-family, and these have priority over those who do not so reside.

The fund of property created by the ancestor is usually supplemented by descendants who create similar funds.[2] This, of course, results in a pool of excess land which is loaned to others and serves to attract other kinsmen to reside in the tumpuk of their patrons. Given the necessary personality attributes, the leader of this group may convert his prestige into village political office for himself and his followers. This further validates the social standing of the members of the descent group, thereby accruing more biik-families to the tumpuk and perhaps increasing the pool of land under their control.

Selako have no distinctive term for a corporate descent group of this kind, perhaps because only a minority of Selako belong to such groups; but they are sometimes referred to as katurunan. At one time or another virtually all biik-families enter into close relations with katurunan of this kind, utilizing their bilateral kin connections to attach themselves to tumpuk dominated by a corporate katurunan.

Some analytical distinctions developed by Appell (1971a; 1974) may be useful in further distinguishing the corporate katurunan as a social entity from the tumpuk which it dominates. Appell distinguishes three different types of social entity—'jural isolates', 'jural aggregates' and 'jural collectivities'—on the basis of the nature of their jural properties. He defines these types as follows: Jural isolates are right and duty-bearing entities in their own right in contrast to jural aggregates which are 'social grouping(s) in which interests are held in severalty by the individual members' (1974:5); and jural collectivities are 'social grouping(s) in which interests are held in severalty by the individual members but whose social existence is recognized by the jural system' (1974:5), thus allowing one of its members to act on behalf of the whole. The distinctions rest on 'the capacity for entering into jural relations' (1974:5), and only the jural isolate has this capacity.

It appears that the tumpuk is a jural collectivity in Appell's terms, while the corporate katurunan, like the biik-family and village, is a jural isolate according to a series of tests devised by Appell (1971a).[3] Individuals may not sell their rights in the katurunan; they are not compensated for their rights if they move away from the group (but neither do they entirely lose them); approval is required from a representative of the group in order to exercise the right to use the land; and a representative of the katurunan adjudicates disputes regarding the use of land.

Control over descent group lands as opposed to rights in those lands is principally lodged in one individual who acts with the advice and consent of other members of the corporate katurunan. Control (*kuasa*), that is, the authority to approve the use of the land by group members, adjudicate disputes regarding the lands, and the authority to lend land to non-members, passes from senior male member to next senior male member within a patrilineal core. Thus, control generally passes from older brother to younger brother regardless of marital residence choices so long as residence is within the village. On the death of the youngest brother the control then passes back to the eldest son of the eldest brother who had first held control. The controller is thus always part of a patrilineal core, connected to the apical ancestor usually by an unbroken line of males.

The tumpuk, in contrast to the corporate katurunan, lacks not only corporateness, but is a jural collectivity rather than a jural isolate. The house elder acts in the interests of the tumpuk when called upon to do so, but he acts only in his capacity as representative of the senior biik-family of the tumpuk, and in this capacity he is only a spokesman for the individual interests of the different biik-families that make up the tumpuk. The jural status of the tumpuk is derived from its component biik-families.

The Village

The Selako village (*kampo'ng* or *kampong*) is a collection of biik-families associated with an area of land. The biik elect and are governed by a common body of officers. Most of the biik in a village are clustered together in several tumpuk, but, at any one time, there is always a substantial minority of biik in isolated houses. The village is a corporate group charged with the management of village lands. It is seen as existing in perpetuity independent of the life of any of its component biik-families.

Villages are bound together ultimately by kinship and political ties and by common territorial interests. Membership in the village is a prerequisite to use of village lands. Ritual and associated activities mediate and structure interaction among its component biik.

Selako define villages in a variety of terms, both implicit and explicit. Elders often note that two related villages are really one village because they feast together. Reference is occasionally made to village sovereignty and exclusiveness—that the people and officers govern within the village, that no one may farm within village lands without permission. Certain rites such as *basangsam* (the annual ritual closing of the village to allow the spirits to roam freely for two nights and a day) and *babuis*, with their associated altars (see below) are seen as symbols of village identity and unity. Most important are the village offices themselves. These are frequently seen as embodying village identity.

The Village Offices

There are eight village offices, although few villages have all eight offices filled. The *sine qua non* of a fully independent village is the office of *tuha kampo'ng* ('village elder'), but if there is a tuha kampo'ng to keep the peace, there are also likely to be most of the other eight offices.

These eight offices are marked by the distribution of packages of cooked pork and rice on ritual occasions when domestic pigs are sacrificed. As noted above tumpuk representatives are identified in the same manner, as are certain kinsmen (see below). There are other village functionaries who provide many services similar to some of those performed by village officers, services such as curing illness, communication with spirits, gods and the souls of different foods, but these positions are not marked by the distribution of such ritual packets and are not seen as symbols of the village.

In order of ritual precedence, the most important village officer is the *tuha binua*.[4] He is the leader of the village men and the administrator and executive of the village. He directs co-operative labour on a village-wide scale, organizes large-scale public activities and mediates disputes on an informal basis. The binua also serves as an intermediary between the people of the village and other important elders (*tuha laut* and tuha kampo'ng) whose role performances are more formal, and therefore more intimidating. Traditionally, the tuha binua was the premier ritual and political officer of the village, but as a result of outside influences, especially during the last 200 years, the tuha laut ('Malay elder'[5]) has become the most important village political officer.

In general the role of tuha binua is very loosely defined, but there are certain duties which are explicitly his. He sets the dates for the two rituals of babuis (lit: 'to make a sacrifice') which occur just after the beginning of the harvest in middle or late March (to ask for the multiplication of the harvested rice) and just before clearing the new swidden fields in late June (to ask the gods to make the seed rice fertile). These offerings take place at an altar in the village guarded by statues of warriors. This altar is used only for these two rituals under the authority of the binua. Offerings are made separately by each biik and jointly by the group of biik participating. Offerings by the biik-families also indicate village allegiance (see below). The separate offerings are heaped together on the altar over which is placed the joint offering, usually several chickens, of the whole group. The binua presents these to the gods. The rituals and this place are most especially the province and ritual property of the binua, and his wife plays an important role here in leading the women of all participating biik to the village altar to make their offerings.

The binua with the advice of other elders sets the dates for other important ritual activities such as *ngarantika*, the beginning of the harvest, and *baantar*, storage of the harvested rice in the drying sheds. He also synchronizes important biik rituals and festivals. The binua shares authority over the graveyard with the tuha kampo'ng. There are few important activities in the village in which the binua does not play a role.

The tuha kampo'ng ('village elder') has ritual functions directed at ensuring the proper relations between the spirit world and the inhabitants of the village. His function as judge or arbitrator of formal legal cases is seen as maintaining the spiritual balance in the village. He presides in formal trials, but is assisted by others, particularly the tuha binua and tuha laut.

The tuha kampo'ng symbolizes the identity and unity of the village more than any other officer. A group of biik with, for instance, a tuha binua but without a 'village elder' is no more than a loose association of biik (quite possibly not even a tumpuk). In one case a group of biik-families from one tumpuk had their own tuha binua as well as their own *tukang sunat* and *pangarah uma* (see below) for a period of six years while they shared their other officers with the rest of the village. It was only after they selected their own tuha kampo'ng that they considered themselves constituting a separate village, and this was at least six years before they selected their own tuha laut. They employed the tuha laut of their parent village during the interim. The tuha kampo'ng has ritual control of the graveyard as well as an altar in the forest and all paths in the village. These areas may not be planted or interfered with in any way. They are village property to the exclusion of any of the component biik. The altar where the tuha binua makes sacrifices may be characterized in the same fashion. Each village has its own forest altar, village altar and graveyard.

The *tuha baiatn* ('shaman elder') is third in ritual precedence. This individual, occasionally a woman, is the traditional Selako shaman. His principal function is a ritual performance (*baiatn*) lasting two full nights and one day during which he journeys to the spirit world in trance. This serves not only to cure the sick and hasten the departure of the dead, but also, at times, to heal serious breaches among kinsmen and neighbours. Even his curing performances often serve direct social ends, as sickness among Selako is often a manifestation of social rather than physiological problems, and Selako explicitly recognize this.

The tuha laut ('Malay elder') conducts village relations with the external political order, District, State and National government. He is always the government-appointed *tua kampong* (a Malay, not a Selako title), but not all tua kampong are tuha laut. Today he is senior in prestige to all others including the tuha binua. In the order of precedence demonstrated in the distribution of packages of rice and pork on ritual occasions he ranks fourth after binua, kampo'ng and baiatn. He is charged by the government with the collection of taxes and fines, the administration of government edicts in the village, and the articulation of the native custom law courts at the Sub-District and District levels with the village-level courts (through appeals or by-passing, in certain cases, the village-level court).

The tuha laut in trying cases sits as the representative of the State and has behind him, at least in theory, the police power of the State, whereas the tuha kampo'ng has jurisdiction of cases, mostly domestic matters, through the parties voluntarily submitting themselves to him. His ultimate sanction today, in enforcing legal decisions, is to refuse the service of his office to an offender and/or to deny him access to village ritual support. The fines which the tuha kampo'ng levies are principally in the form of china plates, although sometimes pigs or chickens are sacrificed or fruit trees paid over. The plates are distributed among village officers or others whom the tuha kampo'ng wishes to honour. The tuha laut, on the other hand, levies fines in Malaysian currency, retaining for himself a portion and passing the remainder on to the State with no distribution in the village.

The State appoints headmen to administer the villages which are geographic units demarcated by the government. All headmen of Selako villages today are of the rank tua kampong or wakil tua kampong (deputy headman). These headmen receive a salary from the government and an effort is made to appoint headmen acceptable to their villagers.

The relation between the Selako office of tuha laut and the government-appointed post of tua kampong is reasonably simple. If the headman is tua kampong in an independent Selako village (i.e. one which has a village elder or a village sufficiently close to that status to consider itself entitled to a tuha laut [see below]) then the tua kampong is ordinarily *ipso facto* tuha laut. Occasionally it might happen that a government-appointed tua kampong is unacceptable to the people of the village, in which case they might not consider him tuha laut, but such a state of affairs would be unlikely to persist.

The four offices discussed above wield most of the institutionalized authority in the village. It is important to note that Selako political organization is not excessively authoritarian, and that these officers serve largely at the pleasure of the people they govern. But most of the institutionalized authority which does exist in a Selako village, that which is not imposed from the outside through agencies other than the tua kampong, resides in these offices and their incumbents.

Participation in policy-making is not solely in the hands of these officers, although ideally the four major officers make policy and the tuha binua executes it. In fact, all men and some women in the village are likely to participate occasionally, especially if the decision is an important one. However, the most prestigious villagers are likely to be office-holders and more weight is given to their opinions. Important decisions today might involve such traditional matters as selection of officers, and community labour projects such as the building of a bridge or the planning of irrigation works.

There are matters where expertise in custom law plays an important part in decision-making. This is particularly true in adjudication of disputes, and here the village officers and a few other respected elders are likely to speak the most. But even here decisions are not handed down from on high. A consensus of sorts is necessary for any decision taken by the village elders that affects their villagers. Neither a tuha kampo'ng nor a tuha laut will render a decision which is not likely to be accepted by all parties to the controversy. One of their important functions is to bring the parties to the point where a decision is acceptable to all. It is this spirit which permeates group decision-making. All those affected by the decision must be reasonably satisfied with it or group action is impossible.

The four offices described above are explicitly senior to and set apart from the other four village offices delineated below. Tuha binua, tuha kampo'ng, tuha baiatn, and tuha laut are the senior elders of the village who participate in all important village decisions and assist in the resolution of disputes.

The remaining four are of considerably less political importance. However, those held by males may be stepping stones to higher office. The four minor offices, in their order of ritual precedence at the distribution of packages of cooked pork and rice, are *bidan*, tukang sunat, *tukang tampa'*, and pangarah uma.

The bidan is the midwife. She is always a woman and is first called to attend a pregnant woman during labour. There are frequently two bidan in one village.

The tukang sunat is the circumciser of boys (actually the process involves superincision of the foreskin along the longitudinal axis of the penis). All boys are circumcised, usually shortly after they attain puberty.

The tukang tampa' is the blacksmith. His work today consists primarily in the tempering of purchased, preformed blanks for the heavy bush knife. It is likely that in the distant past tukang tampa' actually engaged in mining and smelting. Some of the interior ethnic groups of Borneo were making their own steel until fairly recently, but Selako have been in a position to purchase steel tools for at least the past 200 years.

The pangarah uma is the chief ritual officiant over the rice fields. His principal task is a ritual intended to drive pests and evil spirits out of the rice fields. He consults with the tuha binua on the dates for planting, harvesting, clearing fields and other matters related to the calendar of cultivation. He assists the tuha binua in the babuis rituals at the village altar.

Relationship Between Office, Constituency and Village

The eight village offices are significant in any analysis of Selako social organization not only because they are explicitly defined as the most important village roles, involving services to all villagers, individually and collectively, but also because of their symbolic function of designating village unity and division. A single, closely knit village has one set of eight offices which serves the whole village and demarcates it from other similar units. There are many groups of biik and tumpuk in an intermediate position, sharing some offices with the whole group and also having their own independent offices. The sub-group may be, but is not necessarily, a tumpuk. The larger group may be technically one village or two (according to whether a group of biik possesses the office of tuha kampo'ng). Two extreme instances encountered during fieldwork illustrate the range of possibilities. First, it frequently occurs that different tumpuk within a single village share seven officers but employ different bidan. This alone does not indicate a serious division in the village.

A more complex case at the opposite end of the spectrum was encountered where two separate villages that had recently divided shared only the office of tuha baiatn. They were clearly separate villages because they had different tuha kampo'ng, but it was impossible to draw clear geographic boundaries between the two. Moreover, a few biik-families were vacillating in their village allegiances, employing an officer from one village on one occasion and from the other village on another. As a result there were biik-families in the same tumpuk (a long-house in this case) aligned with different villages. It is apparent here that the village is defined by its offices, particularly the tuha kampo'ng, and only in the sense of allegiance to officers and possession of offices can there be said to be two distinct villages. As a function of this close relationship between office and village identity, Selako are frequently required to state symbolically their allegiances to village officers and they do this each time a biik-family sacrifices a pig. Moreover, every biik-family must employ the services of a tuha binua, a pangarah uma and a tuha kampo'ng for various calendrical rituals every year. The need for the assistance from the remaining offices is more irregular.[6]

It should be stated that the apparent possibility of total chaos inherent in defining village identity in this way never comes to pass. Groups of officers are always aligned in factional 'slates' determined primarily by tumpuk and kin loyalties. Thus, two separate groups of officers will each have its own exclusive constituency of biik-families. Each biik-family tends to select a group of candidates for different offices as a unit rather than choosing occupants for each office independently. A few biik vacillate but this is normally in respect of the whole 'slate'.

The political factions which support particular candidates for village office are usually localized in or draw most of their members from one particular tumpuk. Usually this tumpuk backs several of the village offices while a rival tumpuk backs most of the others. Tumpuk thus present and support 'slates' of offices and do not simply support individual candidates. Since the core of the tumpuk is a group of closely related kinsmen, the officers supported by the tumpuk can be seen as representing not only village interests but also the interests of their group of localized neighbour-kinsmen.

There is a continual movement towards village fission in these circumstances. If a political faction is unable to promote successfully its candidates for village office by ousting or succeeding officers of another faction, it may simply select officers which serve only its own faction. Instances of this kind are frequent. The essential point is that the unity of Selako villages is fragile, and most villages exhibit political cracks and fissures which are evidenced and symbolized in a variety of conflicts and compromises over village offices.

Adat Groups

Selako today are divided into two groups of villages: Sangkuku' Selako and Gaje'ng Selako. Selako call these groups '*bansa* Selako', but since they are distinguished by various details of ritual performance, dietary prohibitions and origin stories, they are termed '*adat* groups' in this paper. The adat group comprises a group of villages whose leading families are thought to be more closely related to each other than they are to the leading families of villages outside the group, although this may not in fact be the case because of intermarriage. More to the point is that villages of one adat group share a common adat because of fission from common mother villages. Thus all the Gaje'ng Selako villages in Sarawak are descended from Sedemak which was settled in the 1830s, and the principal officers in many of these nine villages are closely related (Kaboy and Sandin, 1968). Each adat group appears to be dominated by its own core of kin-linked families, and each group has, ideally at least, a leader who is the most prestigious village officer in his own adat group.

Adat group membership in the sense of ritual and customary practice is a biik-family matter, but, since most of the population of a village are closely related, villages are always clearly dominated by members of one adat group. Adat group membership in a political sense appears to be basically a feeling of identification and kinship with prominent Selako leaders and their families. Selako themselves admit that nowadays the differences in customary practices are small, since few families elect to carry out the more onerous dictates of custom.

According to Selako informants, several generations ago there were nine named adat groups. In the mythical past these nine groups occupied villages at different altitudes on the sacred mountain, Bukit Bawa'ng, near Singkawang in Kalimantan Barat. Sangkuku' informants state that their village was higher than the Gaje'ng village, which reflected their higher status. Selako can still trace the ancestry of families to these nine adat groups, but in both Kalimantan and Sarawak only the Gaje'ng and Sangkuku' remain significant groups, these two having absorbed the others.

Kinship

Selako conceive of each individual as surrounded by kinsmen differentiated principally by relative seniority in generation and age, by sex and by degree of collaterality (Schneider, 1974a). In the kinship terminology[7] generation is the only differentiating criterion in generations other than parents', child's and Ego's own. Parents are distinguished terminologically from their siblings and cousins, and children from the children of Ego's siblings and cousins. In most circumstances siblings and cousins of various degrees are not terminologically distinguished, but those younger than Ego are distinguished from Ego's older siblings and cousins, and these last are distinguished by sex. There are occasions when siblings and cousins of various degrees are distinguished, and, in these circumstances, relative age and sex are ignored. Parents' siblings and cousins are categorized by sex and age relative to the connecting parent much as Ego distinguishes his own siblings and cousins (except that parents' younger siblings and cousins are distinguished by sex whereas Ego's are not).

There is a very sharp distinction in attitudes and behaviour towards affinal kinsmen as opposed to consanguines. This is reflected also in kin terminology although some kinsmen by marriage are included within the terms used for consanguines. Parents' siblings' spouses are not differentiated from parents' siblings of the same sex. Siblings' spouses and spouse's siblings are not differentiated from siblings of the same relative age and sex in the ideal system of address. Other affinal relatives are distinguished terminologically from consanguines.

Selako notions of kinship conform closely to the model of the personal kindred (Leach, 1950), but Selako explicitly bound the kindred by excluding kin of their own generation beyond third cousins. The rights and duties entailed in kinship of various degrees within the range of third cousins are not finely differentiated except for incest, but it is clear that the closer the connexion, the stronger the ties are, and siblings and first cousins are expected to co-operate closely.

Categories of kin within Ego's own generation are marked, like the village officers and tumpuk, by ritual gifts of pork and rice on the occasion of the sacrifice of a domestic pig. A single representative from each category of collaterals—siblings, first cousins, second cousins, third cousins—for both of the married pair whose biik-family sponsors the ritual, is presented with a package of cooked pork and rice. The sum of all these ritual distributions can thus be conceived of as a folk model of the Selako social system.

NOTES

1. See Schneider (in press) for a more complete discussion.

2. Note that structurally a long-standing group of this kind is actually composed of several layers of nesting descent groups. There may also be different segments at the same hierarchical level where, for instance, brothers have both created a fund of land held jointly by their descendants. Segmentary relations of this kind are seldom of lasting importance within a tumpuk for reasons which cannot be discussed here.

3. Compare Appell's analysis of Iban, Land Dayak and Rungus social entities (1971a).

4. I am unable to provide a satisfactory gloss for this term since it occurs only in very limited contexts in Selako. I suspect, however, that the translation should involve such concepts as 'land' and, less certainly, 'tradition'.

5. Laut literally means 'sea', but Selako customarily also use it to refer to Malays as well. This office was institutionalized as a means of dealing with the Malay governments on the coast.

6. Tuha baiatn preside at one calendrical festival, but since there was only one remaining tuha baiatn among the Sarawak Selako, it is impossible to make statements about the function of this office in symbolizing village identity and allegiance.

7. Selako Kinship Terms (Reference) are as follows:

ne' moyang	all relatives of the sixth ascending generation
ne' icit	all relatives of the fifth ascending generation
ne' ingke	all relatives of the fourth ascending generation
ne' iut	all relatives of the third ascending generation
nene'	all relatives of the second ascending generation
pa' uha	parents' older brother or male cousin*
ma' uha	parents' older sister or female cousin*
pa' uda'	parents' younger brother or male cousin*
ma' uda'	parents' younger sister or female cousin*
uha	parents' older sibling or cousin*
uma'	parents' sister or female cousin*
bapa'	father
inu'	mother
abang	older brother or male cousin
kaka'	older sister or female cousin
adi'	younger sibling or cousin
gambar kapala	siblings
kadiriatn	first cousins
miadi' nene'	second cousins
miadi' iut	third cousins
kamaru'	all same generation kinsmen out to and including third cousins, or less frequently, all collateral kinsmen, or, rarely all siblings
anak	child
kamanakatn	sibling's or cousin's child
cucu'	all relatives of the second descending generation
iut	all relatives of the third descending generation
ingke'	all relatives of the fourth descending generation
icit	all relatives of the fifth descending generation
moyang	all relatives of the sixth descending generation

bini	wife
aki	husband
datu'	parent-in-law
minantu	child-in-law
imat	child's parent-in-law
kaka' minantu	spouse's older sister or female cousin, or older brother's or cousin's wife.
abang minantu	spouse's older brother or male cousin, or older sister's or cousin's husband
adi' minantu	spouse's younger sibling or cousin, or younger sibling's or cousin's spouse
isatn	sibling's spouse's sibling
sakaminantuatn	spouse's sibling's spouse

* This term is rarely used for parent's sibling or first cousin. Usually a descriptive term preceded by *pa'* or *ma'*, for male and female respectively, is substituted.

4

THE KAYAN

JÉRÔME ROUSSEAU

THE Kayan are a people of central Borneo, where they occupy the middle or upper reaches of the following river basins: Kayan (pop. 1,000?), Mahakam (pop. 1,000?), Mendalam (a tributary of the Kapuas, pop. 1,530), Baram (pop. 7,234) and Baluy, or upper Rejang (pop. 2,508).[1] They all speak the same language, with minor dialectical variations (Barth, 1910; Clayre and Cubit, 1974; Cubit, 1964; Rousseau, 1974e; Southwell, n.d.), and they call themselves Kayan.

Nowhere, however, do they live by themselves; they share their areas of residence with other ethnic groups, such as the Kenyah and Kajang, who follow the same mode of life as the Kayan, and various nomadic or ex-nomadic groups, such as the Penan and Punan (Rousseau, 1975). On the other hand, the Kayan as a whole do not form a group; owing to the nature of the terrain, communications between river basins are very difficult and extremely rare, and those villages within a particular river system constitute the maximal social unit. This study is based on fieldwork undertaken in the Baluy area,[2] and particularly the village of Uma Bawang (Rousseau, 1974a). However, despite regional variations, most of the following description applies to the other Kayan groups.

Historical Sketch

According to legends, all Kayan used to live in the upper Kayan river area (*Apau Kayan*) whence they migrated to the various areas which they now occupy, and to the Baleh, where no Kayan now remain.[3] During the period of expansion, they either displaced or subjugated the populations of these new areas. These conquests provided numerous slaves but the Kayan did not have or develop a unitary political system, and the conquered groups managed in time to regain much of their old independence. The Kayan still play a major role in regional politics. Normally, Kayan chiefs were able to prevent deadly conflicts among themselves, but during the periods of major migrations, there were some wars between Kayan villages, indeed, wars seem to have been both a cause and a consequence of migrations.

Rajah Brooke first extended his influence to the Baluy Kayan in 1863; pacification was complete in 1924, by which time the practice of head-hunting had been eradicated. Control over the Baram had been established earlier, in great part because of the co-operative role of some Kenyah and Kayan paramount chiefs.

Besides the gradual elimination of head-hunting, the major influence of Brooke rule was in regional organization. The administration controlled and limited village migrations; it also nominated regional chiefs (*penghulu*) who were theoretically answerable to the District Officers. This transformation had little effect on local political life.

After World War II, Sarawak became a British crown colony. During this period, the Kayan came increasingly into contact with modern technology. Schools and dispensaries were progressively opened. However, even before Brooke rule, the Kayan had not been entirely isolated. They sold jungle produce, camphor, birds' nests, rhinoceros horns and bezoar stones, in return for brass gongs, beads, cloth, firearms and salt (Burns, 1849).

The incorporation of Sarawak into Malaysia (1961–3) brought further changes. A parliamentary democracy, with elections at the federal and state levels, was established; more schools and dispensaries were built; several Kayan children entered secondary school; and a small part of production is now oriented towards a cash economy. But these innovations have so far had relatively little effect on Kayan life.

On the other side of the border the Dutch lagged behind in establishing control over their area of central Borneo. They eventually did so partly because of accusations by the Brooke government that they were allowing head-hunting to continue, which had very disruptive consequences on the interior of Sarawak. Later on, however, transformations seem to have been more intense in Kalimantan than in Sarawak; a large proportion of the interior groups were converted to Christianity, and many of them are now literate.

Settlement Patterns and Social Relations

The total population of the Baluy area (including all the ethnic groups) is 9,430, that is, a density of slightly more than one per square mile. This sparse population is due to the nature of settlement patterns; most villages are situated along the Baluy river because it is navigable; also, these people are swidden cultivators of rice, and thus need to control large areas of land. In the lower Baluy, villages are on average 2·5 miles apart, in the middle Baluy, 4·5 miles. For most of its course, the Baluy is cut by rapids which make travel difficult or even impossible when the river is high, and this is true even now that outboard motors are available. For daily purposes, each community is thus clearly isolated, and this isolation is a source of local differences in culture, religion and language.

Intercommunity relations may take several forms which are all episodic—informal visits, economic exchanges, harvest festivals, and marriages. Informal visits are possible only if villages are close to each other, which is unusual; trade is very restricted, as every household and every village endeavours to be self-sufficient. Finally, about one-third of marriages take place between members of different settlements. However, we will see that a very high rate of divorce is associated with such unions and this considerably limits their role in the establishment of kinship networks. Because of this isolation, intercommunity relations rest heavily on the chiefs. They normally find spouses of their rank in other communities and thus have wider networks than other members of their village. They are also free from most productive activities and thus have time to promote these relations and visit other villages. Therefore, regional politics take place within this informal network of chiefs. In the last century their roles gradually changed. Previously they had to organize migrations and warfare, but now they try to establish a consensus in their relations with the administration and, more recently with missionaries; they also resolve such conflicts as boundary disputes between villages. However, one must emphasize again that communities are to a large extent autonomous.

A Kayan village typically consists of a single long-house (*uma*) built of ironwood, and divided longitudinally in two parts: the covered gallery (*awa'*), which is unpartitioned, and the apartments (*amin*) separated from each other by walls, with a door leading from each apartment to the gallery. In the Baluy, Kayan villages have an average of 179 inhabitants and 19 apartments.[4] Apartments are more or less of the same size, except that of the chief, which is much larger. The chief's apartment may be located anywhere in the long-house, not only in the middle as was suggested by early authors.

The long-house was strategically important in affording protection against enemy attacks; it has been retained because of its influence on interpersonal relations: it facilitates a higher rate of contacts than would be possible in a village formed by unifamilial residences, and people can visit each other more informally.[5]

The Kayan build durable long-houses; as the building remains for many years in the same spot, it is necessary to make swidden fields further and further away, since the nearest areas have been used and have to be left fallow for one or two decades. Farm areas are therefore far from the long-house, and rather than return there every evening, the Kayan prefer to build less permanent farm-houses on the spot. Situated near a navigable river, these can shelter one or several households. A farm-house is called *lepo'* if it houses a single family and *pura* if it contains two or more. Because of swidden cultivation, it is necessary to build new farm-houses almost every year.

This dual mode of residence has an influence on interpersonal relationships. During the weeding and harvest the long-house is almost deserted, as people start moving into the farm-houses during the sowing. Only a few old people, unable to work in the fields, may decide to stay there. In a farm-house, an individual has very close contacts with a small number of families; the rules of privacy are relaxed, and it is possible to enter freely into each other's rooms. Members of neighbouring farm-houses also visit each other, but not to the same extent. The whole village occupies three or four distinct farming areas, between which relations are limited.

People look forward to the season when they stay in farm-houses; although less comfortable, they allow a more relaxed social atmosphere than the long-house, in which they dwell for the other half of the year. In the latter, interpersonal relations are more superficial, as they meet every day a larger number of people. Because of the concentration of population, the occasions for conflict are also greater. However, religion helps to keep the whole long-house united, as most rituals may only be performed there. The extensive powers of the chief are another powerful element of cohesion. In the past, the fear of head-hunters created a pressure towards concentration in long-houses. Nowadays, this incentive has been replaced by government regulations, which encourage the maintenance of long-houses. In any case, after several months at the farm, people are happy to return to the house, especially to celebrate the harvest festival.

Other social relationships are also based on agricultural activities since all rice cultivation is performed by work teams recruited on the basis of geographical proximity and availability. It is possible, indeed frequent, for members of the same household to belong to separate teams. The composition of a team is usually stable within each agricultural phase of forest clearing, sowing, weeding, harvesting, but this is simply a matter of practicality. A team normally has 10 to 20 members. Its organization rests on strictly balanced reciprocity. To make reckoning easy, team members work a whole day on a single farm in rotation. Co-operation is called *pala dau*, 'to exchange days'. A team has no permanent leader; the only collective decision it has to take is to agree on a rota. The farm owner is the team leader for the day, and he supplies the rice for the midday meal.

Formation and Amalgamation of Communities

Unlike the Iban, Kayan domestic units cannot leave the community without the chief's permission, and units from several villages cannot form a new settlement. A Kayan community can split into two independent sections only if each can find a *maren* ('high aristocrat', see below) to lead them. Fragmentation of villages does not occur primarily because of demographic pressure or land scarcity, but is due mainly to conflicts. The most frequent causes of division are disagreements about migrations, and rivalry for chiefship between two maren. Such partitions are infrequent. In the Baluy area, there was only one permanent division in this century. The power of the chief and the mode of his succession contribute to this stability, and a tendency towards village endogamy has the same effect.

A small community presents many disadvantages; its members have to find spouses mainly in other villages, and as most inter-community marriages end in divorce, this is a major drawback. In a small community, social relations are restricted, and this creates various problems, for instance in the organization of work teams. In these conditions, it appears more practical for a small long-house to establish itself near a larger community. Intermarriages take place, and closer links are developed. The small long-house keeps its political autonomy for a while but is subordinate to the larger one for major decisions. Eventually, its chief may die without a suitable successor, and the minor long-house is absorbed into the other.

The Household

The household (amin) is the only corporate group within the community. It has sole ownership of its buildings, tools and the products of its work. Normally, an apartment contains a single household; there may be two if there has been an economic partition before a new long-house is rebuilt. Except for these transitory forms, the amin is broadly similar to the Iban *bilek*-family (Freeman, 1970). However, it contains more members, recruits a greater proportion of male affines (i.e. uxorilocality is predominant) and is more stable (i.e. partitions are less frequent).

There is an average of eight persons per household, and more than two-thirds of these have a genealogical depth of three generations. The Kayan consider the stem family as the normal form of house-hold organization, and they expect that all married siblings but one will eventually form a separate unit. Two-generation domestic units are either those which have recently split from a larger unit, or where members of the older generation have died before their grandchildren became adults.

Continuity of the Amin

The apartment is called amin; the meaning of the word is extended to designate its inhabitants. But the amin is more than a domestic unit. After a few generations, all the original occupants have died;

most of their belongings have deteriorated and been replaced and, if the long-house has been rebuilt, the original room itself has also disappeared. However the amin still exists. Thus, in talking about an individual who died before the birth of any contemporary member of the village, an informant can readily point out, among today's amin, the one of which the person was a member.

Jurally, an individual belongs to only one amin (*qua* domestic unit) at a time, into which he has been recruited by birth, adoption, incorporation, or marriage. However, an individual who has joined an amin by marriage will normally indicate as 'his' amin that in which he was born.

The amin is thus not only a domestic unit, but also a kinship group, formed by all those who were born in it, even if they subsequently live elsewhere. It is thus structurally similar to the Gilbertese *kainga* (Goodenough, 1955), although it is much smaller in size, and not based on the same economic interests. Members of a kainga control a tract of land; but among the Kayan there is no individual ownership of arable land. Every year, the men hold a meeting to decide in which areas they will make their farms. When this has been ascertained, they establish the limits of their own farms without regard to the identity of the previous occupant, or, for that matter, the previous boundaries. People take as much land as they can cultivate, as there is no land pressure at the local level. On the other hand, a village has exclusive control of its farm land. Members of other communities do not have access to it, and encroachment will bring litigation.

The amin (as kinship group) owns heirlooms (*daven pesaka*), which carry a high economic and affective value. These are automatically transmitted to descending generations within the amin, and this is a reason for the Kayan considering it as an everlasting unit. Those who leave the amin domestic unit, as they marry out, retain their birthrights to a share of the heirlooms. In this latter case, the transfer of daven pesaka takes place only when the out-marrying individual has had children; the gift of heirlooms perpetuates the latter's link with their parent's natal amin. This is why some individuals say that they belong to a given amin, when they refer in fact to their father's or mother's. This is however a metaphorical statement, because they do not have any of the rights and duties established by natal ascription to an amin. What it does indicate, however, is the social recognition of a kinship link.

Partition and Amalgamation of Amin

Beyond a certain number of individuals, the organization of a domestic unit becomes difficult. Married siblings may give preferential treatment to their own children and spouses, or evade their proper share of work. This necessarily leads to conflicts, and it is advisable to divide the household into two independent sections.

However, the sharing of the valuable heirlooms may be a source of quarrels. If the partition occurs while the parents are alive, they preside over it. Otherwise, as the parents become older, and even if no partition is about to take place, they have the duty to decide before witnesses the allotment of the daven pesaka, so that there will be no quarrel after their death. If partition occurs while the siblings' parents are still alive, the older sibling normally stays with them, while the younger one forms a new unit.

With less than three or four members, a household is not viable. The normal course of events is then to join relatives in their room, while remaining a separate economic unit. If the parents of the smaller unit die before their children have become adult, the latter are assimilated into the household with which they live.

Marriage

Marriage is prohibited between individuals who have at least one great-grandparent in common. In other words, one cannot marry a first cousin once removed (i.e. the child of a first cousin or first cousin of parent), or a second cousin; this rule is very rarely broken. Unions are monogamous, although some cases of polygyny have been reported for chiefs (Furness, 1902; Nieuwenhuis, 1904).

Whether for a first or second marriage, there is a strong tendency towards local endogamy: for 63 per cent of marriages in Uma Bawang both spouses were born in the village.[6]

The tendency towards local endogamy is reinforced by patterns of divorce. Only 21 per cent of intra-community marriages in Uma Bawang ended in divorce, while 66 per cent of inter-village marriages did so. At any given time, this reduces considerably the proportion of outside affines. These differential rates are a consequence of the isolation of Kayan communities, which is such that an outsider cannot do otherwise than feel ill at ease; in case of conflict, he has no one to back him up, unless he has relatives in the village, and for daily purposes he is entirely cut off from those who formed his circle of relations during the early part of his life.[7]

In the community described, two-thirds of locally exogamous marriages occur between Kayan. This is a consequence of the ethnic composition of neighbouring villages rather than ethnic discrimination. Geographical distance prevails over cultural ascription in the choice of a spouse; for instance, there have been more unions with people of a nearby Kenyah village than those of Kayan long-houses which are more distant. The only discrimination in this respect is directed against the Penan, whom the Kayan consider as inferior because of their nomadic mode of life. In the lower Baluy, where the population is more heterogeneous, inter-ethnic marriages have a greater frequency.[8] We will see below that stratum ascription also has an influence on spousal choice.

All marriages start by a period of uxorilocality of at least one or two years, and in most cases, this is permanent. In Uma Bawang, 72 per cent of current marriages are uxorilocal.[9] However, this does not mean that marriage cuts a man off entirely from his natal household. Approximately a month after the marriage ceremony, a ritual is performed in the room of the husband's parents, in order to establish their right to some of the work of their daughter-in-law, and at the same time of their son. During the ritual, the husband's parents give to his in-laws some presents (*ku'an*), whose value varies (e.g. for a commoner, it is approximately 50 Malaysian dollars). Until this has been paid, the wife may not enter the apartment of her in-laws, much less cook for them, eat with them, or work for them. From then on, the couple goes to the husband's parents' farm for at most a few weeks every year, to help them in their agricultural activities. As time goes on, they do so more and more rarely. The presence of the ku'an expresses the importance given to the rule of uxorilocality, while at the same time making it more manageable, and reducing the man's anxiety caused by his change in household affiliation.

After a period of adjustment, uxorilocality becomes complete. There are, however, some exceptions; a few couples practise alternatively uxorilocality and virilocality for several years. This transitory arrangement, called *nyayang*, 'to oscillate', usually comes about when the husband's parents temporarily need extra help, for instance if they have several children, and their eldest daughter is not yet married. The wife's parents will accept such a situation for a limited time only.

If the husband's parents have no daughter, their household is in danger of becoming extinct, and they initiate negotiations in order to obtain the permanent affiliation of the couple to their own household. In return, they have to pay a substantial bridewealth (*blian*). The offer of a suitable blian is no guarantee that the transfer will be accepted. The woman's parents have an unconditional right to refuse the proposal.

It may take years before the value of the blian is agreed upon, and the payment is made long after the change of residence, except for one gong, which is given at the outset. This does not weaken the bargaining position of the wife's parents, as they are entitled to call her back if no agreement is reached, or if the payment is not forthcoming; in this situation the most likely outcome is a divorce; there were instances when couples had to part against their will, because of their respective parents' failure to compromise. Nowadays, the total value of the blian is reckoned in dollars, but a large proportion of the payments consists of heirlooms, the market value of which is appraised by some neutral member of the community. For the commoners, it ranges between 200 and 500 Malaysian dollars, for the ruling group, between 2,000 and 3,000 dollars.

Social Stratification

The most striking feature of Kayan social organization is its system of stratification. There are four strata, which are, in decreasing order of status, the maren, *hipuy, panyin* and *dipen*. The panyin form two-thirds of the population, and the maren, hipuy and dipen about one-tenth each. There is a tendency towards stratum endogamy, but intermarriages are not forbidden; in this case, the child belongs to the rank of the parent in whose apartment he lives.[10]

The four strata form two ritual categories: the maren and hipuy are the *kelunan jia* ('superior people'), the panyin and dipen the *kelunan ji'ek* ('inferior people'), the first category being entitled to use some tattoo designs and ritual elements forbidden to the others.

This binary ritual categorization hides a three-tiered social system. The maren, or ruling group, have a monopoly of the chiefly role, and this entitles them to receive regular prestations of work, and to a lesser degree, of goods, from the members of their village, to the point where they have little or no agricultural work to do. This allows them to play a political role beyond their community, as they have time to visit other village chiefs, and in this way maintain a network of political relationships. They also have ample opportunity to undertake some very profitable trading with nomads.

Corvées for the chief are performed by the panyin and hipuy, whom we can call 'commoners'. They are bound to the village by various rules, and cannot leave it to reside elsewhere without the permission of the chief, which is obviously an important element in increasing his power.

The distinction between maren and commoners, which would seem rather difficult to maintain in such small villages, is possible because the maren tend to find spouses of their rank in other villages, and therefore prevent the development of the equalizing tendency that kinship links with lower strata would produce.

While only 24 per cent of all marriages are eventually virilocal, this proportion rises to 64 per cent among Uma Bawang maren. The establishment of virolocality is partly a function of wealth, because of the high values of the brideprice, and the maren are thus in the best position to realize such a goal. They are willing to pay the price because virolocality gives a man a higher status. For the maren, it also makes possible the succession to chiefship from father to son rather than from father-in-law to son-in-law.

Another factor of central importance in separating the maren from the rest of the population is the fact that they, and they alone, can own slaves (dipen). Until recently, the master arranged his slaves' marriages and disposed of their children, and he would own half the children of a slave and a commoner. There are two kinds of slaves: if they are part of their master's household then all their work and its product is directly controlled by the latter; or they can form a distinct household, in which case they have more independence: they cultivate their own fields, of which they keep the product, but have to work occasionally for their masters (in addition to the corvées performed by the commoners) who can also occasionally request from them small prestations of meat or other goods.[11] The position of slave is hereditary; some are descendants of war captives; traditionally, there was apparently no way for a slave to free himself.

It is therefore clear that Kayan social strata have a political and economic basis. Thus, despite the fact that stratum ascription is supposed to be strictly hereditary, there is some mobility. For instance, if a maren family plays only a minor political role, and if its members find spouses of lower rank, the commoners will eventually cease to perform corvées for them; in time, they will lose their maren rank, to become hipuy. Actually, the hipuy category is there primarily to allow a demotion of the 'non-functional' maren without reducing them to the rank of commoners; ideologically, the distance between maren and panyin is too great, and if it were possible to go from one rank to the other, it would then be evident that there is no intrinsic difference between strata. Besides saving face for those maren undergoing downward mobility, the presence of this category thus allows for the maintenance of the legitimizing ideology of class differences.

In the same way, as slaves now become commoners, they stop being called dipen, to become panyin. The backbone of the stratification system is the opposition between rulers and ruled, and the maren can maintain their position because of their strategic role in intercommunity relations (Rousseau, 1974a, 1974b).

Kinship

Kinship plays only a residual role among the Kayan, as it does in Western society. By this I mean that beyond the family it is not the basis of any grouping having an economic or political role. The kinship system is almost closed, in the sense that it only regulates phenomena which are part of kinship. For instance, a rule stipulates that a man and a woman who have at least a great-grandparent in common cannot marry each other; other rules specify how one can adopt a child and so on. Of course, as we will see in a moment, a Kayan can expect the help of kinsmen in times of crisis, but this is so common to kinship relations in all societies that one is justified in saying that the role of kinship in Kayan society is residual. Let us consider the area where it is irrelevant.

Within a village, many people are of course related to each other. For example, in Uma Bawang, approximately 14 per cent of an individual's co-villagers are close relatives, i.e. people with at least one great-grandparent in common. This in fact means that there is a 48 per cent chance that at least one member of a household will be related with at least one member of another household by a similar kinship link (Rousseau, 1974a:307). However, this is not the basis for the existence of a village. Likewise, when every year new farm areas are established, a household's presence in one or the other of these is not influenced by kinship relations, and the same applies to farm-house composition. Finally, there is no correlation between kinship and membership in agricultural work teams. These groupings are established on an *ad hoc* basis, and for a limited period only. Kayan informants themselves state that kinship relations are not important in the formation of these groupings. Their assertion was tested, and it was found that the proportion of close relatives in farm areas, farm-houses, and co-operation teams is that expected of a situation where associations are random in relation to kinship (Rousseau, 1974a:293–335).

For work teams, the irrelevance of kinship is to be expected: if co-operation is on a basis of balanced reciprocity, it is unnecessary to co-operate with kinsmen; moreover, as all farm work is done co-operatively, it would be difficult, perhaps impossible, to recruit enough kinsmen to form a practical work team.

Furthermore, the stratification system reduces the structural significance of kinship. As Godelier (1973:116) noted, 'the appearance of real social classes implies precisely the disappearance not of kinship relations, but of their capacity to be the general form of social relations'. Behaviour is determined on the basis of stratum ascription; among the commoners, forms of leadership develop which are independent of kinship, and solidarity is then partly a consequence of status proximity.

However, the Kayan do recognize that kinship establishes behaviour differentials. In principle, a genealogical link up to the sixth degree of collaterality establishes an individual as a kinsman (*panak*).[12] In practice, few Kayan are aware of the identity of even their third cousins. It is enough to know about one's *panak jeleng* (close relatives), i.e. those who have at least a great-grandparent in common, between whom sexual relations or marriage are forbidden.

Close relatives play an important role only in crises; if a man has to pay a fine or a ku'an, he seeks help from them. When a man receives a ku'an for his daughter, he distributes it among his panak jeleng, or more precisely, these prestations take place among *some* of Ego's close relatives. Some of these relatives live in other communities and have few effective relations with them; even if they live in the same village, there may be personal reasons why they will not activate the relationship.

Even if a man can expect help from his close relatives, this does not imply that they are in any way responsible for his behaviour; their decision to help him or not remains a private matter between them, of no concern to the rest of the community.

People anticipate a friendly attitude from kinsmen, but do not expect their co-operation or association in daily life. This is why knowledge of exact kinship relations is not of central importance and only close relatives are easily identified. However, there were a few cases of individuals who were unable to describe precisely the nature of their kinship links with some of their panak jeleng. Confusion is most frequent in relation to cousins once removed, for which no Kayan term exists. Generally speaking, knowledge of genealogies is not valued, and there are no real specialists in that field.[13] The small number of kinship terms also makes it harder to remember the precise links. There are six basic terms of reference for cognates, which apply equally to lineals and collaterals. Degrees of collaterality can be expressed only for Ego's generation, which is to be expected, as an individual is most likely to marry someone of his own generation. Terminology for affines is similarly minimal, and in part identical to that for cognates.[14] The Kayan also have other terminological systems based on kinship: teknonyms, necronyms and gerontonyms.

Teknonyms may be used both for reference and address by everyone but an individual's children. However, teknonyms are not in common use because they must be abandoned definitely either as soon as any child dies, or when one becomes a grandparent. Even if none of these events occur, most parents are known by their personal name.[15]

An individual takes a necronym, or death-name, when some of his primary relatives die, namely a parent, a sibling, a spouse or a child.[16] If several of these relatives die, no rule indicates which necronym will be used.

As soon as someone becomes a grandparent, he abandons any teknonym or necronym he may have, to prefix his personal name by what we might call a gerontonym.[17] Teknonyms, necronyms and gerontonyms thus give a rough indication of an individual's position in the life cycle, and of his familial situation.

NOTES

1. Population figures for 1970 to 1973. Sources are for the Kayan river, Whittier (1973:19), the Mahakam, Nieuwenhuis (1904:275), the Mendalam, Pastor A. J. Ding Ngo (personal communication, 1973), the Baram, Metcalf (1974), and the Baluy, Rousseau (1974d). I have no contemporary data for the Mahakam. There are other ethnic groups in these same areas, whose population I have not indicated. See Rousseau (1974c).

2. The Baluy area, or upper Rejang, forms the Belaga district of the Seventh Division of Sarawak, Malaysia. At the time of fieldwork it was called the Belaga sub-district of the Third Division. This fieldwork (1970–2, 1974) was made possible by grants from the Canada Council and the Evans Fund.

3. They migrated to the Mendalam (Nieuwenhuis, 1904:56–7).

4. The largest has a population of 324 and 37 apartments, the smallest 61 inhabitants and 7 apartments.

5. I hypothesize that when other Borneo groups abandoned long-houses for unifamilial households, this was a consequence of a change in interpersonal relationships rather than the other way round.

6. Furthermore, for 18 per cent of these marriages, the spouses come from contiguous apartments or from different households in the same room. Kayan young men really are attracted to the girl next door. Such marriages are the most stable, not a single one of these having ended in divorce during the period of my fieldwork.

7. The reader may wonder how it is possible to maintain the exogamic rule prohibiting marriage between descendants of a common great-grandparent while maintaining such a rate of local endogamy in a small community (i.e. about 200 persons). This is in fact statistically very easy (see Rousseau, 1974a:293–307).

8. 'Kayan-Kajang matrimonial alliances ... are extremely common. As a matter of fact, for the last three generations which have reached a marriageable age, the number of Kayan-Kajaman intermarriages, for instance, nearly exceeds the number of intermarriages between the two Kajaman longhouses' (de Martinoir, n.d.).

9. I do not have the space here to discuss adequately the reasons why the Kayan practice uxorilocality, while the Iban and Kenyah have utrolocal residence (See Rousseau, 1974a:260–7).

10. This conflicts with the Kayan overt rule on the subject, which states that a child belongs to his (or her) father's rank. However, this rule is *never* applied.

11. At the time of my fieldwork, the practice of slavery was on the wane and had disappeared altogether in several villages; it could still be observed in an attenuated way in the community where I did my fieldwork. However, most changes in this respect had occurred within the five previous years, and it was easy to get first-hand information on the subject.

12. The Kayan term for 'relative' is panak. As it is formed by the prefix $p(e)$-, expressing commonality, and *anak*, 'child', one would understand it to mean 'descendants of a common ancestor', thus 'cognates'. In fact, it is also applied to affines. If we agree with Freeman (1961:202) that 'kindred' should be used to refer only to cognates and never extended to embrace affines, one cannot translate panak by 'kindred', and there is no Kayan word which could be translated as 'kindred'.

13. This might be one of the reasons why no marriage takes place before a meeting of village elders has considered the appropriateness of the union. Such a general discussion would bring to the surface the presence of close kinship relations between the betrothed. Incestuous relations (*tensi* or *abe*, depending on the kinship distance, the first referring to primary relatives) endanger the well-being of the community.

14. Terms of Reference:

	Cognates	Affines
G+2	sepun	sepun
G+1	taman (male)	taman divan (male)
	hinan (female)	hinan divan (female)
G 0	harin	hawan (spouse)
		hangu (harin of spouse)
(Ego's generation)		
G−1	anak	anak divan
G−2	sau	sau

15. The teknonyms are *Taman* X for the father, *Hinan* X for the mother, X being the personal name of the child, or the words *Bay* or *Binye* which mean respectively 'male baby' and 'female baby'.

16. Necronyms
(X=personal name of survivor)

Dead relative	Sex of survivor		
	Male	Either sex	Female
Father or mother	Uyau		Utan
Sibling of same sex		Hiet X	
Sibling of opposite sex, or spouse	Havan X		Balo' X
First child		Uyong X	
Other child	Akem X		He'et X
Several children		Liwe X	
All children		Lava' X	

Note: Except for Uyau and Utan, the necronyms are followed by the survivor's personal name.

17. *Lake'* for the men, *Doh* for the women (lake' = 'male', doh = 'female'). People who reach very old age usually replace Lake' or Doh by *Uku* (the root word for *muku* = 'old').

5

THE KENYAH*

HERBERT L. WHITTIER

IN the high interior portions of central Borneo live a people who call themselves and are called by others Kenyah. There are about 40,000 Kenyah comprising over forty named divisions and living in over 110 communities. The majority of these are located in the province of Kalimantan Timur, Indonesian Borneo. Here the Kenyah are located along the Kayan, Mahakam and Melanau rivers and their tributaries. The remainder are found along the Baluy and Baram rivers and their tributaries in the Fourth and Seventh divisions of Sarawak.[1]

Kenyah subsistence activities revolve around swidden rice agriculture which is supplemented by hunting, fishing and gathering. Wage labour and cash crops are now becoming important adjuncts to the economy in some areas. The Kenyah traditionally live in multi-long-house villages. Each family in a long-house has its own apartment, but a common verandah joins them all. Kenyah villages are, almost without exception, located at the confluence of two rivers. This provides maximum access to potential swidden land since all transportation is by river or foot.

The Kenyah are not united by a single political office, but they recognize themselves as a distinct people as opposed to their closest neighbours the Kayan and Punan. Although they are frequently lumped together by outsiders on the basis of superficial similarities, the Kenyah consider themselves quite distinct from the Kayan in their language and customs.

Most Kenyah origin stories place their homeland in the plateau

* Fieldwork in Indonesian Borneo was made possible through Public Health Service Research Fellowship 5 F01 MH43246-03 (CUAN) and Field Research Training Grant 1 T01 MH 11023-01 from the National Institute of Mental Health and was conducted in 1970–1. Fieldwork in Sarawak (1973–5) was made possible by a grant from the National Geographic Society's Committee for Research and Exploration and an award from the Department of Anthropology and the Center for Asian Studies at Michigan State University. Gratitude is due to the Lembaga Ilmu Pengatahuan Indonesia in Jakarta and the Sarawak Museum in Kuching for their help and sponsorship. Dr. George Appell and Dr. A. B. Hudson provided many criticisms and suggestions to drafts of this paper which have greatly aided in providing clarity although any shortcomings are those of the author. Finally Patricia Whittier, through her criticisms, suggestions and editorial work, has added immensely to any value this paper may have.

area at the headwaters of the Iwan, Bahau and Pujungan rivers (all tributaries of the Kayan river) in Kalimantan Timur or in the neighbouring Usun Apau (a plateau between the Baluy, Baram, and the aforementioned Kayan river tributaries). Putting the various stories together, it seems probable that the Kenyah were first in the Iwan Iot.[2] From there they split owing to overpopulation and intergroup warfare, with a large segment moving into the Usun Apau proper and other segments moving into the Bahau river. Perhaps 50 years later the Kayan peoples who were living in the Apo Kayan (the plateau at the headwaters of the Kayan river) began to speed up their exodus from that area. Some Kayan went into the Mahakam (where they are known as Busang and Bahau), others into the lower Kayan, and others into the Kapuas and Baluy rivers. Shortly thereafter, the Kenyah who were living in the Usun Apau moved down into the Baram proper and were replaced in the Usun Apau by other groups of Kenyah (e.g. the Lepo Tau, Lepo Jamuk, Lepo Aga and the Lepo Jingan) coming in from the Iwan Iot. At the same time other Kenyah (e.g. part of the Lepo Tau, the Lepo Tukung and the Uma Jalan) moved from the Iwan Iot into the Apo Kayan. From the Apo Kayan some Kenyah groups followed the Kayan to the Baluy and others went to the Baram. The migrations continue today; within the past 30 years large numbers of Kenyah have moved from the Apo Kayan into the Mahakam, Baluy, and the lower Kayan.

One of the largest divisions of Kenyah peoples is the Lepo Tau who comprise more than 4,000 of the total of 40,000 Kenyah and live in ten villages. My own research has concentrated on the Lepo Tau and while I do not claim that they are 'the typical Kenyah', the general principles of social organization seem to vary little between Kenyah groups.[3]

Three Lepo Tau villages will be the basis of the discussion in this paper. Two of them, Long Nawang and its daughter village Mara Satu, are on the Kayan river in Kalimantan Timur. Long Nawang is near the headwaters of the Kayan in the area known as the Apo Kayan and Mara Satu, composed largely of migrants from Long Nawang, is on the lower Kayan a short distance upriver from the coastal town of Tanjungselor. The third village, Long Moh, is near the headwaters of the Baram river in Sarawak.[4] About 200 years ago the ancestors of the people now in these villages lived in a single village in the Iwan. The village split with two of its long-houses moving into the Apo Kayan proper and eight others to the Usun Apau.

The group that moved into the Apo Kayan, after brief stays in various locations, ended up at Long Nawang, where they prospered and increased their numbers dramatically. Their descendants now populate seven Lepo Tau villages, the most recent of which is Mara

Satu. The larger group that had moved to the Usun Apau were decimated by epidemics at least three times. They moved from the Usun Apau to the Silat river (a tributary of the Baram) and, about 50 years ago, came to Long Moh. This is one of two Lepo Tau villages in Sarawak today. In about 1956, twenty-four families moved from Long Moh back to the Silat establishing the village of Long Makaba.

I should point out some major contrasts between the three villages. First, the two areas, Kalimantan Timur and Sarawak, were formerly under different colonial administrations and are now under different national governments with differing policies towards the upriver peoples. Secondly, there have been quite different missionary influences in the two areas. In Kalimantan Timur, the most active and influential mission has been an American fundamentalist group. In the Baram area of Sarawak, on the other hand, both Roman Catholic and fundamentalist missions have been active, with the former primarily influential in Long Moh. The three villages also differ in their relative physical isolation, with Long Nawang the most difficult of access (some thirty days by boat from the coastal town) and Mara Satu the easiest (a mere two-hour boat trip from the town). Long Moh is between these extremes (a day trip from the nearest bazaar and four or five days from the nearest town). Finally, the villages also differ in their duration as recognized units and in ethnic and religious composition. Long Nawang, which has been located at the same site for over 100 years, is composed almost entirely of Lepo Tau, with the minor exception of several in-marrying spouses. The inhabitants of Long Nawang consider the village to be entirely Christian; the majority of the population are members of the dominant fundamentalist sect KINGMI (Kemah Injil Gereja Masehi Indonesia), with a few adherents to another only slightly less fundamental group GPBI (Gereja Protestan(t) Bagian Indonesia). There are a few older people with some doubts but they are nominally Christian and there is no active practice of traditional Kenyah religious ritual.

Mara Satu is a new village, begun about 1968, with a core of Lepo Tau migrants from Long Nawang. They were joined by a few families from other Kenyah groups in the Apo Kayan, namely the Uma Jalan and Bakung, but Mara Satu is generally regarded as a Lepo Tau village. Like Long Nawang, Mara Satu is a Christian village with the majority of its members belonging to the KINGMI sect. It presents a unique situation in that the Kenyah here live side by side with Kayan. Mara Satu was originally a Kayan village and the migrant Kenyah asked and received permission from the Kayan to join them. Although officially one village, the Kenyah and Kayan units operate as distinct villages on a day-to-day basis and are even considered as such for certain government administrative purposes.

Long Moh has been at or very close to its present site for some 50 years. Although usually listed and referred to as a Lepo Tau village, it is actually composed of four groups. What I refer to here as Long Moh or Long Moh proper has Lepo Tau, Lepo Ngau and Lepo Linau components; the fourth group, Lepo Jingan, occupies one long-house at the downriver end of the village. Of the three groups in Long Moh proper, the Lepo Linau have virtually disappeared with only a few old people remaining who claim to be Lepo Linau; their distinct dialect and customs have vanished. The first two groups, on the other hand, are still viable and are, in fact, one basis for village factionalism. They retain certain differences in custom and ritual. Though intermarriage is common, long-houses are considered to belong to one or the other group and may be further distinguished by religious affiliation.

Long Moh is one of the few remaining Kenyah villages that does not consider itself Christian. About 10 per cent of its households are Roman Catholic, 3 per cent (2 households) are fundamentalist Protestant and the remainder, with 2 exceptions,[5] are adherents of the Bungan Cult, a reform version of the traditional Kenyah religion.[6]

The Lepo Jingan long-house (called by villagers 'Long Moh Keabat' or 'the downriver Long Moh') joined Long Moh about 25 years ago because its numbers had been decimated by disease. Their house is entirely Roman Catholic and is separated from Long Moh proper by a small stream. The Lepo Jingan have their own chief and act as a separate village. The relations between Long Moh and Long Moh Keabat are those that would obtain between separate villages even though in the government's eyes they are one village.

Extra-Village Organization

The various Kenyah divisions do not recognize any one individual who has legitimate authority over all Kenyah, nor is there any individual who claims authority over all villages of a particular division. The highest authority is vested in high chiefs of particular river systems or segments thereof. Prior to the European colonial administrations, the positions held by these high chiefs were not formalized offices. Their authority was based on military strength and heredity and supported by alliances with powerful families in other river valleys. Formerly, in both British and Dutch areas, the chiefs were supported and their positions institutionalized and stabilized by the colonial powers. The present national governments continue to support them. In Kalimantan the high chiefs are presently known as *kepala adat-istiadat besar* (lit. 'big chief of customs and traditions') and in Sarawak the lesser title of *penghulu* and the chief title of *temenggong* are used. In both colonial times and at present the government may provide some external guidance in the selection of new high chiefs necessitated by the death of or inadequate performance on the part of the office holder. Although today the chiefs are elected by the village chiefs, the elements of genealogy and social class still play a critical part in most of the selection processes.

In the Apo Kayan area there was one high chief until 1965 when the area was divided into two administrative subdivisions and a second chief created. The Bahau/Pujungan area has had two high chiefs since the 1900s. In Sarawak each of the major river valleys, the Baram and the Baluy, has a temenggong and several penghulu.

These high chiefs do not have regular formal meetings where all attend, but there are occasional meetings to consider specific problems. All the high chiefs, regardless of current national affiliation, are well known to each other and sometimes marriages are arranged among these highest families. For example, in the last generation, a sister of the high chief of the Apo Kayan was married to the high chief of the Pujungan. In the current generation, one of the sisters of the high chief of the Bahau is married to a high chief of the Melanau river area (a Kenyah émigré area in Kalimantan) while a second sister is married to the recently elected penghulu of the middle Baram, a younger brother of the late temenggong of the Baram.

The high chiefs in both Kalimantan and Sarawak are subject to the authority of the district officers (Sarawak) or *camat* (Kalimantan). Theoretically, they are consulted by government officials on any matters pertaining to their areas. They may arbitrate inter-village or intra-village disputes that cannot be solved at the village level. Criminal matters, such as murder, are handled by government courts. However, the line between matters to be handled by the courts and those handled by chiefs is not always clear. In some cases it may be up to the litigants. In most cases there is a definite preference to try to solve cases on the local or river system level, for cases invariably involve fines and redressive measures which all Kenyah feel are best confined to their own system. Cases taken to the courts invariably result in at least part of the fine as well as court costs being lost to the Kenyah.

Intra-Village Organization

The Village (lepo)

Under each penghulu or kepala adat-istiadat besar are several villages. Each village has a chief called in Kenyah *penghabio dalam lepo* (lit. 'big one of the village') or *paran lepo* (lit. 'leader of the village'); today the Malay and Indonesian terms *tua kampong* and *kepala kampong* respectively are used much more commonly than the Kenyah terms.[7] The tua kampong (for convenience I will use one term) is responsible to both the high chief and the district officer or camat. He has to keep order generally in his village and see that his villagers carry out edicts from government officials whether they come to him directly or via the high chief. He represents his village at meetings and is assumed to speak for the general public opinion in the village. As might be expected, one of the ideal characteristics of a tua kampong is that he be an excellent public speaker. Although there are some recent exceptions,[8] the tua kampong is generally from a high-class family. Genealogy certainly plays a part in his selection but the position is not strictly hereditary.

If all goes well, a man is expected to hold this position for life although there have been cases of voluntary retirement in old age. In recent years there seems to be increasing dissatisfaction among tua kampong. Several felt that the rewards were very small and the work too time-consuming; several had also requested or planned to request replacement. Unlike formerly, today's tua kampong are in the government bureaucracy. They are, in a sense, unsalaried civil servants and are sometimes placed in the awkward position of being responsible for carrying out unpopular government edicts. While the work load has increased, the prerogatives formerly accorded tua kampong, such as labour on their fields, have decreased. This adds a new dimension to the selection process: who is willing to serve? It is quite possible that the capable son of a retiring or deceased tua kampong 'does not choose to run'.

Land is considered to be owned by the village and each has clearly defined boundaries for its land which coincide with the boundaries of adjacent villages. In the past, population pressures have not been great and there have been few inter-village disputes over boundaries. In fact, frequently a village will allow near-by villages to use land within its boundaries, but permission must be asked in advance. In the case of the Lepo Tau at Long Moh, their entire holding of land was given to them by the upriver village of Long Sela'an when the Lepo Tau migrated from the Silat river.

Kenyah villages are usually located at the confluence (*long*) of a small stream with a large river; in most cases the smaller stream provides the village with its name (i.e. Long Moh is situated at the confluence of the Moh river with the Baram).[9] Physically, the long-houses are almost always parallel to the river with notched log ladders descending to the river where the banks are steep. At the upriver end of the village, on a hill, are located the *belawing* or sacred poles used during *mamat* ceremonies and village cleansing rituals. Downriver from the village, either on the opposite bank or separated by a small stream from the village, is the *pulong* or cemetery. These are gradually extended downriver as new plots are cleared to accommodate each new death. One cannot cut underbrush or anything within the cemetery proper, so the result is a strip cemetery along the river's edge.

A Kenyah usually describes himself as a member of a particular village; he is not just a 'Lepo Tau' or a 'Badang' but a 'Lepo Tau Long Nawang' or a 'Badang Lio Mato'. Kenyah villages typically consist of several long-houses, as opposed to, for example, Iban practice where one long-house usually constitutes a village. If there is more than one Kenyah division in a village, each has its own house or houses; a house will not be mixed except for intermarriage. In Kalimantan, Kenyah villages are usually composed of only one division: Long Nawang is a Lepo Tau village; Long Ampung is an Uma Jalan village. In the Baram area of Sarawak, however, one frequently finds two or more sub-units in a village. This situation was originally brought about by the decimation of the population through disease and warfare. The remaining members amalgamated with the remnants of other divisions to form villages of viable size such as Long Moh.

The village acts as a collectivity in the timing of tasks in the agricultural cycle as well as in certain ritual and ceremonial contexts. Each separate task in the agricultural cycle (e.g. clearing, planting, weeding) is marked by rituals. No household may begin work until the appropriate ritual has been performed on behalf of the entire village by the specialist in charge of agricultural ritual (*laki malan*).[10] An elder male from each household attends the ritual on behalf of his household. On the day of each ritual the entire village is in a state of ritual prohibition (*malan*) in which no one may leave the village nor may strangers enter. This malan also obtains on the occasion of the death of a villager. A serious delict on the part of an individual (e.g. an illegitimate child for whom the mother refuses to name a father) places the entire village in jeopardy and requires the performance of cleansing rituals on behalf of the village. The village will also act in concert to ritually fence the village from the encroachment of disease from other villages.

The fundamentalist Protestant villages of Long Nawang and Mara Satu no longer perform the agricultural rituals. There is more individualism in the timing of agricultural tasks although for ecological reasons each household performs the same tasks at approximately the same time. Of course, the village-wide malan no longer obtain. There is still some feeling that people should remain in the village on the occasion of a death but the reasons given are social (e.g. 'to help the family', 'to show respect'), and there is no prohibition on strangers entering the village, nor is there ritual danger in leaving it. In Long Moh proper there is a mutual tolerance between the majority Bungan

Cult and the Catholic households. For the more important segments of the agricultural cycle the Catholics hold their own rituals but theirs are timed to be contemporaneous with the Bungan rituals so that all villagers follow the same agricultural scheduling. The Catholic families also observe the malan and many attend the Bungan rituals or, if not the rituals themselves, the accompanying feast and festivities. By the same token, the Bungan people often attend the festivities of the major Catholic rituals at Christmas and Easter.

Emphasis on the rule of consensus in small communities is a time-worn theme in anthropology, but we must bring it out once again in the case of the Kenyah. Some tua kampong are certainly forceful personalities but none rules by fiat. Any decision made on behalf of the village is made by an informal council of male elders. No Kenyah can define exactly what constitutes an elder and there is no one point in a man's life at which he suddenly becomes one. It is a gradual process of greater involvement in village affairs.

For discussion of village matters, the tua kampong may actually call a meeting. In such a case anyone may attend. There may be a few women, particularly elderly ones, as well as children. Younger women may be present if they happen to live in the long-house where the meeting takes place or if they have a particular interest in the matter under discussion. But the seating arrangements and the level of participation make clear who the important voices are. Before the meeting there is usually a good deal of informal talk around the village, so that even the elders in their formal speeches are actually presenting a kind of consensus, combined with their knowledge of other similar matters in the past and the wisdom of their years. The matter of social class is relevant here also. Although any elder has the respect of others, it is the voices of the aristocrats that carry more weight.[11] After everyone has spoken the tua kampong presents his view—actually a consensus view—and if all are in agreement the matter is decided. If not, then the discussion goes another round and another until the matter is settled. On lesser issues the tua kampong may act without such a formal meeting, but even in such cases he will talk individually and informally with various elders before making a decision. This is not to say that a tua kampong needs no leadership qualities. Indeed, by skilful rhetoric and demonstrated wisdom he can often lead a group to consensus.

The Long-house (uma')

Kenyah villages characteristically have more than one long-house. The long-houses usually have 10 to 15 apartments (*lamin*), though there are a few enormous structures like the 65 lamin house at Long Ampung in the Apo Kayan.[12] The separate apartments each have a door opening on to a commonly owned covered verandah (*use*).[13]

The apartments in these traditional structures comprise one large room with, in one area, a hearth, storage for firewood and a place to prepare food. The placement of this area varies according to the inhabitants' taste. It may be partially walled off with a few boards from the rest of the room. The remaining area is open and there coarse mats are spread for the family, fine ones for guests. There may be a slightly raised platform at one side of the room for sleeping or where honoured guests can be fed or wined. A family member who is very old or ill or a new mother is provided with a sleeping place near the hearth.

Many long-houses today are elevated only 4 to 6 feet from the ground but informants say that in the past they were always much higher to help minimize risks from would-be headhunters. Modern style long-houses, more in conformity with the government's ideas about proper housing, are now being built. These are elevated 8 to 10 feet so that the area under the house provides space for storage as well as for activities such as threshing *padi*. This usage is contingent upon compliance with another government idea—that pigs should be in pens or fenced out of the house area and not roaming freely. The other recent innovation provides that kitchens should be several feet distant from the living quarters. As a result, the modern long-house actually comprises two series of rooms, with kitchens separated at the rear, but connected to the main structure by a walkway. In practice this new form seems to result in each household eating, sleeping and 'living' in the kitchen while the front room is used for such things as storage or guest quarters. The new design also uses almost twice as much lumber and other building materials as the traditional one. Consequently, there are new houses that have already been 5 or 6 years under construction. These are generally built of sawn timber and boards: sometimes a man of means may even use plywood. Gone are the magnificent structures supported by uprights 3 or 4 feet in diameter and floored with smooth 4-foot wide planks.

The verandah of the long-house is a public area. Access to the house is usually gained by a notched log at either end of the verandah but some of the 'modern' houses have proper stairs. Much sedentary work such as the splitting of rattan for mats and baskets, sewing and handicrafts, is done on the verandah in the company of others doing similar work. The rhythm of the work is helped along by the easy, casual conversation with neighbours. The verandah is also the place for relaxation. During the day the workers are joined by anyone who wants to rest or by people whose primary task is watching infants. After the evening meal, virtually the entire populace of the house can be found on the verandah enjoying the cool air and the companionship of friends and neighbours. Here the events of the day

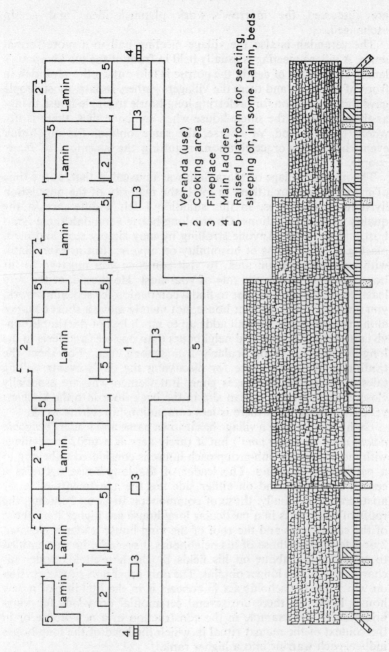

1 Veranda (use)
2 Cooking area
3 Fireplace
4 Main ladders
5 Raised platform for seating,
  sleeping or, in some Lamin, beds

Fig. 1 Plan and Front Elevation of a Kenyah Long-house

are discussed, the morrow's work planned, ideas and gossip exchanged.

The verandah is also the village meeting hall in a more formal sense. A village meeting is usually held in front of the tua kampong's lamin. In the case of death, the corpse is laid out on the verandah in front of his lamin and there the villagers gather. In fact, most people gave this as a reason for preferring long-house to single-house living; as they put it 'In the single-house when someone dies, there is nowhere to sit.' And, of course, the same obtains for any other event, be it crisis or celebration, requiring the assembly of many people.

The migrant village of Mara Satu was unusual in that, at the time of my initial research there in 1971, the majority of the population lived in single-houses. In this situation I felt a difference in the quality of social relations. On the long-house verandah there is no host and no guest. Anyone strolling by may simply stop and chat, placing no obligations of hospitality on anyone. But in Mara Satu, with no such common area, to visit someone you must go to his house, placing him in the role of your host. He should, at the very least, serve a drink. In order to find a companion for sedentary work, you must go out to another house, not merely move a short distance along the verandah. This all adds up to much less of the simple conviviality among friends and neighbours than one sees and feels in the long-house. This is particularly true among men. For them the traditional gathering place for discussing the day's events, telling tales of hunts and travels, is gone. But women who are especially close friends or relatives can slip in the back door into the kitchen; yet even among them there is less companionship during work.

Each long-house in a village has its own name and leader (*pengabio dalam uma'* or *paran uma'*) but it rarely acts as a unit. In a village with more than one sub-group each house is considered to belong to a particular sub-group. The leader of the long-house occupies a central apartment and on either side are the apartments of lesser aristocrats and, finally, those of commoners. In Long Nawang, the roofs of aristocrats in a particular long-house are higher than those of the commoners and the roof of the long-house leader is elevated 2 or 3 feet above those of his neighbours. Formerly, he was entitled to several days labour on his fields by the households under his charge, but this no longer obtains. The only other non-ritual occasion on which the households act in concert is in the building of a new house. However, there are several ceremonial occasions for long-house unity, for example in the construction of a new house or in the context of the mamat ritual in which the head of the long-house inducts each warrior into a higher rank.[14]

In front of each house is a fenced enclosure containing a sacred plant and a carving which is the dwelling of *bali akang* (spirit of bravery). In the rafters of the house in front of the lamin of the long-house chief are the sacred skulls, charms and other ritual paraphernalia, including a large war drum. When a new house is built all these items must be moved to the new house with appropriate ritual. Other occasions for long-house co-operation revolve around the ceremonial activities of the individual households. If the household is a commoner one, other members of the long-house should participate, as guests at least, in ceremonies such as the naming of a child. For an aristocrat, this would be a village-wide affair. To say that the long-house should take part does not, of course, obviate participation by members of other houses. Close kinsmen would be expected to participate regardless of residence.

My informants agreed that it is theoretically possible for the long-house as a unit to be malan just as in the case of an entire village, but none could think of any occasion when this had occurred. As a hypothetical example, one informant, after much thought, offered the example of illness which seemed to be confined to members of one long-house. In such a case, she said, perhaps the spirit medium (*ia on bali*) would perform a ceremony for the house and declare a malan. But, having given this example, she added that illness confined to one house was fairly unlikely and that the ceremony would more probably be performed on behalf of the whole village.

A household may detach itself from a long-house with the permission of its chief and the payment of a fine to the house. In order to join another long-house, it must have the consent of the head of that house. Before granting permission, the long-house head will consult the other members of his house. This is a fairly rare occurrence but during the past 20 or 30 years it seems to have increased due to shifts in religious affiliation. During the period of Christianization in Long Nawang, for example, certain long-houses became 'Christian' while others did not and households moved from one long-house to another in order to be with others of like religious persuasion. In Long Moh proper today the five original long-houses have been torn down and the rebuilding is in process. When complete there will be six long-houses, two of the 'Catholic' houses composed of households from the other five long-houses. It is also possible, and today acceptable but not encouraged, for a household to detach itself from the long-house and erect a single-house. When a household moves out of the long-house it may take with it the building materials in its own apartment, including roofing materials, but not the structural timbers. Nor may it take the flooring or roofing of the verandah section in front of the apartment, even though it originally provided these.[15] If it is to join another long-house, it will build a shack near or attached to the new house. Long-houses are rebuilt every 10 to 15 years and at this time the new household will construct a proper apartment in the rebuilt house.

Long-house membership persists even in the absence of the physical structure. During our stay at Long Moh rebuilding was in process and had been for several years. The long-houses had been torn down and for several years people had been housed in small temporary long-houses of 5 or 6 lamin and in single houses while collecting enough building material for new houses. Even so, each household saw itself and was seen by others as belonging to a particular long-house. For the warrior ranking ceremony during the mamat festival each man returned to his own long-house.

The Household (lamin)

The basic unit of organization for the Kenyah is the household or apartment. The Kenyah term lamin applies to both the physical structure and its members. Lamin vary in their number of members with the average at Long Nawang 7·8 and at Long Moh 9·2. Aristocratic lamin tend to be, on average, slightly larger than those of commoners. At Long Nawang aristocrats averaged 9·9 persons per lamin while commoners averaged 7·2; for Long Moh equivalent figures are 10·0 and 8·8. Almost everyone expresses an ideal for large lamin and the ability to maintain this brings prestige to the head of such a household. And, indeed, it should, for the Kenyah also acknowledge that difficulties in interpersonal relations increase with lamin size; it takes a household head of great diplomatic skill to maintain a large household in harmony.

The following table presents statistics for family types in Long Nawang and Long Moh, for each village as a whole and for aristocrats and commoners in each village.

Lamin Types[16]

	Long Nawang 1970	Long Moh 1974
Nuclear Families	32·15%	41·94%
Stem Families[17]	45·00%	38·71%
Joint Families	22·85%	19·35%
	100·00%	100·00%
	N=100	N=62

Lamin Types by Social Class

	Aristocrats		Commoners	
	L. Nawang	L. Moh	L. Nawang	L. Moh
Nuclear Families	9·00%	37·93%	37·80%	45·45%
Stem Families	52·00%	34·48%	44·00%	42·42%
Joint Families	39·00%	27·58%	18·20%	12·12%

Such statistics, of course, represent only a synchronic picture in 1970 (Long Nawang) and 1974 (Long Moh). Kenyah lamin are not static and the various types are but stages in the domestic cycle. A newly married couple takes up residence in either parental household. The Lepo Tau say that there is no rule of viri–or uxorilocality.[18] The matter is decided at a meeting of both sets of parents. Sometimes the young couple moves back and forth for a few months lending their labour when it is most needed, but by the time there is a child, they should be settled in the lamin previously decided. Occasionally there is an arrangement whereby they will live in one household for a fixed period, then move to the other, but this is an unusual situation (see below). The couple remains in the parental lamin with its growing family. Meanwhile, other siblings marry and some, with their spouses, join the parental household. As numbers increase, so do interpersonal tensions and the lamin may decide to split, with one of the married siblings forming a new household with his spouse and children. There is no rule about which sibling should remain in the natal household (*lamin po'on*). There are a few exceptions, but generally it is rare for married siblings to remain in the lamin po'on throughout their adult lives and most unusual for them to do so after the death of the parents. In the usual course of events siblings move out one by one, either to a spouse's lamin or to form their own household and the lamin po'on is left with one married sibling, his/her spouse and children and the elderly parent(s). The parents then die, bringing the lamin back to the nuclear family stage. One of the children marries, brings in a spouse, and the cycle begins again.[19]

The lamin is the unit of production and consumption. Each married couple in it is expected to make its own rice fields (*uma*) adequate for its needs and those of its children and to accomplish this most nuclear families prefer to make two rice fields separate from one another each year. Likewise any young adult member (person of marriageable age) is expected to make his own field or at least a cassava garden. Thus, most lamin will have several fields each year. But the produce from the various fields goes into a common store,[20] and cooking is done in common. The fruits of hunting, fishing and gathering likewise go into the common pot. Of course, herein lies a source of tension among married siblings, with accusations that one's sibling or sibling's spouse is not contributing a fair share. The introduction of cash crops, primarily rubber and secondarily pepper (throughout Sarawak), and wage labour brings in new complications. Everyone agrees that the cash a man earns from the sale of rubber, pepper or his labour is his (or his nuclear family's) but he can hardly refuse to use the cash for goods such as salt and kerosene that will be used by the entire lamin.

The lamin is the locus of rights to land within the village boundaries. An individual initially establishes the right of his lamin to use a plot of land by clearing primary forest. Control over that plot is then mediated by the head of the lamin. Most frequently the senior generation in the lamin exerts its rights to lands closest to the village, while younger couples go farther afield and fell primary forest, thus establishing new primary rights to land for the lamin. If the individual who cleared the land leaves the lamin the control of the land remains in that household. He retains what we might call secondary right but he must ask permission of the lamin head to use the land. For example, if a man clears primary forest while resident in his natal lamin with his brother and then sets up a new lamin, he must ask his brother's permission before using the land again. Likewise, if a couple is resident in the wife's lamin, and cuts primary forest, then is divorced, the husband returning to his natal lamin loses his primary rights to the land, as do any children who go with him. These children may ask permission from the head of the mother's lamin to use the land but their claims are secondary to the claims of those remaining in that household.

The splitting of a lamin does not create two new households with equal rights in the estate. The lamin po'on retains primary control over all the land rights it has acquired. The 'daughter' lamin can use the land on the basis of secondary rights and it can acquire its own primary rights by felling virgin forest. When people speak of using land to which their rights are beyond the secondary level, they say they are 'borrowing' the land. For example, one man told us he was 'borrowing' land from his wife's mother's brother. The mother had left her lamin po'on (her brother's lamin) so her rights were secondary. Her daughter (our informant's wife) had, in turn, left her lamin po'on (her mother's lamin) so her rights to the land were what we might call tertiary.

The Field House (lubong petok)

The cultivation of swidden fields at some distance from the village has resulted in another Kenyah organizational unit—the *tudo* or *lubong petok* which is a long-house in the field area.[21] It is no field hut but a fairly substantial structure built to last for a number of years. Physically, it is a smaller version of the village long-house, complete with verandah and a lamin for each family, but it differs somewhat in organization and ritual matters, from the long-house proper. Firstly, each lamin usually houses only one nuclear family. The lamin in the lubong petok do not necessarily parallel those in a village long-house, since they may be drawn from several long-houses in the village. Each lubong petok has a leader, chosen by consensus and usually an aristocrat. The position is considered temporary and may last only one or two seasons. His main duties are to coordinate activities when necessary and to adjudicate minor disputes and conflicts in the lubong petok. Secondly, the lubong petok is not a discrete ritual unit. For village-wide rituals its inhabitants must return to the village. For effectiveness most of the village-wide rituals require all members in village territory to be physically present within the village during the malan (taboo) periods. Most charms (*siap*) and sacred heads are kept in the village, and most rituals require the co-ordinated efforts of more than one ritual specialist (even though the actual performance may only involve one person). A few minor rituals can occur at the lubong petok but these are generally family-specific. In the case of illness in several families, a curing ritual might be held for all, or drums might be beaten in case of high winds, but these are relatively small matters.

The lubong petok arrangement seems to point out lines of potential village schism, and indeed this process was close to culmination with one of the lubong petok in the Long Moh area. Over a period of years a number of people had aligned themselves with the Long Lelum lubong petok. Some people had not shared the group's interests and had moved out, while other families had moved in. Most of the eleven remaining families were Christian, and thus not in need of the village ritual specialists. The land they were using actually belonged to another village (Long Seminang) and they (the residents of Long Lelum) had been told that they could have rights to the land if they wished to establish a village. During my stay at Long Moh, two aristocratic families were recruited and asked to join the lubong petok at Long Lelum. The reality of the possible schism became obvious at an adat law case where several members of the Long Lelum lubong petok were fined for planting their crops before the laki malan had opened the first day of planting for the village. If asked directly, most people would deny that Long Lelum lubong petok was considering forming its own village. The value on community solidarity is high and Kenyah are generally reluctant to speculate on or predict future events. But it became more and more obvious that the formation of a new village was in process.

A similar split had occurred 15 years previously when the old adat head gathered at his lubong petok the remaining families to practice Adat Po'on in contrast to the other families which had converted to the reformed Adat Bungan. This small village lasted only a short time; some of the members died of old age, and some of the younger members converted to Adat Bungan. In the end the three remaining families rejoined the village proper at Long Moh and the potential hiving was aborted.[22]

In the fields surrounding the lubong petok and in the fields close to the village where lubong petok are not necessary, there are field huts (*lepau*). These are small structures, ranging from simple lean-tos to off-the-ground structures with floors and bark or thatch walls. The family going out from the village or from the lubong petok to work in the field uses the lepau for shelter from rain, resting, preparing meals and occasionally for sleeping.

Co-operative Labour Groups

The ultimate responsibility for the rice field resides in the nuclear family with both men and women contributing labour, although on some tasks there is division of labour by sex. In the clearing phase of the agricultural cycle men do the work of felling the larger trees while women concentrate on smaller trees and undergrowth. In planting the men make the holes with special dibble sticks while women come behind with small baskets of seeds, depositing 7–10 seeds in each hole. These divisions, however, are not immutable; if one sex is over-represented in the labour force, some individuals may perform tasks generally assigned to the opposite sex.

The labour at certain phases of the cycle lends itself to groups larger than the nuclear family and at these times, exchange labour groups are formed. Clearing, planting and harvesting are the major occasions for this. There are two kinds of group labour organization: *mabe* and *semunyun*.

Mabe is obligatory labour owed by villagers to the village chief and also to the laki malan on specific fields (long-house chiefs supposedly had this prerogative also in days gone by, but not today). While the chief and the laki malan each has his own personal fields, each also has a field which accompanies his office. On this field, each household contributes a minimum of 4 days labour: a day for felling the forest; a day for planting; a day for weeding; and a day for harvesting. On each appointed day each household sends one person. Given 59 lamin in Long Moh proper, then, at each of these events one could expect to find 59 people present. Lamin which for any reason do not send a representative are subject to a fine by the village chief or the laki malan. The yield from the chief's official field helps him fulfil his obligations to host visitors and to contribute heavily to village-level rituals. One chief supposedly sold some of the rice from the office's field and used the money for his personal ends. He came under severe criticism from the villagers and suffered a great loss of influence. The yield from the laki malan's field, on the other hand, is considered to be his and may be seen as a form of payment for the heavy ritual responsibilities he must endure throughout the year. The chief and the laki malan are obliged to provide a substantial noon meal for the workers. The meal should contain meat; if it does not, people feel short-changed.

Semunyun, on the other hand, is strictly reciprocal labour exchange. This is a very popular institution and makes the arduous work on swidden fields seem lighter. Semunyun groups are generally phase-specific. That is, a group may be organized for the felling or planting, but not necessarily endure into other phases of the rice cycle or even throughout an entire phase.

Membership in semunyun groups is by choice based on such considerations as friendship, age,[23] and proximity of fields. There is also concern for the welfare of widows and the elderly; an attempt is made to include them in groups where they will receive the greatest return. Group membership is by individuals, not by lamin; thus, husband and wife may belong to different groups though they are gaining labour for their joint field. Although membership is individual, if a person is ill on one day, he may send someone else from his lamin to substitute for him.

The groups are usually small—6 to 8 persons—but larger groups of 10 to 20 are not unheard of. After the group has made one round of a day each on each member's field, it may dissolve or it may continue on another round.

The host for the day's labour must provide the noon meal and, if possible, he should also provide an evening meal with rice wine to follow. Where the host is a widow, poor, or elderly, less is expected and people may bring their own rice for the noon meal.

A third type of collective labour occurs during the harvest phase of the rice cycle. If a family has a particularly good yield on a large field, it may call people who have completed their own harvest to help. These workers are paid in kind with a portion of their cutting. The amount is not fixed but is usually about 10 gallons per day. This practice enables families with small fields and those who have had a poor yield to supplement their stores. It is also sound practice for the owner of the large field. If his is the only field remaining in the area after all others are harvested, he is likely to suffer large losses from birds and other predators. Also, as the rice becomes over-mature, it may begin to fall or the stalks bend under their load, or rain may come. So, the loss of part of the crop to hired cutters is more than compensated for.

There is another kind of group labour, more often based on kinship, that is not direct exchange. In the cases of widows or widowers with small children, and elderly people, I noted several cases of groups forming for a day's labour without any expectation of direct exchange. This was referred to as simply helping out.

Social Stratification

Social class is a pervasive feature of Kenyah social life.[24] As with many facets of Kenyah custom, the social class system has changed somewhat with the switch from Adat Po'on to Adat Bungan. Under Adat Po'on there were five classes distinguished by differences in adat. These were *deta'u bio* (lit. 'big aristocrats'), *deta'u dumit* (lit.

'small aristocrats'), *panyin tiga* (lit. 'good commoners'), *panyin ja'at* (lit. 'bad commoners') and *panyin lamin* (slaves or their descendants). Under Adat Bungan four of these classes still exist but in fact, only two broad divisions are significant in terms of adat and ritual differences. These are *deta'u* and *panyin*, the latter more generally referred to as *kelunan kado'* or 'the many'.

The deta'u bio (and their families) were and are the leaders of the village and long-houses. Deta'u dumit represent more distant branches of the deta'u bio families who have descended somewhat by marriage with commoners or who have done nothing to distinguish themselves over several generations. In general these aristocrats are considered to be vested with superior knowledge of adat and should also be models to the rest of the community. They control the ritual which maintains the adat as well as redress breaches of customary law. Panyin tiga is also a mixed grouping and may have originated from intermarriage between panyin ja'at and deta'u families, or by individuals who have distinguished themselves over time. Deta'u dumit who have repeatedly intermarried with panyin ja'at may also eventually become panyin tiga. It is most clearly a transitional class. Panyin ja'at are the ordinary commoners. The panyin lamin were originally war captives and their descendants were 'owned' only by deta'u families. Under Adat Bungan and external government policies they are now 'freemen' and are included within the panyin category.

Under Adat Po'on each of the four non-slave classes had adat appropriate to that class. In the agricultural rituals performed by the laki malan on behalf of the entire village, each class was mentioned individually and a sacrifice made for it. During the first two weeks of planting, each class also had special days on which only its fields could be planted. In the ranking part of the mamat rituals and in the mamat itself, each class again had its own sacrifices and parts in the ritual.

Under Adat Bungan there are only two formal ritual divisions, the deta'u and the panyin, except in the case of the planting days in which the finer distinctions are still used. Each lamin, as a ritual unit, is considered to be either deta'u or panyin and follows the appropriate adat. A lamin cannot be mixed; all members follow either one or the other adat. In the case of a deta'u–panyin marriage, the in-marrying spouse follows the adat of his/her new residence. He/she is not considered to have actually changed social class but in ritual matters the adat of the new household will be used. Children belong to the class of their natal lamin. Thus, if a panyin man marries a deta'u woman and takes up residence in her lamin he follows the deta'u adat. His class has not actually changed; people still think of him as a panyin and, indeed, it would be considered unseemly and pretentious if he tried to act as a deta'u in such matters as seating arrangements at meetings. His children, however, are considered to be deta'u.[25]

Obviously, then, there is a certain amount of mobility in the class system, not for an individual but for his descendants over two or three generations. A man born a panyin remains so even though he may distinguish himself but, by judicious marriages and choices of residence, his grandchildren may come to be deta'u. After two or three generations 'genealogical amnesia' sets in and their panyin descent is forgotten in favour of deta'u links.

People who try to 'move up' too soon or with too many panyin marriages in recent generations are generally felt to be 'high in the mind' or presumptuous, as are people who use adat or symbols appropriate to a higher class. According to informants, the incidence of such offences was formerly quite low due to fear of *parib*, a state of ritual impurity which could result in illness or even death.[26] In Long Moh today, however, the fear of parib is minimal. It appears to be one of the aspects of Adat Po'on that was eliminated, along with the omen birds, by Adat Bungan.

In Long Nawang Adat Christian has also eliminated parib as a powerful force. Except for the occasions of birth and death one finds people there using symbols that would surely have resulted in parib previously. One deta'u man in Long Nawang complained that the biggest current problem in village organization is that too many people feel themselves to be deta'u or *paran* ('leaders'). Today, in Long Nawang, it is primarily social disapproval and gossip that remain to keep things in check.

In Long Nawang there is also a tendency to merge the former class divisions into two broad classes and to talk about deta'u or paran and panyin. But, of course, here the ritual distinctions no longer exist. Leaders usually come from the higher class though there are a few exceptions. In the context of the Church organization, there has been a tendency for Church leaders to come from the higher class also, but this seems to be diminishing with the realization that Church leadership offers few material rewards.

Kinship and Marriage

Kenyah reckon kinsmen bilaterally with almost equal emphasis on matrilateral and patrilateral kin, though the naming system, for everyday purposes has a patrilineal cast. A child carries his own personal name plus his father's personal name. Thus, Kuleh the son of Sigau is Kuleh Sigau. It is permissible to use female links in establishing descent lines and in this process one might use the mother's name rather than that of the father. If the Kuleh above has a mother named Bungan and he is establishing a descent line in which she is a link, he will for this purpose refer to himself as Kuleh Bungan. But for common usage, the father's name is used. The exception is an illegitimate child for whom the mother does not name a father.

After an individual marries and has children one rarely hears his personal name used in either reference or address for, at this point, teknonyms are used almost exclusively. After the first child is born the parents are called *Tama Weng* and *Tina Weng* (father and mother of a boy child) or *Tama Aping* and *Tina Aping* (father and mother of a girl child).

After the child receives his name at about one month of age, the parents become *Tama* (name of child) and *Tina* (name of child).[27] When a person has a grandchild, his name again changes and he reverts to his personal name with the prefix *Pe* indicating the respected grandparent status. For example, a man named Sigau Jalong has a male infant. After the birth of the infant he is Tama Weng Sigau (or Tama Weng Sigau Jalong for greater specificity) and is addressed as Tama Weng. After the child receives his name, Kuleh for example, the father becomes Tama Kuleh Sigau. If the child lives and there are no more children and, in due course, Kuleh marries and produces a child, Tama Kuleh becomes PeSigau Jalong.

Interwoven with the system of parental teknonyms and grandparental prefixes is a complex system of death names, names taken by an individual on the death of a relative.

The third system of appellation is kinship terminology. In Ego's generation siblings are *chenganak* but this is heard in reference only. Equally frequent in reference and used always in address (where a kin term is used) are the terms *sekun* (older sibling) and *sadin* (younger sibling). In address, names are more commonly used among siblings than kin terms. Cousins are *chenganak sa'* but the terms sekun and sadin are more frequently applied. Cousins to the fourth degree are recognized kinsmen and precise descriptive terms can be applied: *chenganak sa'* (first cousin); *chenganak sa' dua liwe* (second cousin); *chenganak sa' telu liwe* (third cousin); *chenganak sa' pat liwe* (fourth cousin), but such terms are very rarely used. In discussing a collateral of the same generation, the term chenganak (or chenganak sa') or sekun or sadin would be used. If more precise information were desired Ego would describe the relationship, e.g. 'his grandfather was the elder brother of my grandfather'. A sibling's spouse or a spouse's sibling may be referred to and addressed by sibling terms but names are more commonly used in address. There is a term of reference, *sabai*, which means affine of the same generation but it is rarely used.

The terms *ame* (father) and *uwe'* (mother) are commonly applied to collaterals as well as lineals of the first ascending generation. They are also applied to affines of the first ascending generation. The relationship may be specified slightly more precisely by the term *ame mpe* (for males) or *uwe' mpe* (for females) which may refer to siblings of either parent or their spouses. In address, the terms *ame* and *uwe'* may be extended to any individual of the appropriate generation. For the second generation and above there are differences in usage between Long Nawang and Long Moh. In Long Nawang the term *poi* is used for grandparents and their siblings for both reference and address. It is widely extended in address to almost anyone of the second ascending generation. The term *uko* is used for the third ascending generation and above and may be extended to the sense of 'ancestor'.

In Long Moh the term *poi* is not a kinship term but rather a death name. Members of the second generation and above are referred to and addressed as *uko*.

The term for the first descending generation is *anak* in both reference and address. If it is necessary to distinguish one's own from collaterals' children the term *anak ahong* (Long Nawang) or *anak a'ong* (Long Moh) may be used. It is more usual in address to use the form *anak ke* (my child).

For the second and subsequent descending generations the term *tsu* is used. There are other terms of reference: *tsu siku* (great-grand-child) and *tsu lup* (great-great-grandchild) but these are rarely used. One instance of their use might be to describe a person of great age, 'He has tsu lup', i.e. 'He is very, very old.'

The Kenyah do not have a special term for the grouping of kinsmen that anthropologists call 'the kindred' although the term *chenganak* (sibling) may be extended to the sense of 'relatives'. Nevertheless principles generally associated with the concept of the kindred are important organizational features within Kenyah society. It is from one's kindred that cooperation is expected particularly on the occasion of life-crisis rituals (e.g. naming ceremonies, marriage, death). In Long Nawang, and to a lesser extent in Long Moh, the kindred is drawn together in the production of the highly ornamented *ba' anak* (baby carrier). For a deta'u child in particular the ba' anak requires the assembly of a large amount of wealth and powerful symbols in the form of beads, tiger and leopard teeth and coins. The source of these items are members of the infant's kindred, who are for a time drawn together in their recognition of their new relative and validation of his place in society.[28]

Among the Lepo Tau, marriage is ideally class endogamous, at least for a first marriage. First cousin marriage is permitted for aristocrats with payment of a fine but it is not preferred. For commoners it is prohibited. Brother-sister exchange of the following type: △ = ○ △ = ○ is ideally prohibited though there are occasional cases of it. Both brother-sister exchange and first cousin marriage are considered potentially dangerous and 'hot'; for aristocrats the preference for class endogamy occasionally overrides the fear of first cousin marriage. Marriage with cousins beyond the first cousin is permitted in all classes.

Children who have grown up in the same lamin should not marry even though there is no blood relationship because 'they have lived like siblings'.

Among the Kenyah marriages are seldom arranged without the consent of the couple. According to older informants this has always been the case with the exception of the marriages of very high aristocrats to aristocrats of other villages or river valleys for the purpose of cementing political alliance. Even in these cases the couple had to at least consent albeit they were under a great deal of pressure to do so. Parents can, of course, advise and even exert a little pressure on a son to look carefully at a particular girl, or on a daughter to be particularly friendly and receptive to a certain boy. Most people also say that they would not want to marry against the strong objections of their parents, but pressure can also be exerted in the other direction. The ultimate weapon of a very determined couple is pregnancy; in this case the parents have no choice but to agree to a wedding. In the normal course of events, a boy who has his eye on a particular girl sends a group of his close friends along to sound out the young woman's feelings on the matter. If the friends report favourably, the boy tells his parents and they find a go-between, usually a *kelunan lata* ('elder'), male or female, not necessarily a relative, to visit the girl's parents. The go-between asks the parents whether or not anyone else has already asked for their daughter. If they and the daughter reply in the negative, the go-between states the purpose of the mission and the name of the boy. If the girl and her parents take a favourable stand, the go-between reports to the boy's parents and arranges a meeting of the couple and both sets of parents. The go-between may act as a sort of mediator. It is at this meeting that the all-important matter of post-marital residence is decided. Informants described the discussions as *punan kini, punan kina* (lit. 'to pull here, to pull there') meaning that, given the value on large households and the reluctance to lose a child and subsequent grandchildren, both sets of parents want the couple to reside with them. The Kenyah term is *ngiban* meaning 'to take up residence with one's spouse'. The boy and girl should have got together beforehand and be of one mind on the matter. After the meeting at which the ngiban question is thrashed out, there begins a period of formal *nyadap* in which the boy may come to sleep with the girl at her house.[29] Should a wedding be settled on, the wedding will be scheduled for a convenient time, usually after the harvest. During the formal nyadap period, the boy may give the girl small gifts, such as a sarong, for her own personal use. He should not, during the formalized nyadap, be around the girl's house 'as though he lived there'. His visits should be at night after most people are asleep and he should be gone by morning.

At the time of the wedding ritual (*tebuku taki*) the boy presents gifts to the girl. These are items such as gongs and beads and these vary according to the social class of the individuals involved. At this time the individual who is to ngiban moves with his/her personal possessions to the other's household. If there is a divorce and no children, the boy gets the marriage gifts back. If there are children, the girl keeps the goods for the children.

Post-marital residence is ideally utrolocal. All of our informants said that the Lepo Tau Kenyah, unlike their Kayan neighbours, have no rule of initial uxorilocality; they regard this as a Kayan custom. The matter of post-marital residence is decided, as previously mentioned, in a meeting of the couple and the two sets of parents. There are several factors involved in the decision, including the relative age of the parents, residence of other siblings, resources of the households, whether the union is class endogamous or exogamous and personal relations with others in the households. Of 131 marriages for which I have complete data in Long Nawang, uxorilocality and virilocality are almost equally represented with 52·67 per cent uxori-local and 47·30 per cent virilocal residence. There is little difference between aristocrats and commoners; aristocrats show 54·70 per cent and 45·30 per cent for uxorilocal and virilocal residence respectively and the commoners 48·89 per cent and 51·11 per cent. In Long Moh there is statistically a very clear tendency towards uxorilocality. Out of 111 marriages for which I have complete data 73·87 per cent have uxorilocal and 26·13 per cent virilocal residence. Again there is very little difference between classes. In aristocratic marriages there is 73·33 per cent uxorilocal and 26·66 per cent virilocality, for com-moner marriages the figures are 72·92 per cent and 28·08 per cent respectively.

Marriages between aristocrats and commoners show a difference depending on whether it is the aristocrat or the commoner party that takes up residence in the other's household. In the majority of cases (78·78 per cent or 26 out of 33 cases) the commoner went to the household of the aristocrat and these cases show virtually the same residence pattern as other marriages; for these 26 cases the figures are 69·23 per cent uxorilocal and 30·76 per cent virilocal.

There are only 7 cases of aristocrat-commoner marriage in which the aristocrat moved to the commoner household (21·21 per cent of the total aristocrat-commoner marriages). Six of the 7 cases (85·71 per cent) are uxorilocal; all 6 are unusual in some way: in 4 cases the commoner partner is the last remaining sibling in the household; one is a case of old-age marriage; and in another the husband is in the army and lives with his family on the coast so his 'official' residence is in name only.[30]

In the case of an extra-village aristocratic marriage post-marital residence is in all cases I have recorded virilocal although in the Baram area there is frequently an initial period of uxorilocality lasting an average of 3 years. These marriages, at the highest levels of the aristocracy, require the payment of large amounts of heirloom property by the groom's village to the bride's village. Theoretically, all high aristocrats of the groom's village contribute to the collection of goods. It is received by the bride's father on behalf of his village and is distributed by him among the high aristocrats of his village.

If the couple are divorced and there are no children or if the children return with their mother to her village, the goods must be returned. If the children were to stay with the father, and the mother return alone to her village the goods would not have to be returned. Thus, divorce in these marriages is rare; informants could not think of an instance of it. Women say that the extra-village marriage is very bad for them. The woman is a stranger in the village of her husband with very little chance of escaping if it turns out to be an unhappy arrangement. Only in the case of gross ill-treatment would the aristocrats of her village perhaps agree to return the marriage goods to allow her to come home. Otherwise, she may return only if she leaves her children behind, a proposition most women find unthinkable.

Informants in both Long Nawang and Long Moh state an ideal of utrolocality; Long Nawang most closely approximates this whereas Long Moh shows a clear tendency towards uxorilocality. When I confronted informants with the statistical norms of post-marital residence patterns, those in Long Nawang insisted that utrolocality had always been the rule. Some informants in Long Moh, on the other hand, claimed that in the distant past the ideal rule had been virilocal residence. They could not explain the tendency towards uxorilocality. My research on extra-village marriage showed only one Kenyah-Kayan marriage for Long Nawang whereas in Long Moh there were several such unions. This, plus the history of Kenyah migration into the Baram area, may help to explain the Long Moh tendency towards uxorilocality as opposed to the Long Nawang pattern and the ideal statements in both areas. The Long Moh Kenyah have had and continue to have much closer relations with Kayan than do Long Nawang Kenyah. Members of an earlier wave of Kenyah into the Baram intermarried extensively with Kayan and adapted to Kayan marriage practices. The Lepo Tau arrived later and followed the customs of the more established Kenyah in the Baram.

In a previous section I have discussed the land rights and their relation to lamin membership. Rights in heirloom property are similarly mediated through the natal lamin. Heirloom goods generally remain in the lamin under the control of the lamin head who, after the death of the parents, is the eldest sibling remaining in the lamin.[31] Out-marrying siblings have rights in the goods but all claims are mediated through the lamin head. For example, X has married out and lives in his wife's lamin; his son wishes to marry and needs a gong to be presented to the bride. There is no gong available in the wife's lamin so he goes to his own natal lamin and requests a gong from the heirloom property of his sibling group. Usually such a request will be granted, for all siblings share rights in the goods. The lamin head may, however, refuse the request, claiming some higher priority need for the item. Informants say that disagreements over heirloom property are a major source of quarrels among siblings. Other valuable but non-heirloom property such as shotguns, sewing machines and outboard engines, is divided more or less equally among siblings; frequently the parents make the distribution of such goods before their death.

Rubber gardens, the primary source of cash, are fairly recent. Most rubber gardens were planted by people still living; only in a very few cases have they been inherited. Thus, there are as yet no definite rules about their inheritance. In the few cases where the original planter of a rubber garden has died, his children are tapping the rubber in what they generally refer to as a *kongsi* (a Chinese term meaning a corporation). In practice, this means that each sibling individually taps rubber in the garden which he then processes and sells and the proceeds are his.

This paper has focused rather specifically on Kenyah social organization but it is incomplete without a brief discussion of the notion of adat and the changing nature of the Kenyah concept of adat. Adat and its expression through ritual provide the template for all of Kenyah social organization. Adat is frequently translated as 'custom', including customary law, but the actual meaning is far broader. It includes the whole notion of the proper order and harmony of the cosmos and behaviour of its components. Adat pertains not just to those aspects of Kenyah life Westerners choose to call 'religion' or 'law', it underlies all aspects of Kenyah life including relations to other humans as well as to the natural and supernatural worlds.[32]

When everything is acting according to its proper adat, there is harmony and balance. Wrong action, then, leads to imbalance and sickness, death, crop failure and so on. The imbalance may occur in the world of men in which case redress may take the form of a fine or it may occur against the supernatural, in which case a ritual may be required as well. In some cases men must seek the advice of the spirits to even know the nature of the offence and its proper redress.

This unitary view of adat is in an ongoing process of segmentation. Hudson, in his work on the Ma'anyan (1972), makes the distinction between adat as simply 'custom, tradition' and the adat legal code. This kind of segmentary view of adat now made by the Kenyah themselves was forced by the necessity to articulate traditional systems with the legal and political spheres of the Dutch and British colonial powers as well as Islamic peoples. The process continues today with increasing Christianization and the increasing necessity to articulate with national governments. In my own study of Long Nawang Kenyah (1973), I used a three part distinction: *adat kebiasaan* (custom); *hukum adat* (adat law); and *agama adat* (religious). This distinction was made by my informants and reflects the dominance of Christianity. The Long Nawang Kenyah used the distinction to make it absolutely clear that, although they were still Kenyah in the sense of following Kenyah customs and traditions in most respects, they were not 'pagans', i.e. were not adhering to the religious portion of the adat.[33] Christianity does not necessarily imply a particular social order, whereas Adat Po'on was the social order. To be Christian and also be Kenyah, or to use the courts and also be Kenyah, one is forced to split, and in a sense, weaken the concept of adat. From a powerful set of ideas about harmony and balance in a universe of humans and spirits, it now moves towards a sense of simply 'custom' or 'manner', whether it be legal custom, religious custom, or the details of daily life.

NOTES

1. For a list of Kenyah villages and divisions see Whittier (1973:235–7).

2. Iwan Iot means the headwaters of the Iwan river. This area has also been referred to as the Apo Da'a which is the plateau area at the headwaters of the Da'a tributary of the Iwan headwaters (Whittier 1974:4).

3. I wish to point out that I do not consider my work definitive in reference to the Kenyah as a whole or even the Lepo Tau Kenyah in particular. Comparative material from other Kenyah groups would greatly aid our understanding of Kenyah. I would particularly encourage work with such groups as the Bakung Kenyah, the linguistically distinct Uma Alim, Uma Lasan, Uma Baka and Uma Kulit and the Ngoric, (Morik, Lepuk Aru) and Puak groups. Also of great interest are the Kenyah groups that have been heavily influenced by the Kayan such as the Uma Kelap Kenyah in the Baluy, the Long Tikan Kenyah in the Baram and the Uma Ujuk Kenyah in the Kayan.

4. Population figures and their intercommunity distribution for the study communities include:

Community	Year	Kenyah Population	Long-houses	Long-house Apartments	Single Dwellings
Long Nawang	1970	949	12	104	27
Mara Satu	1971	251	—	—	41
Mara Satu	1975	950	4	98*	—
Long Moh	1975	716	6	74	1
Long Makaba	1975	197	3	24	—

* Combined long-house and single dwellings

5. The two exceptions were a household consisting of an old man and his wife who said they practised the old Kenyah customs (Adat Po'on) and one household consisting of a man, wife and children who did not claim adherence to either Christianity, Adat Bungan, or Adat Po'on, but claimed to practice *adat tengun* (lit. 'own adat').

6. Adat Bungan is a reform movement begun in the Apo Kayan in the mid-1940s (stories vary as to the actual year). The founder of the movement was an Uma Jalan Kenyah named Jok Apoi, who according to most stories, had become a Christian but had experienced a long sequence of bad luck. The goddess Bungan Malan appeared to him in a series of dreams and told him to give up Christianity and follow her instructions. These were basically a simplification of Adat Po'on (traditional religion), eliminating such matters as omen birds, food prohibitions, and other taboos; they dismissed the necessity to propitiate a number of lesser spirits and cut down on the number of rituals and requirements of blood sacrifice. In the Apo Kayan, Adat Bungan apparently never enjoyed much of a following. The aristocratic elders considered it as bad as, if not worse than, Christianity: it was, after all, only the dream of a commoner. Adat Bungan made its entrance into Sarawak, however, with the return of aristocrats who had been visiting the Apo Kayan. Since the aristocrats introduced it, it could be fitted into the class system controlled by aristocrats. Thus, Adat Bungan was much more widely accepted, among Kayan as well as Kenyah groups, in Sarawak than it was in its homeland.

7. In fact, I never heard the Kenyah terms in daily use and had to inquire for them specifically; younger people were quite unfamiliar with them.

8. These exceptions have occurred recently for two reasons: (i) in some areas officials decided that it would be desirable to have literate tua kampong which narrowed the field considerably; and (ii) the position has become less desirable in some cases.

9. For more information on the terminology of village names, division names as well as choice of village site locations see Whittier (1974:3–4).

10. The laki malan is not necessarily an aristocrat although he is an elder. He is frequently a widower and is selected by other elders (*kelunan lata*). The position is held for one year only unless there is a particularly good harvest in which case the laki malan may be asked to serve for a second year but never for a third. It is felt to be a demanding and arduous position the burdens of which should be spread around. In his actual performances the laki malan is always accompanied by some of the elders, usually including the laki malan of the preceding year, who coach the performance.

Informants said that under Adat Po'on the position of laki malan was even more demanding with a number of dietary and other restrictions. The laki malan could not eat salt or, according to some, vegetables, could not live in his lamin but in a special structure on the verandah, could bathe only under certain circumstances, etc. Conley (1973:224–7) has discussed the position of laki malan (also called *dia tena*) under Adat Po'on in greater detail.

11. At meetings one observes that less careful attention is paid when a commoner speaks. In fact, other people will continue to talk, which should never occur when an aristocrat speaks, and adverse comments may be made about his speaking style. Kenyah say that commoners 'do not know how to speak'.

12. At the time that the 65 lamin long-house was present in Long Ampung (1965) there were also 6 long-houses in the village. There are probably less than 20 single

long-house Kenyah villages (of 110 villages). Most have at least 3 separate long-houses.

13. Throughout this paper issues arise which immediately suggest comparison with other Borneo groups; the structure and ownership of the long-house is a case in point. Space does not permit such comparisons here, although I may suggest them when they arise. I am planning several future publications with a more comparative approach on limited aspects of Kenyah organization.

14. The best known ritual and most important to the Kenyah people is the mamat or more properly the *ayau* (headhunting) ritual. In Long Moh today a small mamat (*ayau iot*—small headhunting ritual) is performed before the harvest and a large mamat (*ayau bio*—large headhunting ritual) is performed after the harvest. Part of the ayau bio involves a ranking (*suhen*) ceremony—suhen ranks merely indicate the number of times a male has participated in an ayau bio. As this ranking does not provide the basis for social groupings or action it will not be discussed in this paper.

15. When the long-house is torn down, the original owner may then reclaim all of his materials, including structural timbers and verandah flooring, but he may not take material that would disturb the integrity of the long-house as a structure as long as it is standing.

16. In this table, and throughout this paper the term 'nuclear family' refers to a conjugal pair and their unmarried children or a single adult and his/her un-married children. In some cases such units include other relatives such as an un-married sibling of one of the members of the conjugal pair. 'Stem family' refers to a unit consisting of one and only one conjugal pair in each of at least two suc-cessive generations, plus the unmarried children of each pair. 'Joint family' refers to a unit in which there is more than one conjugal pair in a generation. They are most commonly related by sibling, or occasionally cousin ties.

17. There is variation between Long Nawang and Long Moh in the composition of stem families. In Long Nawang, the distribution of male and female links is approximately equal: 53·49 per cent female links vs. 46·51 per cent male links. In Long Moh, on the other hand, the majority of stem families are female linked: a 75 per cent female vs. 25 per cent male. This reflects the difference in post-marital residence patterns (see below) with virilocal and uxorilocal residence bearing nearly equal in Long Nawang, but a clear tendency towards uxorilocality in Long Moh. The stem family is formed when all siblings but one have either married out to other lamin or have hived off with their spouses and children to form their own lamin, leaving one sibling with spouse and children remaining in the natal lamin. The Kenyah express no ideal preference as to which sibling, by birth order, should be the one to remain in the lamin. In the cases of the sibling sets in Long Moh for which I have complete information, 43·48 per cent of those remaining are eldest siblings, 26·09 per cent are middle siblings, 17·39 per cent are youngest siblings and 13·04 per cent are only children.

18. The Kenyah express an ideal of utrolocality. Throughout this paper, I follow the usage of Freeman (1970:14) in the residence terminology: uxorilocal, virilocal and utrolocal.

19. Of course, the latter two events may be reversed with the grandchild marrying and producing a fourth generation before the death of the grandparents, but statistically four generation households are rare: 5 per cent at Long Nawang and 3·2 per cent at Long Moh.

20. If the field is at some distance from the village, there will be a storehouse (*lepo bung*) in the field area in addition to the lamin storehouse in the village. The

village storehouse is used to store the lamin's valuables and heirloom property as well as for rice storage.

21. In Whittier (1973) I used the term tudo (lit. 'to spend the night') as synonymous with lubong petok. At this point, however, I find it more fruitful to use lubong petok as the field long-house and to refer to the group resident in the lubong petok as the 'tudo family' as opposed to the village 'lamin family'. In comparison see the Ma'anyan *dangau* family/*lewu* family' (Hudson, 1972). The lubong petok system has also parallels with the Iban *dampa* system as described by Freeman (1970) but there are some major differences. Lubong petok are generally larger and of longer duration (20–30 years) than Iban dampa. In terms of organization, the dampa family has the same membership as the village bilek family. What Freeman notes as an exceptional case of the bilek family dividing into different dampa groups (p. 168 n.) is in fact the usual case for the Kenyah. There may also be more than one long-house in a lubong petok area.

22. It should be noted that Sarawak law requires a minimum of 10 lamin ('doors' in government parlance) to constitute an official village.

23. Conley (1973:163–4) refers to *penyuan* groups. *Tuyang* means age mate and, although tuyang do not form formal age grades, there is a general expectation of friendship and helpfulness particularly among the young. For the young, semunyun groups do tend to be composed of tuyang, but this is not the case for adults. The importance of the tie diminishes in later life, although a person may occasionally call his tuyang together for a meal and rice wine, and most adults can name their tuyang.

24. I use here the term 'social class' to describe Kenyah social stratification. The use of the term in this context requires some discussion. Some writers (e.g. Sahlins, 1958) maintain that the term 'social class' applies properly only to market-dominated societies and that social inequality in primitive societies is quite a different phenomenon. I would take issue with this view and maintain that 'social class' applies to the phenomenon of inequality as it is found in Kenyah society. The argument rests not only on strictly economic factors such as control of the factors of production, but must include the ideological component and unequal distribution of ritual prerogatives. Space does not permit me to take up these issues here, but I will do so in a future publication.

25. But the problem of blood is not entirely resolved. It may be called into question if and when problems such as succession to office or marriage arise. In fact, the deta'u dumit category takes in individuals whose panyin ancestry is still in people's minds. Adoption across class lines is likewise possible but infrequent since it poses a similar problem: an adopted child follows the adat of his adoptive lamin and yet he is of different blood.

26. Parib is a term for the state of the individual who has transgressed the proper order. At one level, it may affect only that individual, leading to illness or other misfortune. More serious offences (e.g. incest) may result in not only parib for an individual but also a state of *sial* or general ritual imbalance for the entire community.

27. In teknonyms the forms Ame (father) and Uwe' (mother) may be used in place of Tama and Tina. Thus, Ame Kuleh rather than Tama Kuleh and Uwe' Kuleh rather than Tina Kuleh. In Long Nawang this is almost always the case in present-day usage. In Long Moh the Tama form is maintained but Uwe' replaces Tina in almost all cases.

28. For a detailed analysis of the interaction and functions of this grouping surrounding the construction of the ba' anak see Whittier (1973:190–226).

29. Actually, the boy frequently begins to nyadap before the formal meeting. Nyadap among the Kenyah, however, is not so permissive as the cognate practice, *ngayap*, among the Iban. Continued nyadap of a particular girl indicates a definite plan of marriage. A Kenyah girl with too many partners would be considered promiscuous. Since parents do not generally approve of inter-class marriage, there is a great concern that a child's affairs be with potentially appropriate marriage partners.

30. These latter two cases illustrate the point that the primary significance of post-marital residence in cross-class marriages is for the children of the union. They will belong to the social class of the lamin into which they are born. Thus, in the case of old-age marriage, the matter of residence was of little concern; no children would be expected from the union. Therefore the choice was simply a matter of convenience. The soldier and his wife were returning to the village for an 'official' marriage after living on the coast for several years and having had two children. His family urged him to press for patrilocal residence, citing the children. He refused, saying that he did not want to make a fuss because it did not matter anyway. Privately, he said that he doubted that his children would ever return to reside in the village and in their lives their position in the Kenyah class system would be irrelevant.

31. If the eldest sibling remaining in the lamin is a woman, generally in matters such as public meetings, rituals demanding the attendance of lamin heads, decisions on how to distribute the lamin's fields, her husband acts as the lamin head. But in the matter of control over the lamin's heirloom property, she is in charge; it is she, usually in consultation with her siblings, who decides on the use of the property.

32. As I was independently coming to this view of the nature of the Kenyah concept of adat, I found the work of Jensen (1974) and Schärer (1963) particularly significant in confirming and elucidating my own view.

33. It is notable that they had to use Indonesian terms (*kebiasaan, hukum, agama*) to even make the distinction; the Kenyah language does not make such distinctions.

6

THE LUN DAYEH*

JAY B. CRAIN

THE Lun Dayeh[1] are part of a larger population of as yet undefined linguistic and cultural homogeneity found in the interior valleys and tablelands of northern Borneo where the borders of Sabah, Sarawak, and East Kalimantan come together. The ethnological position of the various groups in this population has been in a state of confusion for a considerable time. This confusion has been the result of: (1) the general use of ethnic names derived from coastal dialects, 'Murut' on the west coast, 'Potok' on the east coast; (2) the presence of groups of this population in all four political divisions of the island which confounded attempts to relate groups in different territories; (3) a lacunae of knowledge about the heartland of the population in the interior of East Kalimantan, and (4) the use of static, external distinctions. Ideally ethnic distinctions should follow from distinctions in dynamic symbolic systems, thus requiring an understanding of each group's categories as applied to individual cases.

The heartland of these peoples is in the Kelabit–Kerayan highlands (Schneeberger, 1945). They are found in East Kalimantan south-east to the headwaters of the Bahau, east to the upper Mentarang, and north-east in the Kemaloh, Raya, and Sesayap; in Sarawak, the upper Baram and Tutoh, the middle Limbang, the entire Trusan valley, the Lawas Damit basin and Lawas area; in Brunei, a few villages along the Temburong and Pandaraun; in Sabah, the Ulu Padas and the entire Mengalong down to Sindumin town (Harrisson, 1959b; Bolang and Harrisson, 1949; LeBar, 1972b). The total population is approximately 34,000, distributed as follows: East Kalimantan (Kabupaten Bulongan)—25,000 (?), Sarawak (Fourth and Fifth Divisions)—7,000, Brunei (Temburong District)—300 (?), and Sabah (Sipitang District)—2,000.[2]

A variety of designations have been used for the entire population,

* Field research among the Lun Dayeh was carried out from August 1968 to May 1969. Support for this research was provided by NIMH Predoctoral Fellowship 1F1-MH 29719-01A2 and Research Grant MH 14226-01. I am indebted to the Sabah Government and the many individuals who assisted us during our stay. I am also indebted to those individuals who have assisted my Lun Dayeh studies over the years, among them Bernd Lambert, Thomas Williams, George Appell, Rodney Needham, Morris Opler and my wife, Nancy Chenoweth Crain.

but all suffer from the confounding use of the term 'Murut', a term applied also to speakers of one branch of the indigenous Ida'an language family of Sabah (Appell, 1968c; Prentice, 1970).[3] Linguistic evidence (Southwell, 1949; Bolang and Harrisson, 1949; Lees, 1959) indicates the dialect with the widest distribution and influence is the Pa Kemaloh.[4] Since Pa Kemaloh speakers refer to their language and ethnic group as Lun Dayeh,[5] I will suggest Lun Dayeh as a useful designation for the entire population and henceforth reserve the term 'Murut' for members of the Muritic sub-family of the Ida'an language family (Prentice, 1970).[6] This designation makes better sense in terms of the indigenous symbolic systems and avoids the traditional practice of viewing the population from only one side of a European-imposed political division.[7] While in the past they did not necessarily recognize themselves as members of any wider grouping than that of the village or perhaps groups of intermarrying villages, the Lun Dayeh today have a number of reasons for employing categories which denote relationships beyond that of village residence and kinship. These include linguistic, cultural, ecological, religious, socio-economic and political similarities. The term 'Lun Dayeh', with a historical connotation of 'interior people like us', seems to have survived as a general contrastive with 'others'.

However, we should not confuse categories (labels) with concepts (notions). There are certainly real, obvious differences between various groups of Lun Dayeh and between the population as a whole and other Bornean societies, but we should not treat the labels used in such circumstances as equally real and obvious. Among the Lun Dayeh, as elsewhere, ethnic labels are applied with differing degrees of specificity and differing connotations by different orders of persons in different contexts. To know what term is used in a specific context tells us about social and other processes in that context, but this does not necessarily tell us something more general about the term itself.

History

Our knowledge of early Lun Dayeh history is scant. Harrisson (1959a:8–11) feels the interior tablelands were first settled in the early centuries of the Christian era, probably from the south-east. In the seventeenth century Lun Dayeh movement south and west into the Baram, Limbang, and Bahau was checked by northward expansion of Kayan and Kenyah peoples (Harrisson, 1959b:58–9). Movement down the Trusan was apparently less contested and the Lawas Damit valley was occupied between 1820 and 1835 (Deegan, 1973:162). In 1858 when St. John began his exploration up the Limbang, he was aware that Lun Dayeh on the Adang had been driven eastwards by repeated Kayan raids (St. John, 1863, vol. 2:12).

At the time of the cession of Trusan to the Sarawak Government in 1885, the Lun Dayeh were a considerable power (Ricketts, 1894–5). Some Trusan villages under Ukong and Dayong, menaced river trade to the extent that a government expedition was sent against them in 1900 (Pollard, 1933:142).

Since Lun Dayeh settlement of the Trusan, Limbang and Lawas brought them into the sphere of influence of the Brunei sultanate, a study of Brunei historiography regarding these areas may shed further light on these westerly Lun Dayeh, but this has not been done.[8] Of the events on the Kalimantan side, nothing is known during this period save some folklore texts (Harrisson, 1967:126–8).[9]

Dutch control did not extend into the interior of East Kalimantan until the early 1930s. A short time later, in the mid-1930s, American missionaries of the Christian and Missionary Alliance (CMA) made large-scale conversions in Lun Dayeh villages on the upper Sesayap.[10] On the Sarawak side, missionaries of the Australian-based Borneo Evangelical Mission (BEM) began work with the Lun Dayeh on the Lawas and Trusan in 1936 (Lees, 1964). By the outbreak of World War II, most Lun Dayeh on both sides of the border were nominal Christians of one of the two varieties.[11]

The Japanese occupation of Borneo from 1942 to 1945 had considerable effects on the Lun Dayeh population. The war brought about the withdrawal of European missionaries from the interior, suspension of almost all trade with the coasts, considerable loss of life in the Limbang and other areas during the Japanese retreat following Allied landings on the west and east coasts, and the arrival of Allied special forces in the heart of Lun Dayeh territory. All these events, and particularly the last, had profound effects and continue to be celebrated in stories and remembrances.

The arrival in February of 1945 by parachute of an Allied party led by Tom Harrisson at Bario, a 'Kelabit' village on the Bah Plain, was the beginning of a major event in the lives of the upland Lun Dayeh (cf. Carter, 1958; Harrisson, 1959a). Within a short time Harrisson's group had managed to assume administrative control over the entire area of upland Lun Dayeh settlement. Hundreds of Lun Dayeh participated in armed raiding or reconnaissance groups, building airstrips, rescuing of Allied aircrews and other activities against the Japanese.

The effect of these Europeans, with their extraordinary amount of food, medicine, weapons, trade goods, etc., was to bring about a level and content of communication previously unknown between various areas of Lun Dayeh settlement. The end of hostilities brought about the end of excitement and the seemingly limitless supply of goods. Some of the inter-communication and the notions of 'Lun Dayeh' remained.

After the war, some groups of families left the interior to move towards the coast, but the major period of migration on the Kalimantan side occurred following the disruption of trade during and for some time after the Indonesian revolution (1945–9). Many of the Lun Dayeh settlements on the Mengalong in Sabah date from this period. Smaller movements followed the period of Indonesian–Malaysian confrontation (1963–6), and still continue today.[12]

In the immediate post-war years, Christian missions in Borneo, as elsewhere in South-East Asia, sponsored the establishment of self-supporting, native-run church organizations. In Sarawak the Borneo Evangelical Mission sponsored the Sidang Injil Borneo and in Kalimantan the Christian and Missionary Alliance sponsored the Kemah Injil Gereja Masih Indonesia Kalimantan Timur (KINGMI-KALTIM).[13] The Lun Dayeh play a dominant role in both of these organizations.

Before the war few Lun Dayeh had any exposure to educational experience. After, through mission and church-sponsored schools and recently in government schools, the majority of Lun Dayeh children on both sides of the border have at least some primary schooling.

Today, the Lun Dayeh recognize their citizenship as Malaysians or Indonesians and in both territories have political representation in a variety of political bodies of a district or regional character.[14]

Lun Dayeh Social Structure

My study of Lun Dayeh social structure[15] has focused on social contexts involving communicative behaviour of the type generally called social exchange (Barth, 1966). Social exchange is a pervasive process in Lun Dayeh social experience,[16] and it occurs predominantly in social contexts of a ritual nature–social contexts which circumscribe behaviours whose symbolic content is highly condensed, redundant, and given dramatic expression.[17]

Social structure is viewed here as most meaningfully expressed as sets of ideas about the relations between persons and groups of persons (Leach, 1954:8ff). Lun Dayeh as 'persons' (Nadel, 1951) express relationships through a series of overlapping relational schema. These schema involve distinctions of village/long-house membership, domestic family membership, cognatic kinship, affinity, generation and sex.

The Lun Dayeh are subsistence agriculturalists and live in small villages with populations of 50 to 150. The village (*kapung*) contains one or two long-houses (*ruma' kadang*), each consisting of five to twenty apartments owned by individual domestic families (*uang ruma'*). In recent times many Lun Dayeh have adopted the single-family dwelling style of coastal Muslim groups and in a few new villages the long-house has been abandoned altogether.[18]

The village/long-house as a social grouping owns no property nor does it engage in any corporate economic or ritual activity. Whatever relationships the physical and social arrangements between individuals seem to imply, the essential features of the village as a residential and social unit reflect the jural exclusiveness of the constituent domestic families.[19]

The domestic family or uang ruma' (lit. 'flesh of the house') is a familial grouping of one to four generations whose members share in the production and consumption of the economic assets according to their particular sex and generation, and utilize a common hearth for preparing common meals. Co-resident domestic families acknowledge social ties of co-operation, particularly in agricultural activities and the elaborate negotiations and exchanges of marriage, but no ritual or jural sanctions compel such co-operation.[20] Rather, co-operation is seen to emerge from the exchange reciprocity between domestic family corporations.

Individuals have jural status within the village/long-house only as members of constituent domestic families. Individuals join the community as members of domestic families and have rights as residents by virtue of domestic family membership. This is not to imply that the Lun Dayeh do not recognize individuals *qua* individuals, rather, jural concerns are domestic family concerns.

Within each village there is a core of domestic families linked by close ties of cognatic and affinal kinship and whose economic, agricultural, and ritual business is greatly intertwined. These core families are descended from the founders of the village and they dominate the political and social affairs of the community. The village headman will invariably come from this core group.

The developmental structure of Lun Dayeh uang ruma' is seen as a function of the nature of the social relations it maintains with similar groups. These are relations of residence, cognatic kinship and affinity. These relations are maintained by activities and sentiments that involve decisions of choice whose foci is centred around the system of prestation exchanges at marriage.

After marriage, a couple normally reside temporarily in the house or apartment of the natal uang ruma' of one of the spouses.[21] In a significant number of marriages one or both of the spouse's natal domestic family will have already dissolved through the death of one or both parents. In these cases the couple will temporarily reside with the uang ruma' of a sibling of the respective spouse's parent. The existence of the couple's respective natal uang ruma' or the conditions of intra- or extra-village unions make no significant difference in the couple's temporary or permanent residence choice.

Unlike the Iban bilek (Freeman, 1958) the Lun Dayeh uang ruma' does not, theoretically, own a corporate estate in perpetuity. In most cases the uang ruma' will dissolve at a point in time, having dispersed its younger members, buried its founders and divided its property. Fewer than 20 per cent of uang ruma' continue to exist for more than three generations.[22] For the majority of new couples, then, the option of succeeding the founders of an existing uang ruma' is rarely exercised. Rather, after the birth of the couple's first child, the couple will establish a separate household.

Post-marital residence is strongly influenced by the attitudes of solidarity between siblings and the positive value of intra-generational co-operation. The latter is most often expressed in agriculture and, most importantly, in providing assistance in the exchange of valuables at each other's marriage. Significantly, the greater the number of siblings (of either sex of either spouse), the more likely they will reside together after establishing their respective uang ruma'.[23]

Attitudes of solidarity between siblings implying interpersonal closeness and expressed in continuing reciprocity are the central foci of Lun Dayeh kinship. The latter, viewed as a system, is cognatic in structure.[24] Kinship terms denoting consanguineal relationships are primarily distinguished by the criterion of generation.[25] In describing relationships the Lun Dayeh utilize kinship terms in two ways. Following Lounsbury (1956: 167–8), we may contrast these two as involving *nominals* which do not designate categories of relationships between kin, but rather identify particular individuals, and *designative* terms. These latter serve to categorize an individual as a member of a class having a distinctive relationship with Ego. This contrast is best illustrated in the context of negotiations leading up to marriage.[26]

Prior to the formal initiation of engagement negotiations, the father of the prospective groom will confer with his close kinsmen. A villager knowledgeable in customary law (*adat*) will be invited to offer advice. In addition to matters of engagement and marriage custom, he will usually expound on the differences between various kinship relations in terms of the exchanges of valuables which dominate these events.[27] By emphasizing that he is discussing the general morality of relationships and not particular individuals, any possibility of offending or shaming someone present is avoided.

Similar discussions take place at the time of the wedding and at the post-marital exchanges. In all these situations, the formal properties of kinship relationships, rather than the incumbents, are explicitly the topic. Designative terms thus provide a set of categories to define and discuss the jural and moral rights and duties that are seen to conceptually distinguish classes of relationship of the type called 'kinship'.[28]

In regular interpersonal situations kin terms are used as nominals in conjunction with the personal name. Such usage serves to delineate particular individuals as members of kinship categories.

It is now necessary to examine the alternative nomenclature that is used in nominal contexts. The choice of particular terms or combinations of terms as nominals depends largely on the necessity of distinguishing between particular individuals or groups of individuals, rather than delineating relationships. This in turn primarily depends on the particular audience and content of the conversation.

Within the village reference is usually made to kinsmen by use of the personal name. Names are prefaced by nominals[29] only when name duplication within the village would make confusion probable. In the not uncommon event that an individual has two kinsmen of the same classificatory relationship with the same name, he will utilize an additional descriptive term to distinguish between them.

The further removed a kinsmen is, as measured by either physical or genealogical distance, the greater the likelihood of name duplication. This is the result of the Lun Dayeh system of naming which utilizes a very limited lexicon (see Crain, 1970a:106–9). The higher frequency of name duplication outside the village has, as one result, the interesting Lun Dayeh practice of making finer distinctions between distant kinsmen than between close ones.

Outside the village, descriptive nominals are used in two situations. In referring to a kinsman in the presence of strangers an individual will usually be quite specific about the genealogical relationship concerned. This is to avoid misunderstanding as to the specific individual(s) referred to. During a visit in Long Semadoh (Ulu Trusan River, Sarawak) a young man from a village in Sabah made reference to his mother's brother by the use of the form *taman fenekan fa dechur* (lit. 'male kinsmen like parent on mother's side'). This was because there were several men in the Long Semadoh area with the same name as his mother's brother. He wished not only to avoid confusion as to the identity of the person about whom he was speaking, but also to make certain it was not assumed that he was a sister's son of one of the individuals in Long Semadoh of that name. Had this last event occurred he would have indirectly shamed and insulted the individuals who shared his mother's brother's name. The young man was visiting in the long-house apartment of a distant classificatory grandfather, an insult to any actual mother's brother in the immediate area.

The other situation where descriptive nominals are employed is quite different. Whereas the usage above is primarily aimed at denying or qualifying a relationship, the second usage involves the establishing of a kinship tie. This practice is related to the Lun Dayeh pattern of reckoning descent.

Descent and Descent Lines

The Lun Dayeh reckon descent ambilaterally over ten or more generations. The depth to which descent can be remembered is partially a function of the system of naming, in which each individual takes the personal name of his or her father as a family name or patronym.

No groupings are formed entirely on the basis of descent, rather descent is utilized to extend kinship to distant collaterals and to determine potential use rights in land.

Genealogies are remembered in straight lines in much the same way as in other Bornean societies (Leach, 1950 : 62). Peranio (1961 : 97) has proposed the term 'descent line' which he defines as a 'straight-line genealogy or pedigree (without collateral ancestors) which may be utilized for various social purposes; it includes both living and deceased members'. Named descent lines occur among the Sadong Land Dayak (Geddes, 1954a : 59–61), Sarawak Bisaya (Peranio, 1961 : 99), and the Oya Melanau (Morris, 1953 : 54, 69).[30]

Leach (1950 : 62) in his discussion of Bornean descent states that 'where such systems differ from the more usual unilateral type is that any genealogical tree of say ten generations or more will contain almost as many persons of one sex as the other'. While females occur often in Iban (Leach, 1948 : 91) and Bisaya (Peranio, 1961: 99–100) pedigrees, this does not appear to be the case among the Melanau (Morris, 1953 : 54, 69).

Lun Dayeh pedigrees are almost exclusively *remembered* in male lines and are recalled by reciting the personal name of each individual in an ascending series. A link with another line can be established through the mother of any of these ancestors and the secondary genealogy then traced up or down through the mother's father. When female ancestors are used in this manner, they are described through the use of descriptive nominals, thus allowing the precise linkage to be stipulated.

In the past such linkages were important in enabling individuals to establish descent from apical ancestors whose descendants were entitled to use of areas for hillside swidden clearings. Today, at least in Sabah, the use of registered land titles and the decrease in mobility following from the change to wet rice cultivation have diminished this particular significance of pedigrees.

On the other hand the use of pedigrees for the purpose of establishing kinship ties is still very important, and this is chiefly due to the importance of kinship ties in the complicated exchange system surrounding marriage.

Marriage and its preliminaries are dealt with at some length in

Crain (1970a:116–88). Here it is necessary only to point out that theoretically everyone in the society is able to participate in a given marriage transaction, provided that a kinship tie can be established with one of the parties. Adoption, fictive kinship, and putative descent are the three ways that Lun Dayeh establish kinship relationships with non-kin. The first two forms will be discussed below.

Every individual of marriageable age can recite his or her patriline pedigree back five or six generations. Given the large number of name duplications, any two pedigrees are likely to contain at least one common name. Individuals may *assume* that the common name(s) are evidence of common descent and proceed to address each other by the appropriate generational term. This is exactly what is done by someone who wishes to participate in the *furut-sulang* transactions of a marriage between parties to whom he is not related. Since the exchanges between families at marriages provide the most valued means to secure major economic assets (money, livestock) and the only means to secure prestige items (jars, swords, beads), families seek to participate in those marriages where they see some economic or political advantage. The use of pedigrees for putative descent enables individuals to put themselves on either side of a particular marriage transaction. Putative descent used in this context is normally limited to the activities and obligations of a particular marriage or set of marriages. Since individuals who manipulate their genealogies in this manner usually live quite a distance from one another, the amount of interaction in contexts other than marriage is limited.[31]

Descent through the manipulation of pedigrees apparently occurred in the past with more permanent and far-reaching effects. A family revised its genealogy when it wished to tie itself to one of the important or well-known families in a village. Here, the common name of an ancestor was assumed to indicate siblingship and, following from this, the original pedigree above this generation was 'forgotten' in favour of the ascending line of the important family.

Affinal Kin

Lun Dayeh affinal terminology consists of six reciprocal terms.[32] All terms are used in both vocative and referential contexts. The criteria by which the six affinal terms are differentiated reflect significant jural correlates in the processes of family formation. The affinal terms distinguish generation and measure degrees of affinal removal (e.g. spouse's sibling or sibling's spouse, spouse's sibling's spouse or sibling's spouse's sibling).[33]

Affinal relationships are generated through and operate primarily in the context of marriage. Affinal terms differentiate individuals who participate either directly or indirectly in various marriages of concern to Ego. These include the marriages of: (1) Ego (2) Ego's siblings (3) Ego's spouse's siblings (4) Ego's children and (5) Ego's sibling's children.

In any given marriage an individual may be involved as one of the principals (the bride and groom), as one of the sponsors (major contributor of furut or sulang), or as an auxiliary (optional contributor of furut or sulang) (see Tables 1 and 2). The only affinal categories that are not extended on occasion to more distant collaterals are *awan*, spouse, and *arum*, the respective parents of *iban*.

TABLE 1

Affinal Categories and Marriages Involving Ego

Category	Sponsor Ego's Marriage: Ego Sponsor's Marriage	Co-Sponsors with Ego	Auxiliaries with Ego
iban	+		
arum		+	
lango	+		
acha'			+
seruai			+

TABLE 2

Affinal Categories and Types of Exchange

Category	Ego Exchanges Directly with	Ego Exchanges at Marriage of	Exchange at Ego's Marriage
iban (ascending)			+
iban (descending)		+	
awan	+	+	+
arum	+		
lango		+	
seruai	+		
acha'	+		

Those individuals who play, as sponsors, a major role in the various marriages involving Ego—e.g. his iban, lango and arum, are those affines with whom marriage is forbidden.[34] These individuals provide the principal amounts of furut and sulang and they have a major say in determining the outcome of a particular marriage negotiation.

Those affines with whom marriage is permissible—e.g. *acha'* and *seruai*—play only an optional auxiliary role in marriages of direct concern to Ego. Their motives in contributing to the exchanges are seen to be more economic than is the case with other affines.

Fictive Kinship Relations[35]

Relationship terms for kin and affines are extended to include unrelated individuals in a variety of contexts. The most important use of 'fictive' kinship occurs within the village. Here, unrelated persons who have established permanent residence are given kinship terms by the other villagers.[36] This is done without ceremony or ritual; the usual practice is for the adults of each household to initiate the use of a kin term in the normal course of daily activities. The application of particular terms to a new household is done with reference to the generational position of the household head *vis-à-vis* the other villagers. The terms used for other household members follow the cognatic pattern appropriate for the spouse and children of a 'real' kinsman.

Fictive kinship within the village involves the use of both terms of address and terms of reference. The former are used reciprocally in the same manner as between real kinsmen. The use of referential forms is classificatory, employing none of the descriptive qualifiers that occur in nominal forms between real kinsmen. This latter feature contrasts with the usage for adoptive relationships, where Ego distinguishes cognates for his adoptive parents with descriptive qualifiers.

After two or three generations, the original 'fictive' character of these relationships may be forgotten. Only on the most formal of occasions, such as the determination of marriageability, will the original nature of such kinship ties be closely examined. What has become important is the economic and social relationships that interrelate the domestic families comprising the village.

The use of kinship terms between unrelated villagers is primarily oriented towards the social relations operating in day-to-day inter-action within the village. Villagers all become kinsmen because the rights and duties between villagers are expressed in the idiom of kinship. While a certain solidarity or social cohesiveness may exist between villagers as residents of a territorial entity such as a village or long-house, the values of living and working together are expressed in terms of kinship sentiment. The only obligations involving villagers *qua* villagers are the recognition of the nominal authority of the village headman, the provision of workers for government-sponsored village work projects, and, in the past, the observance of ritual restrictions placed on the village territory at times of death or epidemic.

A second form of fictive kinship involves the use of parental terms of address as honorifics in speaking to an older individual of a senior generation. In addressing the district chief or the headman of another village, a younger man will use *ama'* ('father, parent's sibling') as a sign of respect. This usage is purely respectful and honorific and the person so addressed uses the reciprocals *asi'* ('son') and *amu'* ('daughter'). Terms of reference are never used in this context.

The last form of fictive kinship involves the use of the affinal term acha' ('sibling's spouse's siblings, cousin's spouse's siblings'). In the past, the fictive acha' relationship was most frequently established between a Lun Dayeh and a Malay or Chinese. It is best described as a ritualized trading partnership. It was initiated and maintained by a series of reciprocal exchanges of gifts. Fictive acha' did not exchange furut-sulang items at each other's marriages. Acha' partners receive and expect hospitality from each other when visiting or travelling through the village. This relationship is rare today. The difficulties and dangers of travel to and from the interior are largely a thing of the past. A coastal trader in the mountains or a Lun Dayeh on the coast no longer needs the protection and support that the acha' relationship provided. A few Lun Dayeh in the lower Mengalong area still have acha' relationships with Chinese shopkeepers, but these involve only old men on both sides and are rarely, if indeed ever, activated.

The fictive acha' relationship is not substantially different in degree from the affinal acha' relationship. Affinal acha' interact primarily in the context of marriage payment exchanges. Acha' are the most marginal of affines. Furut-sulang exchanges between them are often based solely on economic considerations and almost never involve heirloom property.

Kinship Groups

The Lun Dayeh have no groups recruited exclusively on the basis of kinship. The domestic family (uang ruma') recruits its members largely, but not solely, on the basis of kinship. The patriline pedigrees (*inul*) discussed above do not constitute a group, but rather a category.[37]

As Freeman (1960) has demonstrated, the kindred is a cognatic category composed of all the cognates of an individual. The range of the kindred among the Lun Dayeh varies from individual to individual, but exact genealogical relationships are not commonly known beyond third cousin. There is no patrilateral or matrilateral bias in the knowledge of precise genealogical relationships. Presumed cognation, as distinct from demonstrable genealogical relationship, is theoretically infinite. A strong patrilateral bias, reflecting the practice of reckoning relationships through the reciting of the patriline pedigrees, is present in presumed cognation of more distant relationships.

Beyond the regulation of marriageability, the kindred is given no jural recognition. There are no 'kindred-based action groups' as described by Freeman (1961:203).

Although marriage between third cousins or closer is considered incestuous (*sumbang*), and therefore forbidden, no terminological distinction is made between kinsmen within and without this range. The payment of homicide fines (*tued*) and the distribution of furut do not coincide with any internal division of kinsmen, but rather appear to reflect the existence of residential and marital alliances.

An individual lumps his affines together with his consanguines as 'relatives' (*kinanak* or *kanid*) to distinguish them from 'strangers' (*sakai* or *dagang*). This distinction, however, is neither finite nor Ego-centred. Neighbours, as we have seen, become kinsmen. Only the occasion of particular marriages may force a recognition of the non-overlap of the 'relatives' of co-villagers.

Exchange in Lun Dayeh Society

The exchange of affection, greetings, labour, foodstuffs, and other commodities is a pervasive feature of Lun Dayeh society. Exchange, reciprocity, and mutual assistance reflect one of the basic value assumptions of the society—that working together with others is closely related to spiritual and physical health.

Exchanges occur between neighbours, cognates, affines, informally between individuals, and more formally between corporate domestic families. Such exchanges occur primarily in connection with: the organization of labour for the production of rice, clearing of land, construction of houses, and the establishment of conjugal and affinal status (both demonstrable and putative).

Labour Exchange

The methods of organizing labour are described in Crain (1973). The preferred forms of labour arrangements all involve large numbers of families, either directly exchanging labour in the agricultural co-operative groups (*riud*) or working together in the fields of the sponsor of a feast (*musang* or *ngerufan*).

The co-operative groups operate under a leader and are organized according to reciprocity and a rotating schedule. Accounts of debts (by days and workers) are assiduously kept by each member family and are expected to be paid off by the end of the season. Defaulting families are subject to censure in the form of gossip and more overt complaints which question their honesty or good name. These debts are clearly of an economic nature and the attitudes towards defaulters closely approximate those towards economic transactions with Chinese shopkeepers.

A moral component of a different order is also present in the relationships between constituent families of a co-operative group. Although each domestic family technically accrues debts from other families only to the extent that it has provided workers in the latters' fields, there is some competition between families to provide as many workers as possible each day. Differential family size and variations in the size of the fields planted between members' families result in uneconomic outcomes for some families. This situation results from the fact that each family, but some more than others, expends more worker days in the fields of other member families than would be actually required to perform the necessary labour in its own fields.

Families with large fields 'consume' a greater proportion of the co-operative group's total working days than families with smaller fields. The former usually comprise the 'core families' of the long-house. Members of these families dominate the evening discussions about the next day's work schedule and most often are the articulators of the norms of competition, co-operation and exchange that serve to support and define the system of labour exchange. These families are sometimes referred to as *lun do* ('good people'). This term derives from an earlier system of class stratification that according to informants existed until perhaps 60 years ago. At that time, so it is told, most villages in the interior of Lun Dayeh territory were comprised of three classes of family. At the top were the lun do, aristocratic families whose marriages and funeral celebrations were marked by extensive exchanges of bronze cannon, valuable heirloom jars and slaves. Below these were ordinary families whose marriages and funerals involved lesser exchanges of smaller jars and no slaves or cannon. Finally, there were the slaves (*lun demulun*), who were war captives and their descendants. They were primarily the property of lun do families. There was apparently some mobility in the system, as lun do could become disgraced through not showing the grand displays of wealth required, and ordinary families could move upwards by means of the capture of slaves from other groups (notably Kenyah). Today lun do has mostly the connotation of 'successful' or 'meritorious' rather than 'aristocratic' (see Deegan, 1973:86 ff. for a description of these categories among the Lawas Damit Lun Bawang).

It is these same core families who most frequently sponsor the more elaborate agricultural feasts of the ngerufan type. Viewed as exchange, these events serve to extend or reinforce the debt relations of the sponsoring family. Theoretically, a family which attends these events is 'paid' for its members' labour at the feast held upon completion of the work. Actually, the participants leave with a debt owed to the sponsor as a result of the obligation to reciprocate with an invitation to a similar event and the obvious disproportion between the work involved and the magnitude of the feast. The majority of participating families never 'pay off' this debt and thus become, in a sense, perpetually indebted to the sponsoring family. Such a perpetual debt or alliance between families is not given formal or linguistic expression, but debtors are expected to attend events the creditor will sponsor in the future.

These large-scale agricultural feasts are among the most valued events in the Lun Dayeh system, fulfilling the social and economic functions described earlier, and providing vivid examples of the values of health and happiness to be achieved by working together. Those who sponsor such events gain full measure of prestige from their fellows, for the sponsors have redefined and strengthened the norms of the society.

Marriage Exchange

The furut-sulang exchanges, like affinal exchanges at marriage in many societies, involve a rearrangement of the social structure. Unlike a unilineal system, Lun Dayeh marriage exchanges provide, in theory, continual opportunities for the restructuring of interfamilial relationships through the exercise of choice. In practice, however, only a few marriages in each generation appear to involve substantial numbers of very distant or putative kinsmen. These are the marriages sponsored by well-known families (lun do).

The cognatic and affinal relationships of a particular family may be divided into those which are operational, those which are minimal, and those which are latent. Any of these may be actual or fictive, demonstrable or putative. The scale from operational to latent is the function of the frequency and scale of the exchanges (and the accompanying debts) between particular domestic families.

The operational-latent dimension is a reflection of the total interaction between particular families. This interaction is viewed here as a process of social exchange.[38] The actual-fictive dimension is largely a function of residential alignments, themselves following upon relationships previously given definition through exchange. The demonstrative-putative dimension varies according to the size (or skewing) of the kindred range of particular household heads. That is, the kindred, and probably also the affines of well-known families tend to be larger and contain many putative relations. This dimension reflects, at possibly another level, the 'results' or 'values' of the other two dimensions.

The configuration of exchanges (action field) of an average family and of a well-known family differ in two ways. The average family has exchange relationships not only with fewer families, but is more selective about the exchange partners it chooses within the total jural domain of the system. A well-known family has both a larger action field and a more generalized pattern within the total system. The former reflects the number of marriages, agricultural feasts, and other transaction complexes (acha' partners) that both define and sustain the prestige of these families. The generalized pattern of such exchanges reflects the norm-setting qualities of the exchanges of well-known families.

Conclusion

The exchange of goods and services in Lun Dayeh society is a central feature of a system of social relations that allows a wide range of choice. In this system each family is continually a creditor and debtor *vis-à-vis* other families, which are defined for certain social purposes as kinsmen or affines. The creditor-debtor relations are initiated and maintained through a variety of exchanges that centre around the developmental cycles of families and rice agriculture. These exchanges represent the major mechanisms for the circulation of goods and services and are seen to embody the highest moral ethics of the society.

Families differentially participate in this exchange system. Those families which, by virtue of their reputation and wealth, sponsor the ceremonies and activities through which the norms are expressed function in the capacity of moral brokers and receive respect accordingly. This is a matter of degree, for every family sponsors some exchanges. The marriage feasts and agricultural feasts of well-known families have, however, some of the character of 'privilege ceremonies' as described by Firth (1967:79ff). The prestige or privilege accrued to the sponsor is not derived from his display of wealth, but rather from providing the mass performance of symbolic acts which embody the very essence of the system.

Leach (1960 : 124) has argued that 'social structures are sometimes best regarded as the statistical outcome of multiple individual choice rather than a direct reflection of jural rules'. For the Lun Dayeh and perhaps other central Bornean peoples it would seem more appropriate to argue a corollary of this—the jural dimensions of the social structure are themselves multiple, requiring the exercise of option to make them coherent. Rather than obligations and constraints, the Lun Dayeh view their social order in terms of opportunities and incentives. The actions of individuals as representatives of domestic families are conceived and evaluated not against a standard of proper conduct, but rather are seen as unique human events unfolding in a dynamic setting—contrived, but necessary for the continuity of social life.

NOTES

1. Variously Lundaya, Lun Daye, Lun Daie, Lun Dayoh. Orthography for Lun Dayeh here follows Pur (1965).

2. These figures are very conservative estimates. The 1960 Sarawak census (Jones, 1962a) reckoned 5,214 'Murut' and 2,040 'Kelabit'. The 1947 Brunei census (Noakes, 1950) reckoned 296 'Murut'. My own 1968 survey in Sabah found 2,165 Lun Dayeh. The estimated East Kalimantan figure is based on estimates from my own informants and accounts from missionaries and is about one-fourth of the total population for Kabupaten Bulongan reckoned in the 1960 census (Indonesia, 1962).

3. Bolang and Harrisson (1949), Appell (1968c), Cense and Uhlenbeck (1958), LeBar (1972b), Needham (1953, 1955), Pollard (1933, 1935), and Southwell (1949). While these authors have all attempted to distinguish between the Lun Dayeh population and the Ida'an speaking 'Murut' to the north, the use of the category 'Murut' for the more southerly group has presented continuing difficulties (Needham has argued for dropping the term). Firstly, the use of 'Murut' for both populations assumes they have closer affiliation with each other than individual groups within these populations may have, say, with particular Dusun (Sabah) or Kenyah (Sarawak, Kalimantan) populations. Secondly, the greatest concentration of Lun Dayeh live in East Kalimantan, where they have never been known as 'Murut', but rather as Lun Dayeh, Potok, or 'Dayak'.

4. After the Kemaloh River in East Kalimantan, particularly around Long Nuat.

5. This has been used in a number of published materials—*Pejani' Luk Mebaruh*, *Buri' Lun Dayeh* (Edinburgh, R. & R. Clark, 1962), *Nani Lun Dayeh* (Hong Kong, Cathay Press, 1964), and *Kamu Lun Dayeh* by Samuel Labo Pur (Kuching, Borneo Literature Bureau, 1965). Lun Dayeh means literally 'people of the interior'. It is used as the most general and preferred self-referent for all the populations who speak a variant of a common language, 'Lun Dayeh'. It is also employed as an insular comparative to contrast those upriver from those closer to the sea (Lun Lod, 'people near the sea'), and in a contrastive set with Lun Bawang (see n. 7).

6. For a linguistic classification, Hudson (personal communication) has suggested the term Apo Duat (a geographical designation). While this avoids the confusion of such recent terms as 'Kelabitic Murut' (Dyen, 1965; LeBar, 1972b) it lacks any indigenous meaning and is not comparable with such terms as Kenyah, Iban, etc.

7. The popular use of Lun Bawang in Sarawak (Clayre, 1972; Deegan, 1973: 23) does not occur in East Kalimantan, where it has some negative connotation, nor in the Ulu Padas and Mengalong Lun Dayeh settlements in Sabah. Several Lun Dayeh from the middle Mengalong area saw the use of Lun Bawang as a political manoeuvre by Lawas area congregations to assert their dominance in the native church (Sidang Injil Borneo) which grew out of the old Borneo Evangelical Mission centred in Lawas. In any event, the term Lun Bawang does not appear to have been used in upland, interior areas with outsiders (non-Lun Dayeh), but rather in its other meanings (lit. 'people of this place'. It is used in a contrastive set with Lun Dayeh to distinguish newcomers from 'natives'. In the Kerayan and Mentarang rivers of East Kalimantan it has the additional meaning

of 'uneducated farmers'). Historically, the autochthonal connotation of the term may have been meaningful in the middle and lower reaches of the Lawas, Trusan and Limbang due to: (1) the apparently complex ethnic situation (relative upriver, downriver distinctions were vague) and (2) the nature of European interest (Pax Brooke, Pax Britannica) made 'original ownership' claims useful.

8. Harrisson (1959b:57) says there is evidence in comparisons of Brunei and Lun Dayeh folklore to posit a very early Lun Dayeh population in Brunei. These, he argues, were assimilated into the Islamic Malay population.

9. The account of migrations given by Penghulu Balang Siran of Long Nuat, East Kalimantan (Harrisson, 1967:126–8) presents a very complex picture of movements. Ethnohistorical analysis of such texts, together with some external historical data, may some-day allow a reconstruction along the lines of Sandin's Iban research (Sandin, 1967).

10. For a discussion of the records of these events see Crain (1970a).

11. There were, and continue to be, a small number of pagan Lun Dayeh living along the lower Mengalong near Sindumin.

12. For details see Crain (1970a:Table 10, p. 34, Table 12, p. 40).

13. On the establishment of the Sidang Injil Borneo see Lees (1964) and Deegan (1973:274–90). On the history of the KINGMI–KALTIM group see Rudes (1967).

14. Deegan (1973:216-45) has discussed the participation of Lun Dayeh in Lawas District politics in some detail.

15. My discussion is derived from data gathered among the Lun Dayeh villages along the Mengalong and Ulu Padas rivers of Sipitang District, Sabah.

16. This is given linguistic recognition, for almost any action can be expressed as exchange by prefixation of the verb stem to indicate a 'mode of action', e.g. *alap-ne* (to obtain), *fekalap* (to get from each other).

17. The classing of communicative behaviour as ritual follows the proposal of Leach (1966:403). My definition of ritual context is derived from, but not identical with, the ideas of Turner (1968, 1969).

18. The abandonment of the long-house in these villages appears to follow from the greatly increased capitalization of land, rather than labour, in areas of government-sponsored wet-rice projects.

19. The physical and social aspects of the long-house are described in Crain (1970b, 1970c).

20. Forms of agricultural organization are described in Crain (1973).

21. In a sample of 202 marriages, 113 couples (55·9 per cent) resided temporarily with the bride's parents or siblings of her parents and 89 couples (44·1 per cent) resided temporarily with the groom's parents or siblings of his parents.

22. Only 10·6 per cent of couples eventually succeeded to the natal uang ruma' of the bride and only 23·6 per cent to that of the groom. This is very different from the pattern of utrolateral filiation described by Freeman for the Iban (Freeman, 1958:26 f.).

23. Statistical data are presented in Crain (1970a:226 ff.).

24. For other descriptions of Lun Dayeh kinship see Needham (1953, 1954) and Deegan (1973).

25. *tafun*: more than one ascending generation removed; *mufin*: more than one descending generation removed; *taman/tinan*: male/female, first ascending generation; *anak*: first descending generation; *kinanak*: Ego's generation.

26. A transcript and translation of a formal engagement negotiation (*gayum tuduk*) is included as an appendix in Crain (1970a:327–92).

27. These are conceptualized as *furut* (given by kin of the groom) and *sulang* (return valuables from the kin of the bride).

28. Designative terms employ the basic distinctive criteria (see above, n. 25), whereas the nominal use of kin terms utilizes combinations of basic terms, together with various qualifying and descriptive terms (see Crain 1970a:82–7).

29. Kin terms as nominals employ the basic terms (see above, n. 25) with the addition of other terms, viz., *rayeh* ('elder'), *isuut* ('younger'), *fenakan* ('kin'), *fa dechur* ('matrilateral'), and *fa delei* ('patrilateral)'. Thus mother's sister is designated as tinan ('female, first ascending generation'), but a particular mother's sister may be identified as tinan fenakan fa dechur isuut ('mother's younger sister').

30. Peranio (1961:97–9) implies that the Land Dayak *turun* is equivalent to the Melanau *laian*. He is confused on this point. The turun is 'the group of living descendants who [thus] share land cleared by their common ancestor' (Geddes, 1954a:59). The laian, however, is a component stock or line within an individual's total genealogy (*susun*) (Morris, 1953:54, 69). Because of this confusion and the implications about the use of female direct links (see below), the 'descent line' construct appears to have limited use for the analysis of Bornean systems in general.

31. The most common arrangement involves a marriage between families in distant villages. A villager in each village 'connects' with the family in the distant village and thus is in a position to participate as an affine within his own village.

32. *awan*—spouse; *iban*—spouse's parent/child's spouse/spouse's parent's sibling/spouse's grandparent/sibling's child's spouse/cousin's child's spouse/grandchild's spouse; *lango*—sibling's spouse/spouse's sibling/cousin's spouse/spouse's cousin; *seruai*—spouse's sibling's spouse/spouse's cousin's spouse; *acha'* —sibling's spouse's sibling/cousin's spouse's sibling/child's spouse's parent's sibling.

33. The affinal terminology differs from the consanguineal terminology in a number of important ways: (1) generation is ignored in the case of the category *iban*, (2) every term is used reciprocally, (3) sex is never differentiated, (4) referential and vocative usage is the same, (5) the affinal term is always used to preface the personal name, and (6) affinal terms used in reference are always used as nominals.

34. It is said that a long time ago, a man could marry his deceased brother's wife (his lango).

35. The use of the term 'fictive' is purely for the sake of analytical clarity, the Lun Dayeh themselves do not distinguish such usages as a separate order of relationships.

36. Criteria for 'permanent residence' are quite flexible. Many informants used the period of one planting season, but factors of friendship, amiability and prestige are usually involved.

37. Murdock's (1960:5) category of 'circumscriptive kin groups' might apply to the Lun Dayeh *inul* with respect to 'optative' rights to participate in marriage exchanges.

38. The Lun Dayeh themselves describe the content and norms of kin relationships in terms of reciprocity rather than obligation: 'We help my cousin's family, because they help us in return, we exchange (*felibal*).'

7

THE RUNGUS DUSUN*

G. N. APPELL

The Rungus

THE Rungus are an ethnic group of the Kudat District, Sabah. They speak a Dusunic isoglot, one of the many found in Sabah, and identify themselves and their isoglot by the autonym 'Rungus'. In addition to the Rungus, there are, in the Kudat District, thirteen or more such named isoglots, or speech communities, of the Dusunic language family.[1] These isoglots differ to a greater or lesser degree from each other, some isoglots being mutually intelligible while others are not. The customary law (*adat*) of these named ethnic groupings also varies, the degree of difference usually being in proportion to the distance between groupings. Thus, the Rungus have well recognized social boundaries that distinguish them from other Dusunic-speaking groups in the district. These are delineated not only by differences in speech, customary law, and the use of the autonym 'Rungus' but also by dress. In sum, the Rungus form a self-conscious ethnic grouping.

The social organization of the Rungus is cognatic, more specifically bilateral in that the Rungus have no cognatic descent groups. The major social groupings are the domestic family, the long-house, and the village. However, membership in these latter two groupings is not based on establishing a kin link with a present or previous member. Both the domestic family and the village are considered for

* I am indebted to the Department of Anthropology and Sociology, Institute of Advanced Studies, of The Australian National University, which supported fieldwork among the Rungus and the preliminary analysis of data. I am also indebted to the National Science Foundation (Grant GS-923) and the American Council of Learned Societies which have provided support during various stages of the analysis of my field data. I owe a particular debt of gratitude to my wife, Laura W. R. Appell, who participated fully in research among the Rungus as well as in the continuing analysis of data. Religion, with the exception of certain aspects of the agricultural ceremonies, lies in the hands of Rungus females, and without her help it would have been impossible to gather data in this realm, for which she was primarily responsible. I am also greatly indebted to Professor Derek Freeman, who guided my field research, and to Professor John Barnes, who supervised the preparation of my dissertation. Field research among the Rungus was carried out from 1959 to 1960 and from 1961 to 1963. Sociocultural change has been very rapid in Borneo during the past decade, and my description of Rungus social organization only pertains to that time period in which we were in residence.

various purposes as entities, or corporate groupings, in the economic, ritual, and jural realms, but the long-house is never considered as such an entity with but one minor exception in the ritual realm. Traditionally the Rungus as a unit were politically acephalous, although regional leaders did arise in pre-British times. Their social organization is also egalitarian in that there are no hereditary leaders nor is there a hereditary class system. A permeable class system now exists, and existed presumably in the past, of three grades: a wealthy class, a middle class, and a category of poor, the latter probably included in the past a subcategory of 'slaves' as well.

Rungus cultural ecology is based on the swidden cultivation of rice, maize, and manioc. A few families have also experimented with wet rice over the last 50 years. Pigs, chickens and sometimes water buffalo are raised. A large variety of fruit trees are also owned and cultivated. Rights to these are inherited by descendants of the original planter.

In Rungus religion female spirit mediums communicate in trance with their spirit familiars to determine the cause of illness, which is usually the result of the capture of souls by offended malevolent spirits. These spirits are appeased by sacrifices of pigs and chickens. Spirit mediums also officiate at marriage ceremonies, when a pig is offered to appease those spirits that are offended by incest, and at the various village and family sacrifices to promote fertility of people, domestic animals, and the land.

Ethnic Terminology in Northern Borneo

The ethnic terminology of the Dusunic-speaking peoples of Sabah is a highly complex problem for two reasons: first, the indigenous distinctions were almost universally ignored in the colonial period so that ethnic groups were given exonyms (Appell, 1968a; 1968c), that overrode the local categories; second, as a result of processes set in motion during the colonial period some of the original ethnic distinctions were lost and new ones were established on the basis of external factors. For example, the term 'Dusun' is an exonym originally applied to groups of swidden and wet-rice agriculturalists by coastal Muslim from the western section of the Malaysian Archipelago (Appell, 1968c). Later, officers of the British North Borneo Chartered Company continued to use the term 'Dusun' but added a geographical modifier to indicate the location of such peoples in terms of the newly-established district boundaries. Therefore, terms such as Tuaran Dusun, Ranau Dusun, and Penampang Dusun arose. Each of these categories included a variety of Dusunic peoples, with differing social and cultural systems.

The Dusunic speakers in the Kudat District, and perhaps elsewhere as well, refer to themselves collectively in contrast to the coastal Muslim as 'Momogun'. More precisely, therefore, the Rungus should be called the Rungus Momogun.[2]

Because the Rungus are the most visible and largest of the Dusunic groups in the Kudat District, members of other groups are frequently referred to as Rungus. Individual Dusunic speakers may contribute to this misidentification by falsely claiming themselves to be Rungus to outsiders who are not familiar with local distinctions in order to avoid complications.

Population Size and Distribution

The Rungus are found on the southern two-thirds of the Kudat Peninsula and also in the middle region of the Melabong Peninsula of the Kudat District. The Kudat Peninsula is considered to be the original homeland of the Rungus; those occupying the Melabong Peninsula across Marudu Bay first moved there sometime in the last century prior to the arrival of the British. The total population of the Rungus is difficult to estimate, as some Rungus live in mixed villages with other Dusunic speakers along the borders of their main distribution. However, at the period to which we are referring, there were approximately 10,000 Rungus out of a total population of 29,456 Dusunic speakers reported for the district (Jones, 1962b).

The Domestic Family

Social entities which are distinctive, functioning social units in a particular social system I call 'social isolates' (Appell, 1967; 1968b; 1973; 1974; 1976a). If such isolates have the capacity to accumulate assets as a result of their economic activities, I refer to these as 'operating social isolates'.

The Rungus domestic family is the only production, consumption, and asset-accumulating social isolate in Rungus society, and thus is the only type of operating social isolate. Furthermore it is the most important corporate entity in the economic, jural, and ritual realms.

By domestic family I refer to that social unit of close cognates and affines which is originally brought into existence when, after the marriage of the two founders and a short period of post-nuptial residence in the bride's natal household, a separate residence and farming operation is established so that its members:

1. collectively reside in one apartment in a Rungus long-house and use one hearth for the preparation of their joint meals;

2. form a production unit under the direction of the male founders;

3. corporately own the retained earnings, i.e. the accumulated surplus, from the production activities of the social unit and the goodwill established with the spirit world.

Composition of Domestic Family

The Rungus domestic family is ideally and most frequently composed of a husband and wife, who are the two founders of the family, and their unmarried children. The second type of domestic family most frequently occurring includes the two founders, their unmarried children, and the widowed parent of one of the founders. For a short period following the wedding of a daughter, a domestic family may also include her husband (see Tables 3, 4 and 5 for data on domestic family size and generation span in a sample of Rungus domestic families).

TABLE 3

Domestic Family Size

		Number of Members	
Sample Size	Mean	Median	Mode
118	4·52	4	4·5

TABLE 4

Frequency Distribution	Domestic Family Size									
	Number of Persons in Domestic Family									
Sample Size	1	2	3	4	5	6	7	8	9	10
118	3	16	21	23	23	12	10	5	4	1

TABLE 5

Frequency Distribution of Generational Span in Domestic Families

	Generation Span			
Sample Size	1	2	3	4
118	10	92	15	1

Developmental Cycle of the Domestic Family

The Rungus domestic family, like the Iban *bilek* family, occupies a single apartment in a long-house. But unlike the Iban bilek family, which is 'in theory . . . a perennial corporate group' (Freeman, 1958: 24), the Rungus domestic family has a limited temporal existence. A point is reached in the developmental cycle of every domestic family where the decision is made to dissolve it, and the surviving founder or founders move in with the domestic family of a married child. Through analysis of the distribution of family assets at this point it can be established that a particular Rungus family has been terminated. Thus socially as well as jurally the Rungus domestic family has a limited existence in contrast to the Iban domestic family. In order to establish this jural nature of the Rungus domestic family group, it is necessary to consider its economic activities as well as developmental cycle.

Marriage and the Formation of the Domestic Family

When a son of a domestic family wishes to marry, substantial brideprice is provided for him from the accumulated assets (i.e. the retained earnings) of his domestic family. This, as well as the other institutions which lead up to marriage and the eventual foundation of a new domestic family, is justified by the major value premise in Rungus society that all sexual relations are potentially deleterious for the participants, the rest of the society, domestic animals, crops, and the land itself, unless properly entered into through marriage. Because of this, the sexual services of the female are highly valued scarce services; and the explicit and acknowledged purpose of bride-price is the purchase of rights to the enjoyment of these and the reproductive services of the female.

There are no territorial restrictions applying to marriage. But, all first cousin marriages are considered dangerous and are classed as a form of incest. They may only occur if the proper pig sacrifices are made to nullify the 'heat' arising from such a union. This would otherwise have deleterious effects on the marriage, village members, the village area and beyond. Second cousin marriages are not considered incestuous.

For about a year after the wedding, until the next agricultural season, the newly married pair reside with the bride's natal domestic family. They then build a separate family apartment, ideally on to the long-house where the bride's natal family resides.

Production Activities of the Domestic Family

The domestic family's production activities are centred around its swidden and domestic animals.

Each year the domestic family cuts a swidden in the territory of the village where it is resident and plants rice, maize, manioc, and a variety of vegetables. As soon as all the crops in the swidden are harvested and the area begins to revert to jungle, the rights to use that particular area lapse; any other domestic family resident in the village may cultivate there. Thus, in contrast to the Iban (Freeman, 1955a) and Bidayuh Land Dayak (Geddes, 1954a), no permanent or semi-permanent rights over land are acquired by any Rungus social isolate through the clearing of primary jungle.

Each family also raises pigs, chickens, and sometimes water buffalo. Pigs and chickens are used primarily for sacrifices to promote fertility in swiddens, prevent disease or cure it, increase the family's success in the accumulation of durable property, nullify the effects of ritual delicts, and promote the fertility and productivity of the village territory.

Retained Earnings: The Creation of Domestic Family Assets

Surpluses from the domestic family's swiddens and livestock are converted into brassware, gongs, and ceramics, which constitute its major assets. Investment is also made in female ornaments, consisting of ritual clothing, old beads, gold earrings, and brass wire which are coiled around the legs, arms, waist and sometimes the necks of young girls and women.

However, the ability of a newly founded family to create interests over property and accumulate a family estate varies with the particular stage in its developmental cycle. After the year of post-nuptial residence, the two founders establish their own household, plant their own swiddens, and raise their own domestic animals for the first time. But during these early years of marriage their economic activities rarely provide substantial surpluses. The female founder, because of bearing and raising children, seldom accompanies the male founder to work in the fields, and children in their earliest years are frequently ill. This is attributed to the capture of their separable souls by malevolent spirits. To obtain the release of these souls, pigs and chickens must be sacrificed, and these ceremonies are a major expense of the domestic family during its expansion phases. As the eldest female child reaches ten years or so, the female founder begins to transfer more household duties to her and goes into the swiddens with her husband. Then, shortly afterwards, sons begin to play an important role in agriculture, so that by the time they are well into their teens the family economic situation begins to change markedly, and it is able to accumulate substantial surpluses of maize, rice, pigs, and chickens to trade for gongs, jars, brassware, and other durable goods.

However, for any family to build up a sizeable estate, besides success in agriculture and animal husbandry, it must also have a male founder who is skilled in the extended haggling and bargaining that takes place over the purchase of durable goods and who can transform the family's consumables and perishables into durables.

Thus, the only social grouping in Rungus society that may create alienable interests in property is the domestic family. It is the only production, consumption, and asset-accumulating social grouping, and has the most fully developed jural status. This status as an entity is also reflected in the domain of religion (see below).

The Jural Status of the Domestic Family

In delineating the jural status of the Rungus domestic family, the critical question is: Does the family have the capacity to enter into jural relations as a separate entity? To answer this the nature of the family's rights over its retained earnings must be discussed.

Agricultural surpluses are used to purchase scarce goods such as gongs, brassware, and ceramics. These are referred to as *indopuan do nongkob* (lit. 'that which has been purchased and accumulated by the family'). The purchase of such goods lies in the hands of the male founder of the family, or if he is deceased, his eldest unmarried son. Contracts are made with other Rungus, as well as with Chinese shopkeepers. If the male founder contracts to purchase an item by instalments and then dies before the debt has been discharged, this debt is not his personal debt. Except *in extremis* it is not met out of his personal estate, which consists entirely of that property he has inherited from his natal family. Instead, it is a debt of the family as a unit, and hence is amortized from the agricultural surpluses of future seasons.

Brideprice payments and payments of fines also illustrate that the family is a jural isolate in terms of property. When a daughter marries, she brings in a brideprice of gongs, brassware, ceramics, and other items. Prior rights over this brideprice are held by the family to meet the brideprice for sons, to convert into food and clothing in times of need, or to use in the purchase of a particularly fine gong or jar. When a son marries, regardless of his contribution towards the accumulation of family assets, brideprice is provided for him out of these assets. Again, this contract is made by the male founder, but it involves the whole family as a unit and is met by the family regardless of whether the male founder dies prior to its discharge.

Any fine resulting from a violation in the jural realm by a family member is met with family assets, again regardless of the contribution that the offender has made to its accumulation. Any delict committed against a family member yields a fine of property, which is added to the family's assets.

Therefore, as a result of the incidents of ownership, I have termed the jural relationship of the domestic family to its accumulated assets as corporate.[3]

Termination of the Domestic Family

The Rungus domestic family has precise temporal limits. These are delineated by the relationship of its members to its retained earnings. After each child marries, and once this new family has become established, the parents give the child his or her portion of the family assets. This is based on a judgement of how much that child has contributed to the building of the family's assets, order in the sibling set, sex, and his/her character (Appell, 1974). Finally, one child remains, and all things being equal, this last born child will take care of his/her parents when they can no longer actively cultivate their swiddens. If at the time of marriage of this child the surviving parent(s) is no longer able to manage alone, the spouse of this child will move permanently into his spouse's natal household. While this seems to indicate no change in the life cycle of the family, it does signal the termination of the parental domestic family. For, at that point, the retained earnings of the natal family of the child are no longer viewed as the property of that family. Instead they are usually devolved on the child, becoming his/her individual property. Any further accumulation of property by the family, which includes the in-marrying spouse, now belongs corporately to the new domestic unit.

The Ritual Status of the Domestic Family

The domestic family is also considered to be an isolate in the Rungus religious system, since it can enter into relations with the spirit world as a ritual entity.

The domestic family as a ritual isolate is in constant interaction with the spirit world throughout the agricultural year. A number of sacrifices are made to create an enhanced ritual state between the family and those members of the spirit world responsible for fertility in swiddens and fecundity among the family's domestic animals. This ritual state can be destroyed if the ritual restrictions of the ceremony are violated by a family member. However, such violations affect the agricultural success of the family as a unit not only its guilty member.

The status of the domestic family as a ritual entity is also represented in the corporate sanctions on the behaviour of family members. For instance, at the time of the first harvest of rice, only family members are permitted to enter its swiddens; utensils used to prepare rice may not be lent to non-family members for three days; no husked or unhusked rice may be sold or lent to other families. If these sanctions are violated, the family as a unit will suffer since the rice spirits will flee and the harvest will be poorer.

Besides rice spirits there are also a number of malevolent spirits with which the domestic family interacts as a ritual isolate. If a male founder clears an area of jungle inhabited by a spirit, this spirit becomes angry. To vent its anger the spirit may bring sickness on any member of the offender's family, not necessarily the offender himself. To cure a family member a ceremony is held. Pigs and chickens are sacrificed to the offended spirit to create a state of goodwill between the spirit and the family. This state of goodwill may be violated and destroyed if the ritual restrictions entailed in the ceremony are not observed in full. In such a case the spirit attacks the family again. The original patient may not necessarily have a relapse. Any family member may fall ill. To appease the offended spirit another sacrifice must be held, and, if the offender was not a family member, the family sues him for the required pig or chicken.

Finally, if an individual is threatened with a machete, or if his clothing hung out to dry is slashed, his souls will take fright, flee, and he will fall ill. Under such circumstances, the offender must provide the person in jeopardy with a chicken so that he may be marked with its blood and cleansed. If it is the property of the family that is cut, the whole family is placed in ritual jeopardy. For instance, if the family's field house, fences, house posts, or its assets are cut in anger by someone, any or all members of the family may fall ill. To remove this ritual jeopardy, a chicken must be sacrificed and all the family members marked with its blood.

Thus, the Rungus domestic family is considered to be an isolate not only in the jural but also in the religious realm. Interestingly, while the status of the family in the jural realm is mirrored in the religious realm, the religious realm is also supported by the jural. If any transgression against the family is committed by a non-family member while it is engaged in transactions with the spirit world, such as intruding into the family's swidden at the time of first harvest, the family can take jural action to obtain a pig or chicken as a fine. This is then sacrificed to restore the ritual imbalance with the spirit world and re-establish the state of goodwill.

Kinship Terminology and the Network of Kin (see Figs. 2, 3, 4,)

I have argued elsewhere (Appell, 1967) that the Rungus social system does not include the concept of the kindred (but see King, 1976b; Appell, 1976b). The ethnographer, on the other hand, can provide a summary, derived from a number of observed events, or statements about such events, of an individual's kinsmen interacting for a specific purpose, such as a memorial ceremony for the dead. He might class this as a type of kindred, but the Rungus make no such summation themselves, and if it were made by an ethnographer, it would have little significance for them. For instance, the meaning of the term *sangvaris*, which some might interpret as a native term for a kindred, varies with the level of discourse from 'all of one's cognates' to any 'group of cognates' that has gathered together. But there is no delineation of what kin types such a group should consist of for any specific purpose. In activities involving a kinsman the only specification is that parents, children, and siblings, if the siblings are located close by and can be conveniently called, should be present at an individual's terminal illness, his funeral, and his memorial ceremony. If his parents are not alive, a representative of one of them should be called. However, the Rungus have no term for this set of cognates, nor do they phrase the relationship between these and their kinsmen as if they form a distinctive set. The Rungus then do not identify any set of cognates or distinguish it from the total field of 'all of one's cognates' by assigning it to any specific duties,

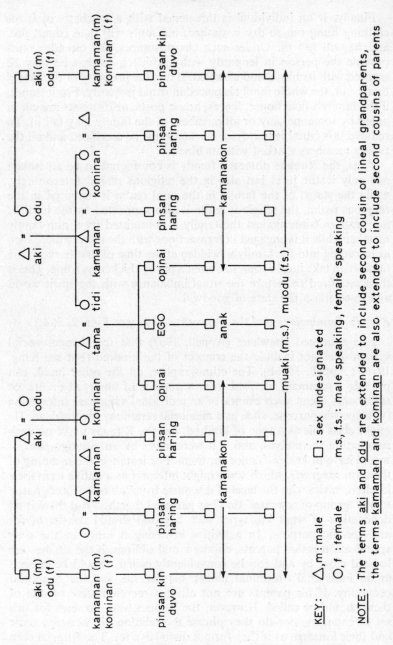

KEY: △, m : male 　　□ : sex undesignated
　　　 ○, f : female

　　　 m.s., f.s. : male speaking, female speaking

NOTE : The terms aki and odu are extended to include second cousin of lineal grandparents,
　　　 the terms kamaman and kominan are also extended to include second cousins of parents

Fig. 2 Rungus Kinship Terminology: Reference System

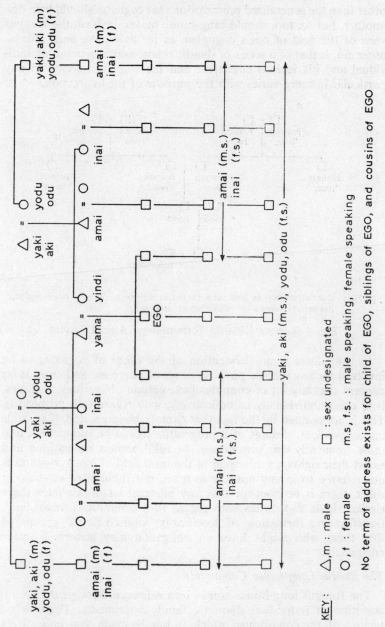

Fig. 3 Rungus Kinship Terminology: Vocative System

other than the generalized prescription that cognates should help one another, but so, too, should long-house mates. Instead, the Rungus view of the field of one's cognates, as far as I have been able to ascertain, is that of a series of dyadic relationships between an individual and his various cognates; and the cognate selected in any particular instance varies with the purpose of the interaction.

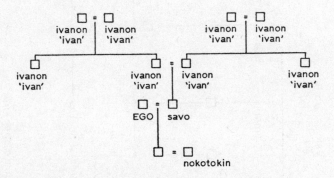

NOTE : Quotation marks indicate terms of address. Where none exist, personal names or nicknames are used.

Fig. 4 Rungus Kinship Terminology: Affinal System

In sum, there is no delineation of the range of cognates to be involved for any specific purpose or set of purposes, and there is no concept that any set of cognates have certain obligations or duties, held either individually or collectively, with regard to a propositus. This is not negated by the fact that parents, children, and, if possible and convenient, siblings of a propositus should be summoned, and most frequently are summoned, to fulfil certain obligations and assert their rights, as this span of the total field of one's cognates is not referred to in any manner as a set, nor thought of as such. In short, there is no concept that any bilateral set of cognates share similar rights and duties with regard to a common kinsman, and, therefore, no formation of specifically 'kindred-based' groups so that those who might have an obligation may achieve it more adequately.

The Rungus Long-house Community

The Rungus long-house comes into existence through the lateral accretion of individual domestic family apartments. There is no section of the long-house which is jointly made and collectively owned by its constituent member families. Physically the Rungus long-house is a series of family apartments cojoined laterally so that the aisleway of each apartment joins on to that of the neighbouring apartment. This forms a long corridor that is open to the use of all long-house members in order to reach their own apartments. At either end of this corridor is an entry ladder to the house. These are moved laterally as new apartments are joined on, and its upkeep is the responsibility of the family in the end apartment.

In a sample of Rungus long-houses in ten villages on the Kudat Peninsula the average number of apartments was 8·9, and the long-house ranged in size from 2 to 32 apartments.

The Long-house Apartment

Long-house apartments are the living quarters of the Rungus domestic family, and as such they are subdivided into various sections each having its own focus of particular family activities. The two major sections of the apartment are the compartment (*ongkob*) and the gallery section (*apad*) (see Fig. 5).

I follow Freeman (1955a) in referring to the separately built and separately owned housing structure of the Rungus domestic family as an 'apartment'. However, for the enclosed section of the apartment I prefer to use the term 'compartment' and not 'living-room', as Freeman (1955a) and Geddes (1954a) have done, since among the Rungus this enclosed section is primarily a 'kitchen' and 'bedroom'. Again I basically follow Freeman (1955a) in using the term 'gallery' to refer to that section of the apartment which is unwalled and which, when joined to other apartments, forms both the corridor of the long-house as well as the open lounging area. But I prefer to specify it as the 'gallery section' of the apartment.

In the compartment the family's meals are cooked and eaten on an area called the *lansang*, and the co-founders, small male children and females of all ages, including female visitors, sleep at night on a raised area called the *tingkang*. It is within this compartment that marriage rites are performed, children born, the sick tended, and the dying pass away. Within the compartment are also found the paramount *rogon* of the Rungus, the *rusod*. The rogon are a class of potentially malevolent spirits inhabiting the natural world. But for each individual there is also his rogon counterpart, a rusod, which dwells in the compartment and, if not annoyed or angered, protects household members from other rogon bent on soul-stealing. A portion of the pig meat of all sacrifices to the rusod as well as rice salt are put in a small bamboo tube and tied up over the fireplace.

It is in the gallery section that the majority of the family's work and leisure activities takes place. It is divided into a corridor subsection which, in conjunction with the other corridor areas of

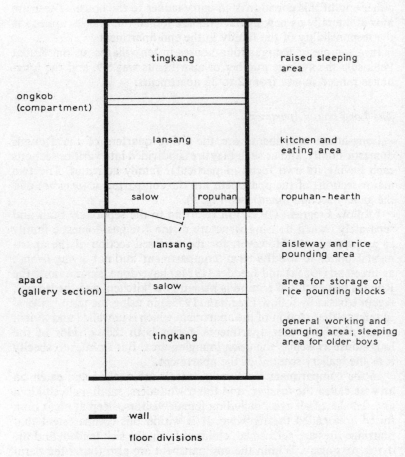

Scale : 1"= 4'0"

tingkang — raised sleeping area

ongkob (compartment)

lansang — kitchen and eating area

salow — ropuhan — ropuhan-hearth

lansang — aisleway and rice pounding area

apad (gallery section)

salow — area for storage of rice pounding blocks

tingkang — general working and lounging area; sleeping area for older boys

▬▬▬ wall

——— floor divisions

Fig. 5 Floor Plan of Apartment of Rungus Domestic Family

member apartments, forms a long passageway that provides access to the apartments from the entry ladders at either end of the longhouse. This subsection is also used by the women when pounding rice. The second major division of the gallery section is the tingkang, the sleeping area for male visitors and young boys. Usually at about ten years old—later if there are no sibling companions, earlier if there are congenial companions—a boy will begin to sleep on the apad in order to minimize the possibility of illicit sexual intercourse within the domestic family.

Web of Social Relations

The domestic families of the long-house are enmeshed in a complex web of social relations based on ties of kinship, apartment position, and need for mutual assistance.

The web of long-house social relations based on kinship consists most frequently of kin ties between parent-child, siblings, and sibling's child-parent's sibling. But irrespective of kinship ties, member families of a long-house are supposed to assist each other in times of trouble as well as in everyday activities. Regardless of kinship ties, apartment position determines the ritual duties that any domestic family must meet with respect to other domestic families. Thus, for example, when a domestic family holds one type of curing ceremony the members of three apartments on either side of that family must observe certain restrictions. These restrictions are lifted according to proximity to the apartment holding the ceremony: after one day for the members of the two outermost apartments, after two days for apartments one removed from that holding the ceremony, and three days for the members of those two apartments that adjoin the one in which the ceremony was held. A complex on-going web of ritual relations is therefore produced in the whole long-house symbolic of the web of exchanges and relations between member apartments in their various economic, housekeeping, and leisure activities.

This web of social relations is the major feature of long-house social organization as there is no formal long-house leader, nor are member families linked in any corporate ownership of property or corporate economic enterprise.[4] The long-house exists as a local grouping primarily so that its members have a ready source of assistance and the companionship of close kin.

Developmental Cycle of the Long-house

The significant feature of Rungus long-houses is that their membership is constantly in flux. In the initial years, after the first apartments are built, additional domestic families may join and build apartments at either end of the long-house. But as a result of illness, a dispute, or the desire to be closer to other relatives or one's swiddens, domestic families soon begin to move out. In time, with perhaps the final departure of several families at once, the hamlet (see below) is abandoned, and the long-houses in other hamlets within the village expand as they gain members from the old long-house. Eventually, after 5 to 15 years, the original location will again attract a group of domestic families, and another long-house will spring up.

Thus, domestic families join on to a long-house for a few years, and then move on to another, taking their house timbers with them.

In a sample of 29 life histories taken to determine length of membership in long-houses, the average length of occupancy of an apartment
was just under three years.

In sum, there is a constant reshuffling of long-house membership
and a constant turnover in the occupation of any particular hamlet
site within the village territory.

The Ritual and Jural Status of the Long-house

While members of a long-house are not involved in any collective
or corporate action in the economic realm, they do take collective,
not corporate, action to protect themselves against the spirit world.
Thus, the long-house is not considered to be an isolate in the ritual
realm, with but one exception (see the ceremony involving the
monginan below). Nor is it considered a jural isolate in seeking
restitution after a ritual delict has been committed against its members. While the status of a jural isolate with a jural personality is
denied the long-house, its social nature is not completely ignored. In
cases of ritual delicts, for example, it is unnecessary for each member
apartment to sue for restitution, but any skilled litigator in the
long-house may sue on behalf of his co-members. The fine distinction
between suing on behalf of one's co-members and suing as a jural
isolate can be illustrated by an analysis of the locus of ritual jeopardy
when a ritual delict has occurred and the manner in which action is
initiated for restitution.

First let us clarify our terminology. Jural rights may reside either
with a social grouping as a unit or with the individual members of
the group. A social group which is considered by a jural system to
hold rights as a unit, I call a 'jural isolate'. When rights are considered
to reside with the members of a group individually, in severalty, there
are two alternatives. First, the social nature of the grouping may be
ignored in the jural realm, and restitution in cases of any violation
of rights must be initiated by each member of the group. Such social
groupings I term 'jural aggregates'. Secondly, the social nature of the
grouping may be recognized by the jural system for certain purposes,
even though the rights are held in severalty. In such cases a member of
the social grouping may be allowed to sue on behalf of the other
members so that each does not have to take action individually. I
refer to social groupings of this type as 'jural collectivities'. These
distinctions hold both for the jural and religious realms.

To illustrate these points, we shall now analyse a few ritual
activities of long-house members.

As the long-house grows entry ladders are removed to the new end
apartments. If at any time a ladder is cut in anger with a machete,
this is considered as a ritual delict. It implies a threat of death against
all users of the ladder and puts them all in ritual jeopardy. However,

it is believed that the end apartment, since it is closest to the scene, is in particular danger. Therefore, it is the duty of the family occupying this apartment to sue for a chicken. This is sacrificed and its blood smeared on the legs of all members of the end apartment to remove their ritual jeopardy. During the ceremony, however, all long-house members are included in the prayers.

If it were the duty in all ritual matters of a member in the end apartment to take action for the long-house as a unit and if this responsibility were vested in a formal office, we might then have evidence that the long-house is a ritual and jural isolate. But this is not the case. Only in delicts involving entry ladders does a member of the end apartment take action. But, while the long-house is not recognized as a jural and ritual entity, as a corporate social grouping, its social nature is not totally ignored in these realms. For ritual and jural action is initiated *on behalf of* all the long-house members by some member, in this case a representative from the family in the end apartment. Since its social nature is recognized for this ritual and jural purpose, the long-house may be considered in our terms as a ritual and jural collectivity.

Let us analyse another example. Whenever a stranger arrives at a long-house, he must ask permission to enter. If a long-house member replies that no gongs may be brought into the house, this notifies the stranger that there has been a death in the long-house and that certain ritual restrictions must be observed. If there has not been a death, then the speaker has committed a ritual delict by falsely implying a death. Since he has not designated any particular individual, he is believed to have placed all long-house members in ritual jeopardy, but not equally so. The family in whose apartment he was present at the time when he made the delict is considered to be in the greatest danger. Consequently, it is that family which sues the offender for a chicken to remove its own and other long-house members' ritual jeopardy. Thus, when the family sacrifices the chicken and marks its own members with blood, the other long-house families are included in its prayers.

Carrying a corpse past a long-house is also believed to imply that someone has died there, and, if this has not occurred, it is considered a ritual delict. The implication of death places all families in ritual jeopardy, but the jural action taken is again not a corporate action of the long-house. It is not a corporate action because it is the member apartments, rather than the long-house as a separate entity, which are put in danger. There is thus no office that involves the duty of representing the long-house in this jural action. Instead it is the male member who is most knowledgeable in litigation who sues the offender for a chicken and certain other ritual objects. These do not belong to the long-house members jointly, nor are they placed in a common fund; they belong to the family of the individual taking the action. This family then sacrifices the chicken to cleanse both its own members and the members of the other apartments. While the long-house social isolate is not entified here either as a jural or ritual isolate, its social nature is not totally ignored.[5] Rather than all members of the long-house taking separate and individual action, one member is permitted to take jural and ritual action on behalf of the others. Consequently, in this matter also the long-house is a jural and ritual collectivity.

The fact that the long-house is primarily considered to be a jural and ritual collectivity is further demonstrated in ceremonies for the 'wandering demons' which bring epidemics. In this ceremony joint or collective ritual activity involving all long-house members takes place and this must be distinguished from corporate ritual activity. To prevent the demons from arriving at a long-house, every family prepares a pinch of husked rice, a betel leaf, an areca nut, and a cigarette for each of its members. The ritual practitioner then goes the length of the long-house and collects these offerings in a basket at each apartment. As he does this he calls the demons to follow him to receive these offerings as provisions to continue on their wanderings. Those family representatives who wish to accompany the ritual practitioner, or who want to sacrifice a chicken in addition, follow the practitioner out of the house to the main trail. There the practitioner calls these demons to come and take the provisions to speed them on their way. In doing this, he mentions the names of all members of the long-house. Then, he returns to the house and inserts a knotted blade of grass into the door of *each* apartment to signify that the family has participated in the ceremony

This is a joint, not a corporate, ceremony held by all member families to prevent illness from occurring in their respective apartments. All perform the same ritual acts for the benefit of their own apartments, not for the long-house as a unit. It is not the corporate ritual of a social isolate; the focus of the ritual jeopardy is not the long-house as a unit but each of its member families. It is the family that is being removed from jeopardy, not the long-house.

While it is not ritually corporate neither is the long-house considered merely an aggregate of member families. Instead, its status is that of a ritual and a jural collectivity, and this is further illustrated by what occurs when any of the restrictions following the ceremony for the wandering demons are broken. The offender is not sued for a chicken by each family in the long-house, but instead action is initiated on behalf of the other members by anyone skilled in litigation. This chicken is then sacrificed at the point where the path from the long-house joins the main trail on behalf of all member families in order to remove their ritual jeopardy.

Ritual Substantiation: The Ceremony Involving the Monginan

A social grouping is considered within a system of cultural logic as a ritual or jural isolate, collectivity, or aggregate, for a specific purpose. But seldom is it considered a jural or ritual isolate for all the activities in which its members may participate. Thus, to refer to a social grouping as corporate we must also know for what purposes it is so considered.

We saw above that in its most frequent ritual activities the long-house is not a ritual or jural isolate but a collectivity. This also has entailments in its social organization. There is no formal leader who has the duty to initiate jural action for the long-house or represent it before the spirit world, with but one exception that we will discuss next. Instead, action for the removal of ritual danger is taken either by the person most skilled in litigation or by a representative from the family physically closest to the spot where the delict occurred.

However, while the long-house is a collectivity in most ritual matters, there is one ceremony, infrequently held, in which the long-house enters into relations with the spirit world as a ritual isolate. This ritual substantiation comes about in ceremonies that involve the monginan.

The first person to build an apartment for a long-house is called the monginan (lit. 'the builder of the body'). If a family cuts timbers for an apartment but fails to join the long-house, a particular species of malevolent spirit (*labut*) comes to live with this monginan. While the first manifestations of these labut are at the apartment of the monginan, soon indications of their presence spread to all apartments. Initially noises are heard at night. Then long-house members are scared by unusual events such as sticks being poked through the flooring from below. Finally, if not appeased, the labut will cause a death in each apartment.

To remove the long-house from this danger, the family that failed to complete its intentions by not joining the house is sued for a pig. This is used in a ceremony to rid the long-house of the labut. The ritual specialist performing the sacrifice takes a stick and goes the length of the long-house, hitting the rafters of each apartment. Simultaneously, he calls the labut at each apartment to go with him to receive the sacrifices. Then he goes beneath the long-house, and, starting with the monginan's apartment, strikes the middle post of each apartment, again calling the labut. Afterwards the pig is killed near the long-house, and its head taken and hit against a house post of each apartment. Following this, the head is given to the monginan to keep, and no stranger may enter the house for three days.

In this ceremony the long-house as a ritual isolate is expressed in several ways. It is in the monginan's apartment that the labut reside; his apartment is the centre of the sacrifice; he keeps the pig's head. The monginan thus represents the long-house as a ritual isolate before the spirit world.

However, it is at most a very weak ritual corporateness. Each apartment must be ritually dealt with rather than there being one ritual focus for the whole long-house. Furthermore, this ceremony does not result in the development of a state of enduring goodwill between the long-house as an isolate and the spirit world. Instead, once the restrictions are over a few days after the ceremony, the ritual relationship between the long-house and the labut is severed.

But for this ceremony can the long-house also be considered a jural isolate? In other words, do jural interests reside with the long-house as a jural entity or with its individual member families? Unfortunately the locus of these jural interests, like those in the previous examples above, are hard to establish since they do not form a prominent feature of the Rungus social system. They are not transacted or converted, which would provide the crucial tests to determine their locus (Appell, n.d.). In fact the jural interests here seem to be split, simultaneously residing in two places. The monginan has a more salient interest in the problem of the labut, but individual member families also have an interest since they too are put in danger. Nevertheless, there is no other evidence to indicate that the long-house here is more than a jural collectivity. For example, there is no designated jural representative for this type of procedure, whose legal powers might provide clues to sort this problem out. Consequently, since for other jural actions we have discussed the long-house does not reach any greater substantiation than that of a jural collectivity, I would argue that the long-house is not a jural entity, with respect to the ceremony for the labut, even though it is a weak ritual isolate in this instance.

On the other hand, it is clearly a jural collectivity rather than merely a jural aggregate, because the nature of the long-house as a social grouping is not ignored in the jural realm. Not all families sue. Instead anyone knowledgeable in customary law is allowed to sue on behalf of the other members.

The Hamlet

The village area is divided into a number of named localities. When one of these is chosen as the location for a long-house, I refer to this physical location, its long-house structure or structures, and its members as the 'hamlet' A hamlet may contain more than one long-house, and it is not uncommon for it to contain two, less frequently three. This is the result of the usual processes of long-house growth and decay. The second house in a hamlet may be built by members of the first moving out because of social friction, decay of the house timbers, or sickness. Thus a hamlet may have one long-house in the process of being abandoned and another in the process of growth.

However, in terms of one's social identity and in terms of jural and ritual elaboration, the most significant social grouping larger than the domestic family and less encompassing than the village is the long-house and not the multiple long-house hamlet. There is no concept of a hamlet founder and the hamlet has no corporate feature in either the jural or ritual realms. There is only one ceremony that encompasses the whole hamlet designed to prevent wandering spirits bringing epidemics. But it should be noted that this ceremony does not distinguish multiple from single long-house hamlets for it is also held in those instances of epidemic threat for single long-house hamlets. Further, as with single long-house hamlets, this ceremony is entered into jointly by all member families as corporate entities and not by the long-houses as social isolates. If any of the restrictions in this hamlet ceremony are violated, one individual may sue on behalf of its other members. Thus the hamlet's social nature is recognized in the jural system, even if it is not given the status of a jural entity. Consequently, we may refer to the hamlet as both a jural and ritual collectivity, but only in a very limited sense. Other than the ceremony to guard against wandering demons, or incidental ritual delicts such as carrying a corpse past the hamlet, it has no economic, religious, or jural function in the Rungus social system. Again, like the long-house, the multiple long-house hamlet serves as a pool of help and assistance, but is of secondary importance to the long-house.

The Village

The Rungus village is the fundamental political unit of Rungus society. It is the only social unit that holds corporate ownership of territory in which its members reside and cultivate their swiddens. These territories usually encompass the drainage area of one of the streams or rivers, including tributaries, that flow from the central hills of the Kudat Peninsula. As a result the boundaries of villages usually follow the watersheds between such drainage systems. Where long meandering streams or rivers occur, village territories may be centred around various sections of the river with boundaries between them based on a natural landscape feature.

A Rungus village may consist of one or more long-houses, usually up to five or six but sometimes more. In a sample of 33 Rungus villages on the Kudat Peninsula population range was estimated on the basis of tax rolls and number of domestic families to be from 42 to 395 persons, with an estimated average of 137·7 persons per village (Appell, 1965).

Like the domestic family, the village is considered to be both jurally and ritually corporate, a ritual and jural isolate. However, the sum total of all its rights and duties are less developed than those of the domestic family. Also unlike the family, the village is not an operating social entity since it does not have the capacity to enter into economic relations with other social entities and accumulate assets. It simply holds the natural assets of its territory, which its members, and not the village as a unit, can use or convert into other assets. It does, on the other hand, have the capacity to increase the state of ritual goodwill between it and the spirit world, to improve the fertility of the territory, and its plants, animals, and inhabitants. Finally, the village is not a kin grouping because membership in it is open to individual domestic families whether or not they have kin resident there.

The Jural Status of the Village: Rights in the Village Reserve

The village has residual rights over its territory, the boundaries of which are actively defended. Domestic families resident in the village may cultivate their swiddens there, but no family from another village may do so without prior permission of the headman. The headman, if he finds a violator, takes appropriate action, but the jural alternatives available to him as the village representative are limited and still in the process of development. It has only been in the last several decades that the population-land balance has become severe enough to cause trespass. The headman may first request the offender to cease. If this fails, he may sue him for a piece of brassware, or more immediately may fire the swidden before the driest period sets in. This results in an incomplete burn of the slash or debris and prevents the swidden from being used.

The village also holds reversionary rights over forest growing back from abandoned swiddens. Thus, the village reserve consists of tracts of forest in various stages of regeneration from previous swidden use by village members. Some but not all villages also have areas of virgin forest where members may gather forest products. If a non-village member takes products from this part of the village reserve without prior approval, the village headman will take jural action against him, and this may involve a fine of a chicken, enjoyed by the headman's family.

All the products of the village reserve, with the exception of certain ritual groves, may be enjoyed by the village members. They also have the right to plant fruit trees there as long as they are not placed in an area particularly vulnerable to destruction by swidden fires. A resident may also use any of the village reserve not under cultivation for the grazing of his domestic animals.

The Ritual Status of the Village

In various Rungus villages a sacred grove may be found under the jurisdiction of the village as a whole. This is the grove of trees where a human sacrifice was made in the past to improve the fertility of the village. It is believed that if anyone cuts into this grove to make a swidden, all the evil influences originally removed from the village reserve and congregated in the grove will be released and will spread in an ever-widening circle. Consequently, the person guilty of such an offence will be brought before the village moot by the headman and asked to renew the efficacy of the sacred grove by giving a pig for the village to sacrifice.

There is also a corporate ceremony held by the village every decade or so in which a pig is sacrificed to renew the fecundity of the village land and the community. During this ceremony the village reserve is closed off to non-villagers. At these times the boundaries of the reserve are explicitly delineated by tying off the inter-village paths with vines at that point where they enter the reserve. A person violating these boundaries is sued by the headman for a pig to repeat the ceremony and re-establish goodwill between the village and the spirit world.

In these renewal ceremonies, in contrast to the long-house situation, the village is considered as a ritual isolate, and not just an aggregate of village families. The village as a unit enters into a ritual relationship with the spirit world, and as an isolate establishes this state of goodwill.

Locus of the Jural and Ritual Rights of the Village

The conclusion that the rights over the village reserve lie with the village as a unit are supported by the following evidence. First, the relationship of the village to its territory remains the same no matter who moves out of or joins the village. Furthermore, on leaving the village, a domestic family does not take any rights in the village reserve with it, nor is it compensated for the loss of these rights; there is also no social mechanism by which these rights to use the village reserve may be transferred to anyone else. They are what I have termed 'derivative rights' (Appell, 1974; n.d.), available only on the acceptance of membership in the village. Finally, the headman is a recognized jural representative for the village, and has the capacity to initiate jural action for it.

In the ritual realm, the locus of rights also lies with the village as a unit as demonstrated by the effects produced by the violation of any of the ritual rules following a village renewal ceremony. First, illicit sexual intercourse by any village member will destroy the state of goodwill between the whole village and the spirit world. Secondly, seeds from family swiddens may not be sold to non-members of the village or removed from the village territory for three years or again goodwill with the spirit world will be destroyed.

Recruitment to the Village: Is the Village a Kin-based Unit?

Is the village a kin-based social unit or one based on contract? First, one of the main processes of recruitment to the village is through birth. The majority of individuals in the villages studied remained in the village after reaching adulthood. An additional process of village recruitment is through marriage. In inter-village marriage males move to the villages of their wives. Finally, there is a great deal of movement between villages by domestic families after they have become established. But whether the village is a kin-based unit depends on whether qualification for membership is based on establishing a kin link with a present or former member of the village.

On these grounds the Rungus village is not a kin grouping. Kinship is not a necessary qualification for membership, although few people would wish to join a village in which they had no relatives. Nevertheless, two instances were recorded in the village where we resided in which domestic families with no kin in the village applied for membership and were accepted by the headman. Instead the criteria for village membership are based on personality characteristics of the applicant. A known fornicator or troublemaker may be refused permission to join a village.

This is not to say that Rungus villages are not in fact composed of overlapping networks of kin usually stemming from one, two, or three major cognatic descent lines with renowned founders. However, in jural terms the Rungus village does not qualify as a kin grouping, nor is it necessarily perceived as such by the Rungus even in non-jural terms. Rungus descriptions of a village may include statements that it is 'where lots of kin gather together'. But descriptions of the characteristics that delineate a village also stress that it is where 'all the members come from a single river drainage', 'all share the same customary law', 'all are comrades', 'have a common marketplace', 'where there are fruit trees', and 'where people visit each other frequently'.

Tree-focused Descent Collectivities

There is among the Rungus one social isolate that is organized on the basis of ambilateral descent. But in terms of its patterns of coactivity it is not a social grouping but a social collectivity.[6] In the jural system this descent collectivity may in certain instances also be recognized as a jural collectivity; but it can also be considered as a jural aggregate, and whether it is a collectivity or aggregate depends on the particular type of tree involved. Trees that require cultivation involve a more developed jural personality for the owners than those that do not and therefore, the holders of rights over a cultivable tree are considered as a jural collectivity rather than a jural aggregate.

Furthermore, in contrast to the other social isolates of domestic family, long-house, hamlet, and village, the descent collectivity focused on trees is not a discrete social isolate, since members may simultaneously belong to more than one such isolate.

Rights to Trees

The Rungus plant a variety of trees and bushes. These include fruit trees, bushes from which rattan may be secured, and trees and bamboos from which flooring materials are made for long-house apartments. These trees and bushes may be planted anywhere in the village reserve, but it is usual to plant them near a settlement site, around the edges of a sacred grove, or in a cemetery site so that they will not be vulnerable to destruction by uncontrolled swidden fires.

The planting of trees does not create rights over surrounding land, and anyone may cultivate up to and around these trees.

In terms of intergenerational transfer, the original planter may divide his trees among his offspring to avoid disputes over rights to them after his death. It appears that this is becoming the more common method. However, fruit and other cultivated trees may be devolved upon all heirs, both male and female without division. The problem here is whether these rights lie with the heirs in severalty or with the cognatic descent isolate that consists of all the descendants of the original planter. But first we must describe more precisely the types of rights to trees.

Certain types of trees require no care or cultivation, whilst others require a small amount of care, including clearing the undergrowth around the tree to improve productivity and sometimes building a rough fence around the trunks to indicate that such trees are not wild but have already been claimed. This is to prevent passers-by picking the fruit before the owners have had access to it. Thus, there are two kinds of rights associated with cultivated trees. First, there is the right to cultivate which entails the right to prior enjoyment of the fruit. Then there is the secondary right held by non-cultivating right-owners to enjoy any surplus fruit.

The person who holds the right to cultivate is usually the person who resides closest to the trees involved. When he has enjoyed the early ripening fruit to his family's satisfaction, he then calls his co-right-holders to come and pick what they want. The more fruit available, the more distant the kin that will be notified both in terms of genealogical and geographical space. Village residence does not restrict the enjoyment of fruit trees except in a practical way. Seldom is the amount of available fruit worth the trip and the problem of transport, and kin living in other villages may only be called if there is an unusually heavy crop. However, other types of trees whose products are used for building long-house apartments and field houses are available to descendants of the original planter only if they are resident in the village territory, because of certain ritual restrictions.

The Jural and Social Nature of the Tree-focused Isolate

The right to cultivate a tree planted by an ancestor must be activated by the interested party. This is done rather informally without necessarily notifying other right-holders. The accepted method is for the person living closest to the trees in question to care for them. Approval for this need not be secured from anyone but, if another right-holder is resident nearby and believes he has not had a fair share in the cultivation right, he will ask the cultivator for a turn. The cultivator also has the duty to initiate jural action on behalf of the tree-focused isolate in disputes with non-members.

The question of the disposition of rights on leaving the tree-focused isolate does not occur for it is *de jure* impossible to withdraw from the social unit. *De facto* the right-holders are lost to the descent isolate as they move away to other villages, and in time they and their children forget their rights.

Sale of these rights is uncommon. When it occurs it must involve all the rights in the tree or trees as a physical unit, not just the secondary rights to enjoy or the primary right to cultivate. Rights are not sold in division. One of the reasons that the sale of fruit trees occurs so seldom is because it is very difficult to get all the right-holders to agree on a price or even to the decision to sell.

When involuntary conversion or destruction occur or when a delict is committed against the property, the cultivator has the responsibility for taking jural action. He contacts the person responsible and arranges for a date to argue the case. The cultivator then notifies all other right-holders of this date, and they decide whether or not they wish to attend. If they do not appear, they receive no part of the settlement. The cultivator receives half of the settlement and the remainder is divided amongst those right-holders present.

The social boundaries of the tree-focused isolate are ill-defined. Right-holders forget their rights if they move away or if there are a large number of right-holders to a stand of trees. This is particularly the case where an individual shares rights to other trees with fewer co-right-holders. In any event, rights over trees are not considered a very important scarce good so that frequently right-holders will not bother to join in jural action for restitution on the destruction of trees.

Finally, there is no jurally recognized representative to enforce sanctions within the group. While the cultivator initiates jural action *on behalf of* the other right-holders, he has no power to enforce any types of behaviour nor has he sanctions to maintain approved behaviour within the group, with the possible exception of failing to call entitled right-holders to share in the fruit. There are thus no real sanctions available to the tree-focused isolate other than those in the jural system at large.

The position of cultivator has no formal title as does the village headman, and there is a certain amount of turnover in the occupancy of this position when, for example, a right-holder moves to another hamlet or village or when his right to cultivate is challenged by another. Most importantly, the nature of interaction within the isolate is very irregular and seldom if ever includes all right-holders at any one time. Only if there is an unusually large harvest are all right-holders in other villages informed, and even then there may well be right-holders in distant villages who do not receive the information about the harvest on time.

I think we can conclude that rights in cultivated fruit trees reside with the individual members of the descent isolate and not with the isolate as a jural entity. This is because the social boundaries of the isolate fluctuate and are blurred; not all secondary right-holders enjoy the harvest equally; and the activation of rights is primarily an individual's decision with respect to his share of the harvest and of the indemnity for a destroyed tree. The cultivator organizes the disposition of entitlements, but he does not represent the co-right-holders as a jural isolate or jural collectivity.

On the other hand the descent isolate is not simply a jural aggregate. The Rungus jural system permits one person to take jural action *on behalf of* the other members. Each person does not have to separately initiate proceedings. Likewise in the jural system of the Rungus the cultivator is given the power to fence off the trees to prevent others using the fruit, and this is done partially on behalf of the other right-holders. Therefore, I conclude that the descent isolate is a jural collectivity.

Finally, what type of social entity is the tree-focused descent isolate? First, in those instances where the trees involved do not need cultivation then we are dealing with a descent collectivity. If right-holders live close by they share the fruit whenever it is available on an informal basis. Each member helps himself without considering other right-holders. This type of tree-focused isolate is only a social collectivity since there is no ordering of interaction in the isolate nor do all members engage in face-to-face interaction. However, jurally, I believe this descent collectivity should only be considered a jural aggregate for there is no role recognized by the jural system that involves the right to take action on behalf of other right-holders.

On the other hand, those descent isolates that involve rights over cultivated trees present more difficult classification problems. At first glance there does appear to be a hierarchical ordering of interaction within the isolate. The cultivator calls his co-right-holders to participate in the harvest or notifies them of the time and place he plans to take jural action after a tree or stand of trees has been destroyed. But since this descent isolate never meets in face-to-face interaction are we dealing with a secondary social grouping? I think not. First, the social boundaries of the isolate are very ill-defined in terms of actual co-activity. Secondly, the cultivator has no sanctions to control deviant behaviour within the social isolate separate from those available to all in the larger jural system. Therefore, I would prefer to class this type of tree-focused social isolate as a social collectivity. But it is also a jural collectivity, since a jurally recognized representative is permitted to sue on behalf of the other members.

In conclusion, I would like to emphasize the amorphous quality of this tree-focused descent isolate. There is no special term in the Rungus language to identify it, nor are these social isolates named. Consequently, I would conclude (Appell, 1968; Appell and Harrison, 1969) that there are no descent groupings in Rungus society. For those who disagree with my analysis and maintain that the descent isolate focused on cultivated trees is a secondary social grouping, they could then argue that the Rungus do have cognatic descent groups. However, let me point out that while these social isolates may play an unfortunately large role in the development of the ethnographer's conceptual tools, they play an inconsequential role in the interests of the Rungus and their economy.

NOTES

1. I have coined the term 'isoglot' to refer to the speech of a group of people who consider their language or dialect to be significantly different from neighbouring speech communities and thus have an indigenous term by which they identify it. Where the exact linguistic status of an isoglot is not known *vis-à-vis* neighbouring speech communities, I find this term preferable to 'language', or 'dialect', or 'communilect' (Appell, 1968c).

2. This term may also be generalized to include all those interior people who eat pork.

3. I argue elsewhere in detail (Appell, 1974) that the relationship between the domestic family and its assets does not involve rights in common or joint rights but instead corporate rights. The relationship does not involve rights in common because under this concept different titles with respect to the same property can exist and survivorship is excluded. Yet when a member of the domestic family

dies, no part of the family estate is distributed; instead the survivor's future shares are thereby increased. The concept of joint rights also does not apply as the incidents of ownership necessary for this classification in the strict sense are not met. Specifically, interests of the tenants are not vested at the same time; there is no unity of possession since prior interests are recognized in terms of an individual's contribution to the creation of the estate. Thus there is no unity of interest since each member of the family does not have estates of the same type and duration.

4. But there is an informal leader whose main function is to help minimize disputes between apartments in the long-house.

5. 'Entify' is defined in the *Oxford English Dictionary* as 'to make into an entity, attribute objective existence to'.

6. A social grouping engages in co-activity as either a primary group or a secondary group. A social collectivity, in contrast, refers to that class of social isolates in which the members never engage in co-activity although they share a similar body of norms and a similar sense of moral obligation to fulfil certain role expectations with regard to a propositus. With respect to the concept of the kindred, I have suggested (Appell, 1967: 204) that a kin isolate should be classed as a kindred under the following conditions: (1) cognates of an individual are specifically designated as holding in severalty identical rights and obligations to perform with respect to him; (2) the characteristics of such a social isolate should include the recognition by the members that they share these norms and obligations with other individuals in the isolate, even though the whole body of members may not be known to each other; and (3) the recognition that others have similar norms and obligations that result in various members of this isolate, or a significant portion of them, coming together at pertinent times to form 'kindred based' groups in order to discharge more adequately their individually held obligations.

8

THE BAJAU LAUT*

CLIFFORD SATHER

The Bajau

THE Bajau are a diverse, culturally fragmented population, numbering some 72,000 persons in Sabah, spread unevenly in scattered villages and hamlets along the eastern and north-western coasts of the state, and so southward to Kimanis Bay on the west. An additional 90,000 Bajau are present in the southern Philippines and a further 30,000 to 40,000 in eastern Indonesia, chiefly in coastal Sulawesi.

Like most other north Borneo peoples, the Bajau speak dialects of a Philippine-affiliated language, not all of which are mutually intelligible. The term 'Bajau' was originally applied to the group by the Brunei Malays with whom those living on the west coast maintained intermittent contact, sometimes hostile, especially during the eighteenth and early nineteenth centuries. The Bajau refer to themselves as *a'a sama* or by dialect variants of these terms. *A'a* means simply 'people' and its use implies recognition of common cultural links and the use of a shared language (*ling sama*). The Bajau have never constituted a unified political entity however, and prior to European penetration local communities in Sabah and the southern Philippines were under the tenuous jurisdiction of the Sulu Sultanate, and in eastern Indonesia, Buginese, Makassarese, and lesser political units, most of them dominated by non-Bajau rulers or their local political agents.

Within this complex, variegated social world, the Bajau have historically occupied a special niche, as island or strand-dwelling fishermen, shoreside farmers and marine collectors, and', while pronounced local differences exist, most settlements remain heavily dependent on the sea for subsistence, trade and outside contacts. In Sabah the Bajau comprise more than two-thirds of the indigenous fishing population.[1] But economic patterns vary. Along exposed

* Field research among the Bajau Laut was carried out in 1964–5 with the support of a NIMH fellowship and research grant (MH 10159-01). An additional brief visit was made in April 1974. I wish to thank the headman of Kampong Bangau-Bangau, Penglima Tiring, and his family, with whom I lived during my initial stay, and my other Bajau Laut friends, too numerous to mention by name, for their generous hospitality. I am also indebted to Dr. G. N. Appell for reading and commenting upon earlier drafts of this paper, some parts of which, in a very different form, were read at the annual American Anthropological Association meetings, Washington, D.C., 1967.

sections of the ~~western~~ coast fishing is supplemented annually by occasional farming, wood-cutting and casual trade, and in the heavily settled Tuaran and Kota Belud Districts most Bajau live inland from the immediate coast and practice a mixed farming based primarily on wet-rice cultivation and cattle-rearing. Because the ~~western~~ coast is more sheltered, particularly from the south-west monsoon and intermonsoon, fishing is more reliable and the irregular, embayed nature of the coastline, and the existence of extensive offshore islands and reefs, permit more specialized fishing adaptations, of which the Bajau Laut represent an extreme example.

The Bajau Laut

The Bajau Laut are the most maritime of all Bajau-speaking groups. In the past they relied exclusively on fishing and the exchange of fish and other sea products for their livelihood. As a group they were, and remain, almost entirely without farmland or other property ashore, except for burial sites which belong in common to several neighbouring communities and represent their principal point of land connection. Until 1930 the Sabah Bajau Laut lived wholly in boats. Since then most families have built pilehouses for themselves over the sea, and only a few, less than 20 per cent of the total population, remain permanently boat-dwelling. At the same time barter exchange with more sedentary groups ashore has been replaced by the disposal of fish through commercial market channels, resulting in the breakdown of political clientage by which the Bajau Laut were previously bound to the neighbouring groups with whom they traded.

At the present time the Bajau Laut occupy two relatively large pilehouse villages, Bangau-Bangau and Labuan Haji, with a combined population of some 1,300 persons, located near the extreme eastern tip of the Semporna Peninsula in south-eastern Sabah. Additional, widely dispersed settlements, consisting either of pilehouse villages, or, less often, of houseboat flotillas identified with fixed, recurrently occupied anchorage sites, are found throughout the Sulu Archipelago of the Philippines and over a wide area of eastern Indonesia (cf. Sather, 1971, 1975; Sopher, 1965). The Semporna Bajau Laut are part of a smaller regional group that includes six additional communities in the Sibutu Island cluster of the Philippines. Individual settlements within the region vary in size from three to four households to more than 100 (e.g. Sitangkai) and are interspersed with and sometimes interpenetrated by the villages of other coastal and island peoples, chiefly Tausug and other Bajau-speaking groups. The Bajau Laut identify themselves locally as the *sama laut* or *sama mandelaut*, the 'sea Bajau' or 'maritime Bajau' (*sama*), and are linked, on an interpersonal level by ramifying ties of kinship and intermarriage, by frequent visits and occasional participation of families from different villages in large-scale fish netting drives (*ambit*).

The Local Community

Families from the two Bajau Laut villages in Sabah fish the off-shore reefs, coral terraces and shoals that fringe the Semporna Peninsula and outlying islands of the Sulu island shelf. Because of the distance and scattered location of their main fishing grounds, fishing is done primarily in the course of extended voyages lasting from one or two days to several weeks or longer. Voyages are under-taken by separate conjugal family boat crews (*dabalutu*), the members of which live for the duration of each voyage on board a small sea-going vessel belonging to the family head and equipped with a portable sleeping quarters, foodstores and hearth. While at sea, family members carry on their everyday domestic activities entirely afloat, putting into shore only to collect additional firewood, to dry nets or take on food or water supplies, and their association with other families is limited to those with whom they are sailing or hap-pen to encounter at sea. While fishing the conjugal family thus forms an independent productive and capital-bearing unit, and its members enjoy exclusive control over the disposal of whatever catch they land except for a small share reserved for their own consumption and for distribution among housemates and neighbours in their home village.

Owing to the constant coming and going of village families, the local settlement (*lahat*) is a relatively fluid grouping, with few corpor-ate characteristics, and the fundamental social and economic units are large, multi-family households (*luma'*) and household clusters (*ba'anan*). Village households typically contain several conjugal family fishing units whose members live together in joint occupancy of a single pilehouse dwelling belonging to a common 'house leader' (*nakura luma'*) for as long as they remain in their home settlement. Fish reserved for consumption (*pamillah daing*) are pooled primarily within the luma' and the larger, more inclusive cluster. Here too are focused most significant social relations and daily interaction. House-hold clusters are organized around alignments of related house leaders and consist physically of tightly aggregated groups of adjoin-ing pilehouses.

Together, households and clusters are largely autonomous groups, united, in making up the village, in loose confederation from which withdrawal, and to which the entry of additional families or house-holds coming from other settlements, is possible at any time, largely as the heads of these groups see fit. While various ties of friendship, economic convenience and personal kinship and affinity unite village members, there are no enduring ties, such as common descent, that attach these groups to one particular settlement rather than another; movement between communities is relatively common, and is easily possible, provided newcomers are acceptable to their village neigh-bours or, if they join existing domicile groups, to their senior house leaders. A large proportion of the members of any village are ordinarily related as cognates, or by marriage, but settlements are not kin groups, either ideally or in practice. The village is rather a local community, corporate only in the limited sense that its members share a common *addat*, safeguarded by its headman and other senior household elders. The fishing grounds exploited by village members are unowned, and overlap with those exploited by the members of other settlements, with the result that those who have newly taken up membership enjoy the same rights of use to these grounds as established villagers. Moreover the community as a whole never functions as a corporate economic unit, either in terms of co-activity, or as a group with control over resources.

Political leadership within the village is vested in the senior house and cluster leaders and no strict separation at this level can be made between domestic and politico-jural relations. Jural support is marshalled within the household and among ba'anan allies. The leaders of these groups have responsibility for securing the political interests and formal jural rights of their followers (*tindug*) and of acting on their behalf as spokesman, or counsellors, in the event of litigation with members of other domicile units. In the ritual sphere, house leaders are recognized as the formal sponsors of all major rites involving household members, primarily marriage, circumcision, burial and rites of thanksgiving (*magmaulud*), and the household, rather than the village, forms the principal congregation that comes together in the performance of ritual. An official village headman, recognized in office by the State and given the Malay title *orang tua*, is chosen by the villagers from among the heads of the largest household clusters in the settlement. Within the village, his role is confined chiefly to convening village moots, or mediation sessions, whenever an open breach of addat or a serious dispute arises between households that cannot be settled informally by the principals involved. He commands very little authority, except by dint of personality, outside his immediate luma' and ba'anan, and cannot impose a decision or judgement on the community without the full concurrence of its other household elders. Thus, positions of leadership are bound up with familial statuses and a person's relations with the members of his own and other village households.

Kinship

The Bajau Laut trace kinship bilaterally and assign equal importance to relations between the father's and mother's kin.[2] The total field comprising all of an individual's known, or presumed, cognatic kin is termed his *kampong*. Within the kampong are numerous descent lines, called *turunan*, leading back to particular ancestors. Recognition of ancestry is generally shallow, and is rarely reckoned beyond four or five generations, but when collateral branches are added to these lines, acknowledged cognatic relations ramify widely. All descendants, through both males and females, of an individual's two sets of grandparents constitute a narrower cognatic category, called *dampalanakan* or *dampo'un*, the members of which are counted as 'close' (*magsekot*) kindred in both social and genealogical terms. All cognates are additionally placed in a limited set of terminological categories, defined primarily by sex, generation, and collateral distance, to which are attached specific social rights and obligations that, in total, provide the individual with a guide to the behaviour expected between himself and his different classes of relatives.

Neither the kampong nor the dampalanakan is a kin group, as such, and both exist only in reference to a particular individual. However, dampalanakan ties, and relations between primary kin (*taianakan*) within the category, provide the basis on which the cognatic members of households and clusters are recruited and the scheme of rights and obligations that govern their behaviour towards one another. The significance of households and clusters is that they impose a form of 'closure' within each individual's personal field of cognatic relations, singling out those cognates, and by extension their spouses, with whom an individual is joined in continuous, daily transactions based on long-term expectations of mutual support (*nabbang*), sanctioned by moral values and the authority of group elders. While neither the household, conjugal family, nor cluster coincides entirely with Ego-centric categories of close kindred, cognatic ties outside these groups may be only selectively recognized, or even ignored entirely in specific social situations. Relations between members, however, are constantly in play, and support for one another can only be withheld by revoking membership itself. Thus the categories by which the Bajau Laut order cognatic relations reflect not only their individual social behaviour, but provide the framework within which cohesive groups—families, households and clusters—emerge as part of the basic structure of their society.

The presence of large, extended, or multiple family households, and their association in kindred-based residential groups, has not been adequately described for cognatic societies.[3] The extended family, in particular, is frequently thought to presuppose some form of lineal or descent group organization. Thus Murdock (1960) treats extended family households, for example, as minimal units in societies internally divided into corporate descent groups, and, on this basis, takes their presence or absence as a typological feature in classifying cognatic social systems.[4] Descent is not, however, a significant feature of Bajau Laut social organization, and the structure of village domicile units—households and clusters—is fully consistent with the bilateral nature of Bajau Laut society, nor does the presence of these groups preclude the functional importance, particularly in the context of sea voyaging, of the conjugal family, as a separate social unit.

The Conjugal Family

At sea the minimal, and only permanently constituted, social unit is the conjugal family boat crew (dabalutu) consisting typically of a fisherman, his wife and their dependent children. Married women regularly accompany their husbands, except on very brief voyages, or occasionally when pregnant or with new-born infants to look after. The longer the voyage, the more important a wife's presence becomes, not only domestically, in preparing meals or caring for younger family members, but in the arduous work of cleaning and splitting fish for preservation by salting or sun-drying. New crews are formed at the time of marriage and family members work together as a single fishing team as long as the group persists, using a boat, drift nets and other gear belonging to the family head, either alone or with other family crews, under the husband's supervision. Decisions regarding when and where to fish, and with whom, are made independently by the head of each family, in consultation normally with the other family heads in his village luma', and are arrived at in terms of the immediate needs of his family, as well as the decisions of their other partners and reports of landings being made by returning fishing parties.

The intensity of fishing activity, and the pattern of movement of village fishing teams, is governed primarily by wind and tidal conditions and the seasonal appearance of pelagic fish at known netting sites within an area of some 40 miles radius surrounding each settlement.[5] While the intensity of fishing varies, there are no well-defined periods in which netting is totally suspended, except for brief, irregular intervals, rarely of more than one or two days' duration, during local squalls or rainy weather. Most families spend roughly a third of each year at sea, divided between some 20 to 50 voyages. Driftnets are the chief gear used and allow considerable variation in the deployment of labour. A single length of net may be used alone, or it may be tied by the head and footline to additional lengths of net belonging to other families to form engulfing or encircling structures, the largest of which may be several hundred feet across and require as many as 50 to 60 family crews, possibly drawn from four or five separate villages, to set in place and operate. Most netting is done by smaller teams consisting of from two to six families, but the pattern of fleet alignments is highly variable and single families may equally well fish alone or in temporarily assembled parties, occasionally of considerably larger size and possibly recruited across village lines.

Each family head has a small circle of some 5 to 12 fishing partners, or frequent 'companions' (*sehe*'), with whom he and his family repeatedly join to form these smaller, recurrently assembled netting teams. For each family head, these persons comprise a personal roster from which he repeatedly selects team-mates; thus it emerges as a relatively lasting 'quasi-group', or action set, formed specifically for co-operative netting. Relations between roster members are relatively stable and are based primarily on close cognatic kinship and affinity. Partners are most commonly men of the same generation, most often brothers or husbands of sisters, although a younger man may join the roster of his father or father-in-law until he is able to form sufficient partnerships among his own related age-mates. Although roster ties are relatively stable, the smaller teams mobilized on this basis vary in size and rarely have precisely the same composition for more than two or three consecutive voyages. Moreover, not all members of an individual's personal roster are necessarily members of each other's rosters, although most team-mates have at least one frequent 'companion' in any party they join. Alignments are short-lived and teams disband at the conclusion of every fishing venture. Although they may regroup at the next opportunity, individual families may also fish alone, or with others, some or all of whom are unrelated by roster ties. Thus, for the individual family head, his personal roster grades into a wider periphery of more casual, irregular alignments entered into out of a short-term need for labour, pooled gear, or through the fortuitous presence of other family crews at the same fishing site. The constituent family is the only permanent group which persists as individual parties are repeatedly formed and disbanded; reflecting its fundamental independence, the landings realized through co-operative fishing are divided equally between each participating family crew regardless of its size or the tasks performed by its members. On the other hand, alignments between families are highly fluid, with the result that fishing parties of varying size and composition can be rapidly assembled, or disbanded, as landings alter and the main centre of fishing activity shifts from one site to another.

The Village Household

Exchange and the distributive aspects of the economy are organized, in social terms, along quite different lines than those of production. At sea the conjugal family is an independent productive unit, and its members, even when aligned with others, fish chiefly for themselves, using gear belonging to the family head. At the same time each family is bound by generalized obligations to assist others within its home village, and, as a result, production is geared to a system of communal consumption and mutual support centred in the larger village households and kindred-based clusters. The importance of these groups is that they attach each family to a set of larger, more enduring · social groups, the members of which are joined by long-term commitments of mutual political support, food pooling and shared access, through reciprocal lending and gift exchange, to the material assets, monetary resources and labour help of their separate members. As a way of consolidating ties, endogamous marriages are frequently arranged within household clusters, so that these groups additionally supply their members with a pool of preferred, potential marriage partners.

Of these two groups, the household (luma') is the most important. Minimally, a household contains a single conjugal family or, more frequently, a set of closely related families or partial family units whose members live together in a single dwelling under the authority of a common house leader or nakura luma'. In describing the household, the Bajau Laut lay stress on the criterion of co-residence and use the same term, luma', for both the house, as a physical structure, and the group of housemates who occupy it. In everyday speech, the latter are spoken of as *siga* . . . or *kami daluma'*, 'those . . .' or 'we of one house'. Despite this emphasis on co-residence, luma' membership is restricted to persons who are primary kin of the house leader or his wife, or are the offspring or spouses of the couple's primary kin. In other words, the luma' is also a close-knit unit in a genealogical sense. Structurally it most often contains what Murdock (1949:35) has termed a 'bilocal extended family'. This he defines as a family that 'unites the nuclear family of a married couple with those of some but not all of their sons, of some but not all of their daughters, and of some but not all of their grandchildren of either sex'. In the case of the luma', however, only a minority of households actually contain the nuclear family of a grandchild or grandchildren of a still living nakura luma', and, as we shall see presently, the group lacks Murdock's further criterion of 'indefinite continuity over time' (1949: 33). In Bangau-Bangau, the largest of the two Bajau Laut villages in Sabah, 60 per cent of all village households contain three- or four-generation extended family units, and the remainder either smaller stem (21 per cent) or conjugal families (19 per cent) (cf. Sather, 1976). The luma' is also a domestic group and its members additionally prepare and eat their meals in common, contribute to a joint budget and share responsibility for everyday domestic chores and for the upkeep of the dwelling, its attached boat landing platform (*pantan*), hearth (*kusina*), and the plank walks, if any, that join it to neighbouring houses.

(a) *Household structure*

The village household is characteristically a large, structurally complex family unit. In Bangau-Bangau mean household size is 12·2 persons; the mode is 9, and the range is 6 to 22 persons. Two basic features underlie its structural composition. The first is that newly married couples never establish a separate household of their own, but begin their married life as dependent members of an existing household headed by a senior house leader, ordinarily the husband's or wife's father. It is only after a number of years, when the pair has established their own family of procreation, and their eldest children have reached, or are approaching, marriageable age, that the couple is likely to secede from the parental household and set up an independent luma' of their own with the husband as founder and house leader. Because secession is delayed, the couple's eldest children will begin to marry, in the normal course of events, shortly after the new household is founded. While some may marry out and so become members of other luma', at least one child, and more often several, will remain to rear their own families in the newly established luma'. Thus, the household rapidly grows into an extended family unit containing, in addition to the senior pair, their still unmarried children and the families of those of their married offspring who have chosen to remain in their luma'. At this point, once dependent families are added to the group, its continuance, unlike that of the conjugal family, is no longer wholly dependent on the stability of the house founder's marriage, and the household is usually large enough to function as a domestic group even if divorce or death occurs in its senior generation. The household thus becomes a more stable group in the sense that its continuance is no longer bound to the survival of a single conjugal unit.

The second feature is that the household is only temporarily self-perpetuating. As the house founder and his wife reach old-age and their grandchildren come to maturity, their children ordinarily depart to found new luma'. By the time the last of their children is ready to make good its independence, the original dwelling is usually abandoned or dismantled. When this occurs, the family unit initially established by the aging pair is dissolved. Occasionally a house may be inherited by one of the couple's children, preferably the youngest (*anak kebangsuan*). But this is only a temporary measure, adopted until the remaining husband to whom control of the dwelling has passed is in a position to build a new house and found a separate household to which the parental couple, if still alive, will normally attach themselves as dependents.

Following its establishment the household thus undergoes a regular cycle of growth, fission and dismemberment ending with its eventual dissolution and replacement by similarly constituted groups headed by persons who were once dependents in households now undergoing dismemberment or dissolution. Structural continuity is achieved not by the perpetuation of individual households, but rather by the constant cycle of development they undergo and the permanent processes of group recruitment and fission that underlie it. These give the household, throughout its major developmental phases, a stable structural form despite changes in its personnel.

Under ordinary circumstances the conjugal family emerges as an independent domestic unit only for a brief interval at the time a new household is founded. Following the marriage of the eldest of the house founder's children, the luma' enters a 'phase of expansion', which continues as each of the couple's remaining offspring takes a spouse. With the subsequent birth of grandchildren to those children who remain in the household, the luma' enters a 'procreative phase'. At this point the household loses the original unity it possessed as a single conjugal family and becomes an internally differentiated, extended or multiple family unit.

This internal differentiation foreshadows the eventual partition and ultimate secession of component families in a final 'hiving-off phase'. Every man should ideally head his own household some time before the end of his wife's childbearing years, provided the couple are able to form a stable, fruitful union. Most couples achieve this goal, with the result that all luma' containing more than one dependent family undergo eventual partition. The ultimate lines of cleavage along which secession occurs are evident from the moment the first in-marrying husband or wife joins the household. Following marriage and the birth of children to the house founder's dependents, relations between the nakura luma' and his children, and among the heads of the dependent families under his authority, come into sharp focus as adult housemates acquire new, and at times diverging, interests and responsibilities. For a number of years the nakura luma' is generally able to contain conflict within the group, but other factors also work to delay partition and preserve close, amicable relations, even after secession takes place. For one thing, the dispersal of separate conjugal families on fishing voyages provides a periodic escape from household tensions, and, for another, young married men are often economically dependent on the house founder or other, older more experienced fishermen until their children are old enough to assist them actively at sea. But most importantly, the potential for conflict within the luma' is reduced, and the movement of persons in and out of the household is made relatively easy, by the lack of a corporate estate controlled by the group, or administered by the house leader, that might otherwise have to be divided or left behind by those who secede from the group. The household as a whole is not a property-owning unit, and each married couple holds whatever property they acquire subsequent to marriage, or receive through inheritance, independently of both the house leader and their other housemates. When secession occurs, the departing couple simply removes its belongings to the new dwelling which the husband has built with the help of his former housemates. It is usual for the nakura luma' and his wife to settle property on their children as they leave the luma', either at marriage or upon the completion of their family of procreation. As a result, by the time that all but the last-born child have departed, most of the older couple's heritable possessions (*pusaka*) will have been bestowed, except for the house and a small residual share of property reserved for the youngest child. Property bestowal is thus closely keyed to the process of partition. In addition, the lack of a corporate estate vested in the household as a whole, particularly in the form of land or other durable, productive resources, means that there are no compelling property interests that might otherwise preserve the authority of the aging house leader or justify the continued membership of his dependents in a common household once they and their families are able to form viable domestic groups of their own.

The final result of partition is the termination of the original household. This occurs upon the abandonment of the dwelling initially erected by the house founder. Most houses can stand for 30 or 40 years, or as long as their piles (*tu'ut tambelian*) remain sound and capable of supporting the upper structure. Less durable materials, however, such as flooring or wall planks, require periodic replacement. In the course of renovation, the structure itself may be enlarged, or parts of it dismantled, with the result that the house, as a physical structure, closely reflects the numerical strength and material resources of its occupants. And eventually every dwelling is pulled down or abandoned, marking the final dissolution of the domestic group established by its founder.

Thus the household is, in neither a social nor physical sense, a self-perpetuating group persisting from generation to generation, but, rather, each takes its identity from a particular dwelling and varies in membership with the changing circumstances of its leader and the cycle of growth, fission and dissolution to which his own and the families of his dependents are subject. But even as it gains or loses members, the household retains the same basic structural form. Founded by the nakura luma' and his wife, most households expand, to contain the families of those of their married sons or daughters who have not married out nor yet seceded from the group, the couple's residual family of procreation, plus possibly other persons, with or without offspring, chiefly children, grandchildren or siblings who have joined the household following the break-up of conjugal links in other domestic groups. In most families at least one or two children will marry out, and, because of differences in the age of those who remain, older children often make good their independence by the time younger brothers or sisters are beginning to marry and rear families of their own. As a result, few luma' contain more than two or three dependent families at a time. Additional persons may occasionally be incorporated in the household, or later on rejoin the group after having once relinquished membership, but its basic structural form remains the same. It is essentially that of a pyramid of interlocking conjugal families, each family or married pair typically at a different stage of maturity, with the house founder and his wife at the apex, and extending through three, occasionally four, generations each of which is linked successively by parent-child or filiative ties.

Clearly the household is not a descent group, minimal or otherwise. Although the house leader and his wife are typically its senior members, their position depends, not on descent as such, but on the leader's role as house-owner, his familial status within the group and position as its spokesman. Moreover, eligibility to household membership is established, not by successive genealogical affiliation, but primarily by means of marriage and bilateral filiation. Furthermore, neither marriage nor filiation alone automatically ascribes membership, but rather they provide the basis for claims to eligibility which must, in the case of adults, be asserted and acceded to by the house leader and be accompanied by actual residence sustained over a prolonged period of time.

(b) *Filiation*

Every Bajau Laut child is by birth a member of one particular luma' which may as equally well be the luma' of the father as that of the mother. In practice, it tends more often to be the latter, particularly if the child is the first-born. Uxorilocal residence is the norm during the first few years of marriage, or until the birth of the couple's first child. Statistically 60 per cent of all couples continue to reside uxorilocally until they eventually establish a household of their own (Sather, 1976).

However, regardless of which household a child is born into, it does not usually come to maturity in its natal luma'. Generally its parents leave the group unless they stand to inherit the original dwelling. By accompanying its parents the child relinquishes membership in its natal household and becomes a member of the newly founded household established by its parents. It is normally into this luma', or the similar group founded by its spouse's parents, that its own children are born and acquire their initial household affiliation.

By right of birth a child may belong, then, to the parental luma' of either of its parents. The choice is made by its parents, together with the heads of the respective households in which they live prior to marriage. While a degree of option is involved, once a particular residence decision is taken, it is, in Firth's terms (1957:5), *definitive*, i.e. it assigns an individual to membership in one, and only one, specific luma'. However, the choice is always *reversible* (cf. Firth, 1957:5) and an individual is never permanently bound to it, but may, and regularly does, change his group membership several times during his lifetime. The first change regularly occurs in childhood when his membership is transferred to the new household established by his parents on their secession from his natal luma'. Membership is thus acquired at birth, or is later transferred as secession occurs, by means of bilateral filiation. Following Freeman (1956:87–8; 1958:26–8) the system is more specifically one of utrolateral filiation, in that membership is established initially in *either* the husband's or wife's parental household, but *never in both*. However, the Bajau Laut system of filiation differs from that of the Iban described by Freeman in that neither of these households is ordinarily either spouse's natal luma'. This is because filiation is not only optionally reversible, but is regularly and systematically reversed in each generation. This difference in filiation is of fundamental structural importance. What it means is that household membership is transferred in every generation from an existing group to a newly founded one, with the result that, from the perspective of the original household, there is an inevitable break in filiative links between successive generations. While this break may be averted temporarily by the short-term inheritance of the household by the house founder's successor, affiliation is, nevertheless, eventually transferred to a new luma'. The difference can best be summarized by saying that the Bajau Laut system is one of *discontinuous*, as opposed to *continuous*, filiation. Thus the luma' is a self-replicating group but, unlike the Iban *bilek* family, is never a self-perpetuating one.

All children have identical rights of membership in the luma' into which they were born or grew to maturity, except in so far as the youngest or last-born daughter, has a superior claim to succeed the house founder or his wife upon their death or retirement. The emphasis in defining these rights is on parentage and the central relationships that unite luma' members are those between parents and their children and between siblings. Collectively these persons are termed taianakan and relationships between them form the relational core, not only of the luma', but of every permanently constituted social unit in Bajau Laut society. As the household expands, successive filiative links, and their collateral extension through relations of siblingship, are temporarily incorporated in its make-up. Incorporation is relatively short-lived, however, as filiative links of membership are eventually revoked or transferred to other luma' in the ensuing process of partition and with the ultimate dissolution of the household. Relations traced maximally through three successive filiative links define, both ideally and in practice, the effective limits of eligibility to luma' membership. No one outside these limits is ever accorded full household membership with the exception of in-marrying spouses.

What needs to be stressed is that not all persons related within these limits are necessarily members of the same household or even of the same household cluster. Filiative ties establish rights of eligibility but membership of both the luma' and ba'anan additionally requires prolonged residence and acceptance of the responsibilities that membership entails. Furthermore, filiative links provide an individual with multiple and overlapping rights of possible admission to more than one set of domicile groups. Choice is made in terms of specific residence decisions, and once an individual elects, or accompanies his parents or spouse to take up residence in a particular luma' (and ba'anan), his membership is unambiguously defined, even though it may be revoked later on and transferred to another group. As a consequence, the combined outcome of numerous individual acts of choice is the emergence of concrete, relatively stable domicile groups. At the same time, the overlapping nature of these rights provides each individual with a field of potential claimants and sponsors through whom alternative lines of affiliation may be sought or accorded, as domicile groups change in personnel.

(c) *Marriage*

Residence is, therefore, of central importance in determining both household and cluster membership. Marriage is crucial in this regard since it constitutes the principal occasion on which a residence choice resulting in a change of household membership is made. By and large, filiative claims to membership are established by birth, or are transferred from one luma' to another in the process of household partition. While some additional reshuffling of personnel may occur, chiefly due to the break-up of marriage or the incompatibility of housemates, such occasions are relatively infrequent. Moreover, those who take up membership are in many cases former housemates who, in doing so, rejoin a group to which they previously belonged by right of filiation. An additional, but very infrequent form of household recruitment is by adoption. Unlike many other Borneo peoples, the Bajau Laut do not regularly practice adoption, except, as a rule, in the event of the death of a child's parents. But, when it occurs, adopted children acquire the same status in the household as natural children born into the group.

Marriage requires that one marriage partner leaves his parental luma' and takes up membership in the household of his spouse's parents or some other senior cognate. From the point of view of the household, the decision is a vital one since the group is typically founded by a couple past or near the end of their childbearing years and at least one in-marrying spouse must be added to assure the group's continuance. As a result, conflicting pressure is frequently brought to bear on newly married couples by their parents or other senior kinsmen anxious to secure their residence within their own particular domicile group. To minimize pressure, and prevent dissipation of resources among unrelated households, particularly in the form of bridewealth (*dalaham*), marriages are often arranged between children of allied families residing in the same ba'anan. Also a permanent residence choice is usually deferred for a number of years. Following a one- or two-year period of uxorilocal residence, most couples alternate for a time between the two parental households before settling permanently in one or the other luma'. Recently married couples are therefore allowed an opportunity to discover which set of housemates they find most compatible and their parents are given time to reconcile themselves to their final decision.

A first marriage is ideally arranged by the couple's parents, their related cluster elders and other senior cognates, but sometimes the union is precipitated by elopement or the girl's abduction by a young man and his friends. Later marriages are generally contracted directly by the couple themselves. The rules that apply to marriage primarily concern alliances between cognates. While non-cognates (*a'a saddi*) may marry, their union is neither frequent nor favoured, and cognatic marriage is the norm, both preferred and actual. For cognates, marriage and sexual relations are prescribed as incestuous (*sumbang*) between: siblings, both full and half; immediate patrilateral parallel cousins; and all cognates, in practice through the range of second cousins, who are not of the same generational level.

The most stringent prohibitions apply to relationships within the conjugal family and between children and parents' siblings; under no circumstances may such persons marry. Outside these limits, intergenerational unions, and marriage between patrilateral parallel cousins, may be allowed, although the latter in particular is strongly disapproved, provided ritual fines are paid to negate the spiritually deleterious consequences. The children of brothers are said to be, like full brothers and sisters, *dabohe'*, 'of one (seminal) fluid' and their union is therefore incestuous, as *anak kasumbang*, although more distant patrilateral ties are ordinarily ignored. There is also an inherent role conflict that is likely to arise in the event of their marriage, since the bride's father's brother is, in most cases, expected to act as her *wakil*, or guardian, and be witness (*saksi*) to the pronouncement of the marriage formula (*batal*) and transfer of bridewealth on the occasion of her marriage.

With this exception, all other cousins of whatever degree are strongly preferred marriage partners. Approximately 80 per cent of all unions in Bangau-Bangau are between kampong (presumed or actual cognates) and nearly all of these are between *magkaki*, persons related, or presumed to be related, as cousins of some degree. First and second cousin marriage is particularly important structurally as it serves to maintain and further consolidate relations between close cognates within the category of dampalanakan. There is no marriage prohibition within either the luma' or ba'anan, provided that it is not incestuous, and while intra-luma' marriage is highly infrequent, that within the ba'anan is common and often arranged by the elders (*mattoa*) of the group to prevent the attenuation of ties among their followers. While a single union may suffice, a double marriage is sometimes arranged between a son and daughter of a pair of sisters or of a brother and sister. Such double marriages not only consolidate the cognatic networks linking ba'anan members, but ensure that one couple will reside post-nuptially in each intermarrying household, and have the further advantage of requiring only a token bridewealth exchange.

Marriage is also a major means of household recruitment. Persons marrying into a household attain full rights of membership, including in the case of an in-marrying husband, the right to inherit the dwelling and succeed the original house founder. The only way in which marital rights differ from those established by filiation is that they are contingent upon the continuance of the marriage relationship.

Statistically it is more often the husband than the wife who moves at marriage. The principal reason for this is the strong pull normally exercised by mother-daughter ties and secondarily by relations between sisters. These ties are typically close and, in addition to their strong affective content, come to the fore, in particular, on the occasion of childbirth. At this time a woman's mother and sisters have customarily prescribed obligations to assist her delivery and attend her and the new-born infant during recovery. As a result of the strength of these ties, few women will consent to be removed from their parents' luma' as long as their mother is alive, or from the ba'anan in which their sisters are living, and most husbands are satisfied to leave the final residence choice to their wives. Also, ties between related women are important in that all exchange of cooking fish within domicile groups is handled by women. Consequently, their composition tends to be markedly matrilateral, and uterine ties, by and large, are the predominant genealogical relations between luma' and ba'anan members, even though they have no special jural status, as such.

The Household Cluster

Every household is aligned with one to five or six others, generally in a tightly aggregated group of pilehouses, to form a 'cluster' or ba'anan. The largest ba'anan in Bangau-Bangau contains seven luma', including that of the village headman, or a total of 101 persons; the smallest consists of only two luma' or 15 persons. Most others contain some three to five households or 35 to 50 persons. Cluster formation is linked to the process of household partition. As a household undergoes partition, the seceding families generally build houses in a group surrounding the original dwelling. Alignment is generally maintained, at least for a time, with the cluster to which the original house founder belonged. But, if the group is large, or able to attract additional allies, fission may occur, and the group formed as a result of partition may split off, possibly bringing others with it, to form an independent cluster. The core members of most clusters tend to be related not only as close cognates and affines, but also as former housemates and the relations between house leaders on which cluster alignments are based are generally the same as those that maximally unite household members. In each generation alignments centre, in particular, on one, or possibly several, sibling sets, linked, in the latter case, by marriage or close cognation. Occasionally the siblings or parents of an in-marrying spouse may be brought into the ba'anan, but as children are born, and often as additional marriages are arranged with established members, affinal ties are converted in time to consanguineal ones, with the result that each individual's personal network of cognatic relations is densely focused and heavily interwoven within the cluster to which he or she belongs. Thus every ba'anan member, with the possible exception of in-marrying spouses, belongs to the personal kindred of every other, and the group as a whole has the nature of a dense node, or 'cluster' (Barnes 1968:118), of tightly interwoven cognatic and affinal ties.

Like the household, the cluster is not a permanently enduring group of constant membership, but undergoes repeated shifts of personnel, related ultimately to changes in the membership, and the formation and dissolution of its constituent households. While every cluster is typically organized around a core of married siblings and tends to split along sibling lines when fission occurs, affiliation of house leaders is possible on the basis of any of the same cognatic or affinal links that confer eligibility to possible household membership. As a result, the cluster similarly affords multiple lines of possible affiliation, graded as far as their likelihood of being utilized is concerned, in terms of social and genealogical closeness (*magsekot*). Its concrete composition tends to alter in each successive generation, as established households dissolve and new ones are founded, or as relations between members become attenuated or ruptured by death or enmity. Additional changes may occur as house leaders reorient themselves around the luma' of dependable allies, newly emergent sibling leaders, or men of wealth or forceful personality.

The senior house leaders and their wives generally make up an informal body of elders (mattoa) who exercise strong collective influence over their ba'anan followers, mobilize their assistance on occasions when common action or material aid is called for on a greater scale than a single household or family can supply, or when the economic or political interests of the group are challenged or in need of assertion. Assistance is called forth and rendered on the basis of personal cognatic or affinal ties. While similar ties extend outside the ba'anan, those within the group are particularly binding and the cluster constitutes a highly cohesive support group.

Conclusion

Choice, as Firth observed, is a fundamental aspect of cognatic social systems. Both at sea and in his home village, the Bajau Laut faces choice in his permanent group affiliations and in forming more ephemeral associations among his kindred or those related by local ties or convergent interests.

At sea the conjugal family head must repeatedly choose partners for voyaging or co-operative netting, and through repeated selection, a relatively stable personal roster emerges, drawn primarily from among his close collateral cognates and affines of the same village. While partnerships are recurrently brought into play, the specific need for which they exist is short-lived and intermittent, so that fleets formed on this basis are variable in composition and disband at the end of every voyage or briefer fishing venture. Moreover, the need for pooled gear or co-ordinated labour may at times surpass that which roster members alone can supply, while family crews themselves are largely interchangeable with the result that roster partnerships are periodically supplemented, or replaced, by more ephemeral, contractual alignments between family heads without regard to prior kin or village ties.

Within the village, family production is geared to a system of distribution that centres in larger, more enduring households and localized, kindred-based household clusters. Both households and clusters are cohesive support groups, represented by senior house leaders responsible for overseeing the political interests and internal domestic affairs of their dependent housemates. While house leaders are generally senior in generational terms, the strength of domicile alignments, like the strength of roster partnerships, depends upon collateral, rather than lineal relations, particularly those of sibling-ship. This is due to the economic nature of these groups. The prime concern is with the contribution of economically active families. Property, on the other hand, is owned in severalty by individuals and acquired separately through the efforts of single conjugal families, and never that of the household or cluster as a whole. The boats, nets and other capital assets required for fishing are within the means of most family heads and are ordinarily supplied to the husband by his father at the time of his marriage. Moreover, they are not highly durable, but require repeated replacement and repair. Similarly the major form of village investment, the pilehouse, is ultimately dismantled or abandoned, generally near the close of the home founder's active lifetime. As a result, the authority of individual house leaders rapidly declines with their advancing years, and in the absence of a possible corporate estate in which their dependents and future followers might share a continuing interest, households are dismembered and eventually dissolve.

Thus household membership continually changes and, as old households are dismembered and new ones founded, so too does the composition of the larger village clusters. An element of choice enters as single individuals, families or entire households transfer membership from one group to another. However, choice is made, in contrast to the more ephemeral alignments at sea, in terms of affiliation in relatively enduring groups, and occurs within the circumscribed limits of eligibility defined by ties of marriage and bilateral filiation. These ties afford possible entry to more than one group, so that some must necessarily be left dormant, while others, which may for a time come into play, are later revoked. Choice itself is made by taking up actual residence within a particular household or cluster under the sponsorship, or by invitation, of a specific house leader or senior married pair. The factors determining individual choice are complex and include, in addition to the pull of kinship and marriage ties, the numerical strength, resources and solidarity of possible sponsoring groups and the quality of political or moral stewardship exercised by their senior leaders. However, individual decisions have little effect on the structural make-up of domicile groups, since choice is made within well-defined limits mirrored in the basic categories and relations defined by the kinship system, and the groups that take form as a result of many single acts of choice preserve a stable structural form, even as they undergo partition, dissolve, and are replicated.

NOTES

1. See Sather and Chua (1975). In 1974, working with Fisheries Department personnel and survey data, I estimated the number of Bajau fishermen on the east coast at 3,095, out of a total east coast fishing population of 4,780 (Sather and Chua, 1975: 238). Adjusted for family dependents, roughly 16,000 persons, or a third of the Bajau population present in east coast districts, derive their major income from fishing or related marine activities. A considerable number of others engage in casual, occasional fishing. No comparable data exist for the west coast, but all available evidence suggests an even greater marine dependence.

2. The Bajau Laut system of kinship terminology is basically similar to that of other Borneo peoples.

(a) Kin are classified by generation, and, excluding primary kin and affines, are designated by six basic terms: grandparents and collaterals of their generation (*mbo'*); parents' siblings and all collaterals of their generation (*bapa'*) male, and (*babu'*) female; cousins (*kaki*); children of siblings and cousins (*kamanakan*); own grandchildren and all children of kamanakan (*mpu*).

Special terms exist for eldest (*anak sulong*) and youngest child (*anak kabangsuan*) and birth order is specified by numerical terms; an orphan is called *anak dodos* and an adopted child, *anak i'ipat*.

Degrees of collaterality may be specified in the case of cousins by the use of numerical terms, *mente'dda*, *mendua*, *mentellu'*, literally 'once', 'twice', 'thrice', and so on. The terms *mbo' koktu'ut* (knee grandparents) and *mbo' kengkeng* (toe nail grandparents) may be used to indicate generations removed from Ego for lineal great-grandparents and great-great-grandparents, respectively, and *mpu koktu'ut* and *mpu kengkeng* for the offspring and grandchildren of Ego's own mpu.

(b) Ego's primary kin are set apart by special terms: father (*mma'*); mother (*nngo'*); sibling (*denakan*); child (*anak*).

In addition siblings may be referred to according to relative age, as *siaka* and *siali*, older and younger sibling, respectively.

(c) Kinship terminology is basically of an Eskimo type (Murdock, 1949). Outside the nuclear family, collaterals, and in the case of mbo', ascendants, and of mpu, descendants, are merged in each category as far as relationships can be traced. The term *kampong* is used for all persons to whom Ego acknowledges a cognatic tie, whether the precise genealogical nature of the tie is known or not. The category thus forms, in Freeman's sense, a 'kindred' (1961), or perhaps better, Ego's 'cognatic kin of recognition' (Peranio, 1961:95). The limits of the category are indefinite and are set by the recognition of the individual at its centre; those outside are negatively described as 'other people' (*a'a saddi*).

The term kampong is rarely used for close personal kindred within the range of first cousins; instead, such persons are referred to as *dampalanakan* or *dampo'un*. Ego's dampalanakan comprise a bounded sub-set of cognates, and, although there is some variation in individual usage, the category refers essentially to an Ego-centred network composed of the members of the two stocks formed by an individual's lineal grandparents. By stock I mean 'all the descendants of a man and his wife counting descent through females as well as males' (Radcliffe-Brown, 1950:22). The dampalanakan is thus a bounded category or network circumscribed by reference to a set of truncal ancestors' of a defining Ego, and is socially significant as defining Ego's 'close kindred' and those cognates maximally eligible for membership in his household. Within the dampalanakan primary kin are set apart terminologically, whether they live together in the same domestic family unit or not, and are referred to as *taianakan*. Taianakan is a centrally important kinship category, as taianakan relations constitute the recruitment core of all permanently constituted social groupings in Bajau Laut society (cf. Sather, 1971:267ff).

(d) Affinal relatives are consistently distinguished terminologically from consanguineal kin, and the principal affinal terms are seven in number: parents-in-law (*mato'a*); siblings-in-law (*ipal*); spouses of siblings (*bilas*); child-in-law (*ayuwan*); husband (*hella*); wife (*handa'*); co-parents-in-law (*ba'i*).

Affinal terms, except for those used between spouses and between their parents (ba'i), are regularly extended to spouse's relatives. Thus all cognates of Ego's spouse in the first, second, or further ascending generation, regardless of their sex or degree of collaterality, are referred to as mato'a. Wherever possible, however, such persons are included in an appropriate category of cognatic kin.

Given the preference for endogamous marriage between cognates of the same generation, this is frequently possible, and keeps the number of affinal relations recognized by most persons to a minimum. A descriptive marker, *tili*, is used to designate step-relationships, e.g. *anak tili*, step-child.

(e) Terms of address are limited and reflect generation, relative age and respect: grandparents and elders generally (*mbo'*); father (*mma'*); mother (*nngo'*); parents-in-law (*mato'a*); parents' siblings (*si'it*); eldest brother or eldest son (*oto'*); eldest sister or eldest daughter (*arung*).

In general, the members of senior generations, including parents-in-law, should not, out of respect, be addressed by personal names. However, there are no formal speech or name avoidances. The position of those addressed as oto' and arung is especially important, as upon the death or senility of one or both parents, they are expected to assume responsibility for the well-being of their younger brothers and sisters.

3. Evers (1969:120ff) has discussed the failure of anthropologists to deal with the presence of the extended family as an alternative form of household unit in lowland Thai society. A similar point might be made with regard to bilateral societies generally. His argument is that the conceptual assumptions of the discipline, particularly with regard to the 'loosely structured' nature of Thai society, has caused them to ignore the not infrequent existence of corporate domestic groups larger than the nuclear family in an otherwise fully bilateral social system.

4. In this paper I follow Murdock's original definition of an 'extended family' (1949). In 1960 Murdock altered his definition to require that an extended family contain 'two or more married siblings in its senior generation' (1960:4), and he introduced a number of alternative family classes, including the 'lineal family', which he acknowledged as misnamed and which most closely approximates the structural form of the Bajau Laut luma'. It should be added that it also corresponds to the great majority of 'extended families' in the ethnographic literature. Here, I would argue, Murdock has sought to classify his way out of a theoretical impasse created by his insistence that an 'extended family' exists in perpetuity through recruitment by lineal descent. Owing to this definitional requirement, his 'correlation' with descent organization is hardly impressive. In contrast, a major point made here is that domestic groups based upon an extended family, by Murdock's original definition, may be self-replicating, without long-term persistence; that is, their structure may persist, but not necessarily the individual groups themselves. Part of the difficulty in Murdock's discussion arises from his failure to distinguish between 'descent' and 'serial filiation', a point well clarified by Scheffler (1966). See also Sather (1976). In terms of his classification of cognatic societies the contrastive criteria Murdock uses with regard to family organization are 'small domestic units' and 'extended families' (1960:14).

5. Fishing grounds are an unowned resource, and with the minor exception of artificially constructed underwater coral moulds (*tumpuk*), neither individuals nor villagers enjoy exclusive rights of use to particular sites within these areas.

9

THE MALOH*

Victor T. King

THE Maloh, numbering approximately 11,000 souls inhabit the
Upper Kapuas region (Kabupaten Kapuas Hulu) of the province of
West Kalimantan (Indonesian West Borneo).[1] They are mainly
found in various tributaries of the Kapuas river, including the
Leboyan, Embaloh, Lauh, Palin (Nyabau), Sibau, Mendalam,
Mandai, Peniung and Kalis, and also on the upper Kapuas river
itself above the administrative centre of Putus Sibau.

This interior region is remote from the coastal provincial capital
of Pontianak situated at the mouth of one of the major Kapuas
distributaries, and by trading boat it can take up to two weeks' travel
along the main river to reach the Maloh area. Maloh do undertake
journeys down the Kapuas to some of the important trading centres
such as Bunut, Selimbau, Semitau, Sintang, and occasionally to
Pontianak; but more frequently they cross the nearby watershed into
Sarawak for purposes of trade and work. The journey from the
Embaloh river to the market at the Sarawak border settlement of
Lubok Antu takes only some two to three days on foot, and more
often than not the range of goods available is greater and terms of
trade more favourable on the Sarawak side.

The upper Kapuas area is bounded on three sides by jungle-
covered, rocky and in some places steep-sided upland. To the north
the Upper Kapuas Mountains divide interior West Kalimantan from
Sarawak, although passes through these uplands adjacent to the
Kapuas lakes and the upper Embaloh river facilitate Maloh movement into Sarawak. The Müller Mountains in the east and south-east
form the boundary between the provinces of West Kalimantan on
the one hand and Central and East Kalimantan on the other. The
Madi Plateau in the south divides the Kapuas river from the basin

* The fieldwork (1972–3) on which this article is based was made possible
by grants from the Social Science Research Council, the Evans Fund (University of Cambridge) and the British Universities Student Travel Association.
My thanks are also due to the staff of the Sarawak Museum and the Indonesian
Institute of Sciences (*Lembaga Ilmu Pengetahuan Indonesia*), as well as to the
numerous Indonesian govenment officials and Maloh residents of the upper
Kapuas who assisted me during my stay in Kalimantan.

of its major tributary, the Melawi. There are stories of past Maloh journeys and head-hunting raids across the mountainous divides to the south and east, but the main Maloh orientation, has been, and still is northwards to Sarawak.

Unlike a number of other interior indigenes the Maloh are characteristically lowland dwellers. Their villages and rice-fields are situated mainly on the extensive and, in some places, fertile alluvial flood-plain of the upper Kapuas, although their economy is still based largely on the swidden cultivation of dry rice. The risks of frequent and persistent flooding are minimized to a certain extent because Maloh settlement is, in general, located on slightly higher and undulating land away from the main river. Besides rice, Maloh also grow a variety of vegetables and fruit, principally for local consumption, and they supplement their agricultural production by hunting, fishing and gathering. The main sources of cash and items of trade are rubber, various jungle products such as rattan and, in the past, locally made adornments from gold, silver and copper. Some Maloh, particularly those in the Embaloh river, also make 'red sugar' from the juice of the aren palm, and this too is sold or traded.

The low-lying Maloh environment means that there is little relief from the equatorial sun. The extensive areas of swamp and lakes and the chaotic drainage, although providing plentiful supplies of fish, are also breeding grounds for mosquitoes. However, the cycle of rice cultivation and other economic activities are dictated to a significant degree by the pattern of rainfall. There are very few reliable statistics of rainfall but the average annual rainfall is high, somewhere in the region of 4,300 mm. There are two main rainfall peaks coming approximately in the periods October to January and April to May and these are interspersed with a short dry period from February to March and a longer dry season from June to September.

The rather flat terrain alongside rivers and frequent Maloh rice surpluses, obtained, in part, because of the fertile alluvial soils, have permitted a comparatively dense population by Bornean standards, concentrated in particular regions of the upper Kapuas. Within these relatively confined stretches along rivers Maloh villages are close together and a number are heavily populated. Among the largest are Sungai Ulu', Melapi and Siut, each containing more than 500 people. In the past some of these larger villages also consisted of more than one long-house. Most of these concentrated groupings are some distance from each other either by river or land, so that those Maloh in the Leboyan and Embaloh regions, for example, rarely have contact with those in the Kalis, Sibau and Mendalam areas. This distribution has implications for the degree of cultural dissimilarity which is exhibited between the three main Maloh divisions of Taman, Embaloh and Kalis (see below).

Complex, Division and River-based Grouping

An individual Maloh sees himself as belonging to a variety of groupings, each different in their nature, size and extent. First, by way of general introduction let us look at levels of identification above that of the village.

The Maloh as a whole distinguish themselves from their close neighbours the Iban, Kantu', Suruk-Mentebah, Kayan, Ot Danum, Punan and Bukat. Maloh are identified over a large part of Borneo by their distinctive skills in copper-, silver- and gold-working. Itinerant Maloh smiths frequently visited long-houses in Sarawak, particularly those of the Iban, and stayed there for long periods of time making various adornments such as earrings, belts and bracelets for the local population (Harrisson, 1965:237, 241–2; King, 1972:98). In return Iban would trade their woven blankets, skirts and jackets. More recently this Maloh craft has experienced a significant decline in its fortunes largely because of a fall in indigenous demand and competition from imported and Chinese-made goods. In the Iban mind the term 'Maloh' or sometimes 'Memaloh' is virtually synonomous with 'metal-smith', and, in fact, 'Maloh' is the Iban appellation for this complex of culturally similar upper Kapuas peoples.[2] Very rarely do the Maloh themselves use this general term, although they accept that it is a valid designation indicative of a broad sociocultural unity which distinguishes them from other Bornean peoples. This term commonly appears in the Sarawak literature, and occasionally in early Dutch writings, and I choose to retain it in the present paper.[3] Nevertheless there is no agreement within Maloh circles on an internally-derived name appropriate for them as a whole.[4]

Important and distinctive features of Maloh which mark them off as a partially separate ethnic grouping (*bansa*) are their language, customary law, various beliefs and rituals surrounding marriage, death, sickness, rice cultivation and augury, and certain items of material culture such as dress, long-house design and basketware. Finally, although a number of Maloh social features show similarities with those of other Bornean peoples, in their particular combination they serve as a further means of demarcation.

A second lower level of identification divides the Maloh into three units or divisions which are referred to as Taman, Embaloh and Kalis. Those people grouped together as Taman are found in the region of Putus Sibau in the Mendalam, Sibau and Kapuas rivers. The Embaloh division comprises individuals in the Leboyan, Embaloh, Lauh and Palin rivers as well as those further south in the Mandai and Peniung who migrated from the Lauh region in the 1870s

(Enthoven, 1903:67). Finally, the Kalis division is found principally along the Kalis river, a tributary of the Mandai. These divisions have some territorial foundation, being more or less localized in three easily demarcated regions. They are also distinguished by differences, some quite marked, in language and custom. But the basis of the three-fold division must be sought in Maloh oral tradition, and it is by reference to this that these divisions, within an overarching sense of 'Malohness', are maintained and perpetuated. All Maloh are in general agreement that they are of a common stock. This is demonstrated, for example, in various origin stories. However, in the distant past people ancestral to the Maloh apparently divided, in a context of migration, into three main groupings. It is the disagreement among Maloh about the actual process of division which goes some way towards explaining the maintenance of distinctions.

The people of the Embaloh division claim an origin from the coasts of West Borneo. They say they migrated along the main river as far as the point where the Embaloh and Palin rivers flow into the Kapuas. There they divided, the Taman and Kalis splitting off from the Embaloh parent branch. This story is used to give support to Embaloh notions of superiority and their claims that other Maloh divisions should be called 'Embaloh'. In contrast learned Taman individuals point out that the name 'Taman' should be extended to all Maloh, and believe that the upper Kapuas is their place of origin, and that Embaloh and Kalis are offshoots of Taman. Finally Kalis hold to an origin somewhere near or in the Madi Plateau area to the south, stating that Embaloh and Taman are branches of them and are, in fact, called 'Kalis' (King, 1974, 1975a).

Genealogical evidence does little to clarify these differences of opinion since the genealogies which I collected, in some cases extending back between 15 and 20 generations, refer to a period when the general outline and divisions of Maloh settlement in the upper Kapuas had already been established. These internal divisions lead me to suggest the term 'complex' for Maloh as a whole, since this does convey a sense of diversity within an overall socio-cultural unity.

The third kind of grouping above the village, based largely on the criterion of territory, embraces those people inhabiting a particular river and its tributaries. Each grouping takes its name from the river along which it lives. Thus, a man from the Leboyan river will refer to himself as *orang* or *tau Labian*[5] ('a Leboyan man') or collectively as *Ikam tau Labian* ('We of the Leboyan'). Rivers are a vital means of transport in Borneo, and, as a general rule, water unites and land divides. People living along the same river embrace certain common historical traditions, customs and linguistic usages which, in detail, mark them off from other rivers, and finally, they have closer ties of kinship and friendship. In the head-hunting past, raiding generally occurred between villages in different river-systems and allies were found in one's own river. Nevertheless, long ago it appears that on occasion enmity did arise between villages along the same river, although this dated back to a time when distances between upriver and downriver settlements were much greater, particularly on the main Kapuas (King, 1975a).

What I have referred to as a 'river-based grouping' is equivalent to the Iban 'tribe' as defined by Freeman (1970:126); but the lack of political cohesion within these particular units and, in some cases the blurring of boundaries makes it difficult to apply the term 'tribe' in Borneo in any meaningful sense.

In the following discussion the major concern is with some of the general principles which serve to give form to Maloh social life. The fieldwork data are derived mainly from the Embaloh division and, in particular, from the Leboyan, Embaloh and Palin rivers. This is supplemented by observations made during a short stay among the Taman on the main Kapuas and interviews with various Kalis informants. Such items as kinship terminology and details of bride-wealth are those of the Embaloh and may not apply in all respects to Taman and Kalis, but it is assumed that certain organizational principles and social units are common to all Maloh.

Household, Long-house and Village

The family group (*kaiyan*) occupying one of the separate apartments (*tindoan*) of a long-house (*sau*), constitutes a household and is one of the most important social units in Maloh society.[6] In some areas, particularly in the Embaloh river, the abandonment of long-house domicile has given way to the dispersal of these household units into separate dwellings. However, a number of long-houses still exist in other rivers, and in these each kaiyan has its own apartment, consisting of a living area (*tindoan*) which also gives its name to the apartment as a whole, a kitchen (*biringapi* or *biringdár*) at the back of the house and divided off from the main area by a thin bark wall, a section of outer covered verandah (*tanga' sau*), a loft (*tago*) for storage purposes, and a platform (*ando*) below the long-house which serves as a support for rice storage bins (*tarinoan*).

The kaiyan is a genealogically simple and numerically small unit. Out of a sample of 119 households in the Leboyan, Embaloh and Palin rivers there was an average of 6·32 persons per household, with a range of one to 16. Kaiyan membership varies, but it normally comprises a husband and wife and their unmarried children (nuclear family), and sometimes includes a married child and spouse, and their children (stem family). Other types are those which also contain unmarried collateral relatives of either husband or wife, and not infrequently a surviving parent or parents. On the other hand it is rare for there to be two married siblings with children living in the same apartment. If this does occur it is usually a temporary measure until one of them accumulates enough resources to set up an independent household, although there is evidence to suggest that it was much more permanent in the past. Freeman terms this process of division of collateral families among the Iban 'partition' (1970:41).

First and foremost the kaiyan is a household unit. It is demarcated by the occupation of one apartment of a long-house, or a separate house in villages where there are no long-houses. Common residence is intimately related to and reinforced by close ties of kinship and affinity within each household. Maloh are generally monogamous and in most cases it is the conjugal bond between husband and wife which constitutes the central focus of the household and by means of which it is perpetuated. Divorce is relatively low and out of a sample of 184 marriages just under 9 per cent had ended in divorce. The head of the household (*toa tindoan, kapala tindoan*) is almost invariably male, whether he be a natal or in-marrying member, and acts as the representative of the tindoan in legal and other matters. Thus household unity is expressed in the form of the toa tindoan and recognized in word and action by the Maloh themselves. Despite the predominance of males as household representatives the member of the tindoan through whom rights to property are obtained is usually a woman. This follows from the tendency for post-marital residence to be uxorilocal. Out of a sample of 175 first marriages 125 (71·43 per cent) were initially uxorilocal residence, and 50 (28·57 per cent) were virilocal.

There are various spheres of activity, domestic, economic and ritual, in which the household is manifest as a defined entity. Household members share a common meal and undertake everyday chores for the benefit of all. They sleep together in the tindoan, although in the past, young boys slept outside on the verandah. They usually farm particular plots of land together, and food and other resources are obtained on behalf of the household. The possession in common of certain items of property accumulated during the lifetime of its members also serves to define the tindoan as an allodial unit. Nevertheless, there is a wider social grouping (*kapulungan*) which shares rights in inherited property. Finally, the household is a ritual unit in that it possesses certain charms, carries out its own agricultural rituals and shares the main burden of financing curing and death ceremonies for its members.

However, it is by no means always the case that the kaiyan is equivalent to the household unit described above. For example, where the kaiyan comprises parents and unmarried children plus a married child with spouse and children, it may divide temporarily.

This is usually prior to the eventual separation of the married child from the parental household. The process is seen most clearly in the context of the rice cultivation cycle. The married child may decide to occupy an independent farm-hut (*kadampé*) or an apartment in a smaller version of the long-house (*pambutan*) situated near the rice-fields. Thus in the busy agricultural periods this family, also called kaiyan, forms a separate residential, domestic and economic unit. But after the harvest it frequently happens that this family reunites with its previous tindoan members in the main long-house and pools part of its food supplies. This occurs until the married child is ready or forced to secede from the natal apartment.

Individual households identify themselves with a particular village (*banua*). The village is principally defined by the criterion of territory and is not considered as a kinship unit, although numerous village relationships are comprehended in a kinship idiom. Any stranger can affiliate with a village provided he obtains the consent of the headman and villagers concerned. Every household has equal rights of access to virgin forest and unclaimed land inside its village boundaries. Therefore, the Maloh concept of a village combines the notion of a territory containing dwellings, farm-huts, farms, gardens, fruit and rubber trees and rivers with that of people. Interestingly the 'commoners' or ordinary villagers in the Maloh ranking system are also referred to as banua.

Maloh maintain that initially each village comprised one long-house. In the past, these were massive structures high off the ground and built on heavy ironwood stilts. Today, however, villages present a bewildering variety of forms. Some consist of one long-house, either built in the traditional style such as Sungai Ulu' in the Palin river or more modest in size such as Ukit-Ukit in the Leboyan. Others have more than one long-house as in the case of Bakul, also in the Leboyan. There are villages in the Embaloh river which have no long-houses and are comprised of individual family houses. Finally, some Taman villages such as Siut are made up of a hotch-potch of independent family dwellings intermixed with long-houses of different shapes and sizes. All, however, are called banua.

The present-day settlement pattern is the cumulative result of a number of interrelated factors and processes. An increase in population within a long-house or disagreement between its inhabitants sometimes led to the formation of another house which might have remained in close proximity to the parent settlement, or have moved some distance away and eventually established its own autonomy as a separate village under its own headman. On the other hand after the decimation of the population by an epidemic or in times of extreme insecurity independent long-houses might amalgamate under one headman. In the past individual family dwellings were rare, unless as a temporary expedient following, for example, a serious fire in the main long-house. But since the decline in feuding and head-hunting the need to remain in a long-house has lessened and encouraged the increased splitting off of individual families into their own houses. Official Indonesian government policy, based on the assumption that the long-house is insanitary and a fire-risk, has also been directed against it as a viable form of habitation.

For reasons of space only a general description of the long-house as a village is included. However, these features are also appropriate to a village of independent family dwellings, although in the latter case the feeling of community, formerly centred on the common long-house gallery, has decreased. Where a village comprises more than one long-house it exhibits certain differences in organization which will be mentioned in passing.

Each village has its own territory and its members have equal rights of access to unclaimed village land. Any individual who wishes to clear land under the jurisdiction of another village has to seek permission from the headman of that village. These prior rights of exploitation of land shared by village members also extend to other village resources such as wild game and various jungle products. Ownership of land in perpetuity is established by the clearing of virgin forest, and once land is opened for farming it is removed from the village inventory and rights to use it are theoretically shared by all the descendants of the original pioneer. Yet if an individual has inherited rights in land in his natal village but is no longer resident there, he has to ask permission from and consult with the custodian of the ancestral land in that area. These rules therefore establish the important principle and defining characteristic of a village, namely that residence gives village members prior rights and control over village resources. In a village of more than one long-house this principle also applies.

The long-house members own certain man-made structures in common. These are the access ladders to the long-house (*tangka'*), the raised plankwalk (*panto*) running from the river bank to the main house entrance, the floating wharf (*lanting*) and, on occasion, the locally built primary school (*rumah sekolah*). Finally, the death-house (*kulambu*) in which the coffins of the dead are stored is built and owned by the village as a whole and any resident has a right to place his/her dead in this structure. This is with the exception of smaller kulambu which are only shared by a few households, usually of aristocratic status.[7]

Common constructional work such as the building of a new long-house or a death-house has a significant religious component, and in this the ritual unity of the village is manifest. All village members co-operate in the erection of a new death-house (*mulambu*) and in its ceremonial inception. Furthermore in the building of a new long-house it is incumbent on all residents to contribute labour and materials and to participate in rituals surrounding the placement of the main support posts and the house-warming (*mamasi sau*). The recent decline in long-house domicile has meant that individual kaiyan are solely responsible for the construction of their own houses, perhaps with the help of a few close relatives, and this has obviously resulted in a decrease in co-operative work and community ritual.

The long-house is also seen as a relatively safe area in relation to evil spirits which inhabit surrounding forest and fields. All members must have due regard for the delicate balance which is maintained between human society and the supernatural world. In this sense it is recognized that certain transgressions such as incest (*kudi'*, *salaka*) can affect the ritual well-being of the whole house. If a household wishes to leave the long-house and move elsewhere it also has to pay a quittance fine to the headman to ensure that the ritual integrity of the house is maintained. To the same end ritual protection is strengthened by the observation of certain taboos and prohibitions by all inhabitants during times of crisis, particularly when death, sickness or some other misfortune occur.

In the past, the ritual unity of the house was also embodied in the position of the headman (*samagat*). The headman was invariably from the aristocratic rank, also referred to collectively as samagat, and by virtue of his descent from powerful ancestral spirits, his possession of various charms and his knowledge of ritual formulae, he played an important part in village ceremony, and in the regulation of village activities, particularly during the agricultural cycle. For example, after the samagat had selected a propitious site for his farm, all the members of the village would gather at this spot to make offerings to various deities and spirits. Usually it was the task of the headman to provide the offerings, deliver the prayers and contribute substantially to the accompanying feast. However, he was sometimes replaced by an elder (*tamatoa*) well-versed in ritual address. Following this everyone would contribute one day's work in clearing the samagat's swidden (*sa'ason nana samagaten*). Only after this was done could others proceed with their work. This same pattern occurred before planting and harvesting. With few exceptions such as among Palin villages, these community rituals and co-operative work on behalf of the samagat have all but disappeared at the present time, and in consequence village unity, although still observable, is less marked.

Privileges attached to aristocratic rank have been eroded by both Dutch and Indonesian government policies and the general changes attendant on, for example, the introduction of education. Now the headman, referred to more commonly by the Indonesian term *kapala kampong*, which has no connotation of rank, is democratically elected by all village members. He is entitled to wear a uniform supplied to local government workers and is paid a nominal salary. This process of democratization has also meant that upper-ranking individuals no longer monopolize the office of village headman, although a number are still found in this position. The traditional props of village leadership, particularly in ritual, have also been removed.

Nevertheless, it remains true to say that the position of headman, in a somewhat modified form, is still an expression of village unity. In the past he was the custodian of customary law (*adat*), and, assisted by a council of elders, was the main arbiter in intra-village disputes, as well as representing his villagers in matters involving them with outsiders. Despite the gradual removal of certain legal issues from the jurisdiction of village authorities the headman can still be regarded as a juridical warden and the representative of the village as a whole.

Finally, common residence provides a social space within which close interaction and intimacy are possible. Particularly in a long-house context, the common covered verandah brings people together on both a formal and an informal basis. For any individual the local community probably contains some of his closest kin and best friends, although this is not to suggest that conflict of various kinds is absent from the long-house. On the contrary it too is an all-pervading social phenomenon.

In the case of villages which have more than one long-house, each house is identified by the name of its headman, or by its position relative to others. Thus an upriver long-house will be referred to as *ulu banua* ('upriver village'), one downriver as *banua ilaut* ('downriver village') and so on. Formerly, each house, led by its own samagat, would undertake its own rituals and settle disputes between its members. In the construction of a large building such as a new house or kulambu the onus would fall on the particular house in question, although help and materials were sometimes obtained from other nearby houses. There were no common activities embracing all long-houses within a complex, apart from participation in head-hunting raids in the past and in rituals to drive out sickness, misfortune and evil spirits.

Each house had its own headman but one of these (*indu' banua*) was recognized as the representative of the whole village in inter-village matters, and the main arbiter in disputes which could not be solved at the house level. In the present situation the long-house still retains most of its functions, and embraces the most intense feeling of community. However, among members of a long-house complex there is also a sense of belonging to a particular banua by virtue of rights in a common territory, close residential proximity and the existence of a village representative in the shape of the indu' banua.

Aside from the various territorial, social and ritual aspects which serve to divide Maloh into recognizable village communities, certain village co-operative labour enterprises have also been mentioned. However, in a productive sense, apart from key work projects such as constructing a new long-house or death-house, economic activities are performed by individual households or by co-operative work groups (*suang bár*) based on labour exchange between households.[8] The overriding principle in the organization of work teams for various agricultural tasks such as clearing, burning, planting, weeding, harvesting and threshing is one of strict reciprocity. Of course, an individual may prefer to work with close kinsmen and to the extent that relatives may be farming close to one another, any given work group may well contain a significant component of kinsmen. But it should be noted that, under the terms of labour exchange which demands that a day's work is repaid by an equivalent day's work, kinsmen are treated like any other individual.[9] Indeed in a number of observed instances work teams did not comprise close kinsmen, and on occasion a household would choose to work alone. Furthermore, the close proximity of villages in, for example, the Embaloh river, meant that sometimes membership of work teams extended beyond the confines of any one village.

Finally, there are dwellings within a village territory, apart from the main long-house, which also provide a basis for social interaction and which deserve to be dealt with as separate and definable entities within the village as a whole. These are the pambutan, smaller long-houses built close to rice-fields.[10] In any one year kaiyan farming land distant from the main house, and in the same general area, may decide to come together under one roof. Pambutan range in size from a membership of two kaiyan up to ten, but the main criterion of formation is propinquity. This is complicated by the existence of close kinship ties among pambutan members, since in a relatively closed village community a large number of individuals are kinsmen and farm adjacent lands. Nevertheless, to my mind, close kinship was not a prime influence in deciding pambutan membership, although it was certainly a factor. It was rather considerations of proximity and convenience which determined the content of field-house organization, modified by each person's preferences concerning the people with whom they would wish to co-operate. This in itself was influenced by kinship but it was the option of each family whether they wished to take advantage of these ties or repudiate them. In some cases an individual family would construct a separate farm-hut or kadampé rather than move into a field-house.

Social intercourse is obviously intense within a pambutan and this social unit itself to some extent shapes work-team membership. But residence in a field-house is never permanent. The very nature of swidden cultivation means that kaiyan are forever changing their pambutan affiliation, and are brought into other relationships elsewhere. Hence social interaction, centred on pambutan, is not a basis for the formation of enduring social groupings.

Kinship, Descent and Rank

The various social units described above are defined principally in terms of locality and residence and certain shared rights and activities. The Maloh themselves recognize these as elements in their society and, in most cases, name them. It now remains to discuss the ways in which Maloh categorize their social life by reference to the principles of kinship, descent and rank. These principles are contained within and cross-cut the social units of household, longhouse and village, providing an underlying social coherence to Maloh society as a whole.

Maloh kinship is bilateral and a given individual recognizes a universe of consanguineal and affinal kin.[11] Consanguineal kin are reckoned on both the father's and mother's side and are more or less given equal weight in social relations. Kinship terminology indicates that affinal categories are lineally and laterally less extensive than those of consanguines, and that there are two main structural components within this categorization. First, there is that of genealogical level which in ideal terms embodies notions of deference and respect of junior toward senior generations. In return lower generations receive protection, help and advice. Within generations these patterns of behaviour, although milder in form, are regulated by the principle of relative age and expressed in the distinction between kaka' and adi'. The hierarchical generational segments are themselves preserved by the practice of lateral extension of particular kinship terms and by the ruling that these terms are never used outside their own generation. Furthermore, teknonymic designations also reinforce these asymmetric social categories.[12] Generation, particularly in the case of collaterally close consanguines, also influences sexual accessibility. An individual on pain of fine is not allowed to indulge in sexual relations or marry the categories of kamo'/ampé', baki'/piang and kamanakan. However, even more serious and supernaturally dangerous are incestuous relations within the kaiyan.

The other component is that of collateral distance. Close collateral kinsmen up to and including fifth cousins are termed *sundaman* or *saparanak*.[13] However, the extent of recognition of close consanguineal kinsmen varies. In the Embaloh river a limit of third to fourth cousins was usually set, whereas in the Palin it was extended to fifth cousins. Beyond sundaman are distant kinsmen (*sundaman bajau*) said to include seventh cousins. These are distinguished from individuals with whom no kin tie is traceable but who are considered as friends (*kawan*), and are usually close neighbours; these in turn are marked off from strangers (*tau bokan*).

These collateral distinctions are a guide to marriage preference. There is an expressed ideal and a marked tendency for marriage within the category sundaman. In addition, there is a general preference for third cousin marriage, and in the Embaloh and Leboyan rivers a marked disapproval of first cousin marriage, although this was possible with the payment of a ritual fine. Perhaps the dislike of first cousin marriage is a result of Catholic influence in this area, since elsewhere in Maloh country, and particularly within aristocratic circles, this type of marriage is perfectly permissible and not finable.

The consanguineal category focused on a given Ego and called by the Maloh sundaman or saparanak would appear to be equivalent to the anthropological term 'kindred' as defined by Freeman (1961). Nevertheless, I have argued elsewhere that Freeman's conceptualization of the kindred is in some important respects problematical (1976b). After employing the term in a flexible way (to include both consanguines and affines) in my earlier papers on Maloh kinship organization (1974, 1976b), I have since decided against using the concept. The variety of definitions and uses of the term tend to confuse rather than clarify the description and analysis of Maloh kinship relations.

In the Maloh case if one asks any individual to provide a list of those kinsmen whom he recognizes, he will list the various consanguines mentioned above (see note 11). He also extends the term sundaman to include the various categories of affinal kin. The spouses of consanguines and, if Ego is married, his spousal kin fall within this circle.[14] Maloh agree that although terminologically they differentiate consanguineal from some categories of affinal kin, in terms of behaviour, address and obligation these affines are generally treated like consanguines.[15] The inclusion of spousal kin within the Maloh sundaman is explained by the Maloh rationale *Namin siala lakunyai sama diri* ('After marriage husband and wife are the same'). A man enters his wife's kinship circle and vice versa.[16] Thus in certain cases the conjugal pair can also be conceptualized as a focus of kinship networks (cf. Smart, 1971:113).[17] Of course, initially the relationship between various affinal kin is likely to be restrained, particularly between Ego and his parents-in-law, but in the opinion of the Maloh this is no different in nature from the early stages of a relationship with a close blood relative whom Ego has never met.

For reasons of space it is impossible to describe the different kinds of behaviour which Maloh generally agree are appropriate between the various categories of kinsmen. However, there is much individual variation and such factors as personal preference, compatibility and, perhaps more importantly, place of residence influence behavioural patterns and social interaction.

An individual can obtain assistance and advice in certain activities from his pool of consanguineal and affinal kinsmen. There appear to be no particular obligations marking off consanguines from affines, and although there are mutual obligations between various categories of kin, these are mediated by the factors mentioned above. Outside the immediate family there are no jural norms underlying kinship obligations, rather participation in activities depends very much on situation. In general terms, the strength of obligation tends to decrease with increasing collateral distance, but this does not imply that only close consanguineal and affinal kin are called on in any one instance. In addition, in observed situations in Maloh society the refusal to co-operate with kinsmen was not automatically greeted with social opprobrium. Ultimately no individual is forced to honour his obligations to relatives since his decision is obviously influenced by context, personality, residence and the strength and nature of the kinship tie.[18]

Kinship ties are activated in a wide variety of situations, in life-cycle rituals, agricultural work and other enterprises such as hunting, fishing or canoe-making. Nevertheless, it should not be assumed that because some participants may be kinsmen that this is the prime reason for co-operation. There may be any number of other reasons operative, and ties of friendship, and more importantly, relations based on rank are also significant.

The *ad hoc* groupings formed occasionally and temporarily on the basis of kinship ties are hardly suitable for transmitting rights in property. Instead inheritance and ownership of property are regulated by the principle of descent. Maloh have a 'property-based descent category' (kapulungan) which is defined principally by shared rights in certain kinds of property such as land, fruit-trees, long-house support posts and valuable heirloom items.[19] In reality, the term 'kapulungan' applies to the non-partible estate, but the collection of people who share rights in the estate are also designated by this term.

If an individual clears virgin forest, plants fruit-frees, accumulates valuable heirlooms such as gongs, jars or cannon, or erects support posts for his long-house apartment, then, on his death, rights to these are transferred to his spouse or, if she is incapacitated or unwilling to act as supervisor of the estate, to his children. These are then passed on to their children and so on. In other words the kapulungan comprises all the descendants of a given ancestor traced through male and female lines, and a given individual belongs simultaneously to a large number of kapulungan. Rights to property are ideally shared equally by the children (*sama mamiara*), but the one who remains in his parents' household and looks after them in their old age (*anak panuntui toa*) invariably becomes the custodian of the estate (*toa kapulungan*). Property such as personal belongings, clothes, less valuable jars and gongs and other equipment is divided, although the custodian acquires the largest share. An individual may be disinherited if he is unruly and disobedient to his parents.

It must be noted that not every Maloh belongs to a kapulungan. This is particularly so for some individuals of slave descent who have had little opportunity to accumulate or inherit resources. Furthermore, I would argue that, in general, kapulungan are not corporate descent groups. The sharing of rights in property does not necessarily lead to the regular coming together of kapulungan members, nor does it follow that the membership will develop common aims and a sense of identity. This is primarily because a given individual may well belong to a number of different kapulungan, and, in consequence, the activation of his rights in a particular estate is dependent on a range of considerations which are not directly related to the principle of descent.

First, claims on the undivided estate, particularly the land, vary in strength, since opportunities to exercise rights are influenced by place of residence. In other words, in general terms the custodian has prior use rights, another child still living in his natal village has secondary rights, and a child who marries into another village has tertiary rights. Demands on kapulungan land are minimized because at any one time some members, who are living elsewhere, do not activate their rights in the estate. Second, on marriage an individual acquires usufruct rights in his spouse's various kapulungan property, and if he marries into her village he will often take advantage of these. Third, for reasons of personal advantage an ambitious person may decide to stress his links with a particular ancestor at the expense of others. Fourth, since an individual probably belongs to many kapulungan his membership in some of them may be allowed to lapse and over time these links are forgotten. Thus, in practice membership in kapulungan is often vaguely defined, and over a period of time an individual may co-operate and interact with different people from different kapulungan.

A household is usually alone responsible for informally selecting and activating the rights in the kapulungan property of its various members, and an individual has to decide himself whether he wishes to join with other kapulungan members and the custodian in a dispute against outsiders involving the property of one of his kapulungan. But where a plot of land is claimed by two members of the same kapulungan the custodian is called in to resolve the dispute. The toa kapulungan is also important in any decisions affecting the use of heirloom property. Presumably if pressure on land was great then one would expect there to be a significant degree of common interest on the part of kapulungan members in preserving the estate. But until recently shortage of land has not been a problem for the Maloh, and therefore, I would suggest most kapulungan have not developed strongly corporate characteristics. However, the degree of corporateness of kapulungan is influenced by the remaining important organizational principle in Maloh society, that of rank (see below).

Membership in a rank (*ranakan*) is inherited from parents and traced through various lines of descent. Ranks are ideally endogamous which logically results in close kinsmen, both consanguineal and affinal, having the same rank position.[20] Most villages comprise a full complement of ranks which are: *samagat* ('aristocrats'), *pabiring* ('middle-ranking villagers') and banua or *suang sau* ('commoners'). Formerly there were also *pangkam* ('slaves') made up of war captives, debt-slaves, orphans and those born into slavery. The Dutch, however, gradually stamped out this institution and along with it the practice of sacrificing slaves on the death of their owners or in ceremonies connected with the building of a new death-house or long-house. Although today those of slave descent are still recognized and certain behavioural patterns and choice of marriage partners are to some extent guided by this fact, it is becoming less important in village affairs. In addition, overt discrimination and addressing someone in public as a slave are subject to fines. Increasingly those of slave descent have merged with the banua.

In the past the aristocratic rank, which in each long-house probably accounted for no more than about three households, apparently held the monopoly of economic, political and ritual power. Therefore to maintain the principle of rank endogamy and their superior position in the village, and to avoid incestuous unions, samagat frequently married outside their natal community. Maloh settlements are thus linked by a complex web of upper rank marriages. Headmen always came from the samagat rank; it was the aristocrats who often acted as war-leaders and led various communal rituals; it was they who had the most slaves. Samagat households were always located at the upriver end of the long-house, and their apartments were usually more spacious to accommodate the greater number of slaves. The possession of these slaves to open forest and farm on their behalf also meant that aristocrats could establish rights to more land and had more leisure time to organize trading and war expeditions.[21] In fact, Maloh oral tradition frequently mentions impressive journeys of adventure led by famous samagat ancestors.

A further system which worked in favour of the samagat was that of differentials in fines and bridewealth according to rank. Fines for various transgressions were graded such that a commoner who was accused by an aristocrat had to pay a fine appropriate to the samagat rank. This was much larger than fines due to commoners. In addition a samagat could expect a larger amount of bridewealth if his daughter married a commoner (see below).

The samagat rank carried the responsibility for a number of political, legal and ritual tasks. Aristocrats were the main arbiters in inter- and intra-village disputes. They could impose fines on their followers in certain instances. It was they, and particularly the headman, who had to find resources to entertain guests and who usually supplied a large proportion of the food and drink in communal ceremonies. Where aristocrats within the same village belonged to the same kapulungan then their close co-operation in political, economic and ritual matters and their common interests in maintaining their social position and estate may have resulted in their descent categories taking on much more corporate characteristics. In this sense their kapulungan could be termed 'corporate descent groups'. However, these common aims and activities have recently decreased with the decline in the importance of rank ascription as an organizational principle.

The decline in the traditional stratification system has been partly caused by the increasing influence of modern education and Christian and democratic ideals. But perhaps one of the most serious blows to the superior position of the samagat was the abolition of slavery. In economic terms this tended to set aristocrats on a par with other villagers. In addition, increasing opportunities for young people to live and work in coastal areas and the availability of white-collar employment, even in the interior, has called into doubt the value of superior rank position. In the Embaloh river, for example, where missionary and governmental influence has been of long duration customary law has been reformulated and differentials in fines and bridewealth have been virtually eliminated. Nevertheless, the older generation of aristocrats still attempts to cling to its position by upholding, where possible, the rule of rank endogamy; but even here parents meet with opposition from their children who demand more freedom of choice in marriage.

Ranks are still recognizable and they do regulate certain kinds of behaviour. But because of increasing marriages between ranks and the decline in the significance of these inherited positions the situation in practice is complicated, since given individuals frequently differed in their opinions about their own rank position and that of others. However, in the Palin river in particular, rank differences are still quite marked and this is seen most clearly in negotiations about bridewealth payments and marriage. The pre-marriage discussions (*panaju*) concerning the suitability of the two people to marry are largely phrased in terms of descent and rank. The parents' main concern is still the rank position of the prospective spouse of their child, and rank is ultimately expressed in the nature and amount of bridewealth which is finally decided upon. In very broad terms the following bridewealth amounts (Emb: *panyonyok* or Palin: *kéningko*) are appropriate to each rank. In the past bridewealth was generally reckoned in terms of slaves or *kalétau*, but the equivalent value in the form of cannon or gongs was also acceptable.

Marriage within samagat ranks required the payment of four kalétau or a cannon (*badil*) of one pikul weight or four gongs (*garantung rá*); between pabiring two kalétau or 50 katis of brassware or two gongs (*garantung rá loloé*) were necessary, and for banua one kalétau or 25 katis of brassware or one gong sufficed, although usually banua payments were made in the form of special jars (*bakam*). Different amounts, types and sizes of gong, more ornately decorated cannon and extra ceramics such as jars and plates could also be demanded, depending on certain internal rank gradations. Within the samagat rank there were *samagat tutu* who claimed pure aristocratic descent, and *samagat rá* who had mixed samagat and lower-ranking ancestry. In the past gradations also depended on whether the samagat in question was an indu' banua, a headman or a war-leader. In pabiring ranks internal differentiation depended much more on whether an individual could trace fairly recent links with samagat, in which case he could demand more bridewealth, or whether he had been a pabiring of long-standing. Finally, a true commoner (*ulun mám*) of unmixed blood was in a better negotiating position than one with slave ancestry.

In certain instances traditional items of bridewealth are still used in the Palin river, but these symbols of rank have been increasingly undermined by the introduction of money. In the Dutch period 15 silver guilders came to be equivalent to one kalétau, and today paper money is becoming even more popular. 1,500 rupiahs are now equal to one kalétau. A further problem in maintaining symbols of rank has been the influx of new items such as outboard motors and sewing-machines. These are now valued more than hierloom property, and gongs and jars are frequently exchanged for them. This means that in some villages the items which traditionally symbolized rank differences are no longer available for bridewealth.

Social mobility between ranks is not a new phenomenon, although it has probably increased over the last 50 years or so. There is an ideal system, and this is still largely followed in the Palin river, which sets out the various bridewealth payments required for inter-rank marriages. In detail the system is complex, but as a general rule and by virtue of the fact that bridewealth flows from groom's to bride's side, the children of an inter-rank marriage usually take the mother's rank. This is also reinforced by a tendency towards uxorilocality in these marriages.[22] It is the children who benefit or suffer from a marriage between ranks and not the husband or wife since theoretically they remain in their respective ranks.[23] Perhaps a few examples from the Palin will illustrate this process. The bridewealth values below were also used in the Embaloh river up until 1970 when an adat conference standardized bridewealth payments in all inter-rank marriages at four kalétau or Rp. 6,000.

In the case of a man from the banua rank who wishes to marry a samagat woman he has to pay the usual bridewealth according to *adat samagat*, which is four kalétau. But he also has to find an additional eight kalétau 'to buy rank'. This enables his children to become samagat (*mambiti*). The man is not recognized as a samagat and is not addressed as such, although he goes to live with his spouse. However, an increasing practice in the Palin is for the man to pay the bridewealth of four kalétau and omit the rest; this results in his children becoming pabiring. On the other hand if an aristocrat marries a commoner woman he merely pays one kalétau and his children become banua. The process of falling in rank is termed *rapéan dara'*, and the use of this term itself reveals an important feature of this kind of marriage. 'Rapéan' is commonly used to refer to the partial breaking of a tree-branch; it is not a clean break since the branch is left hanging. This is analogous to the situation of the samagat; he partially breaks his aristocratic ties since his children are destined to become banua, but he himself retains his rank.

The decline in the importance of rank in Maloh society has also led to a gradual merging of ranks. Today in some villages no one is considered as a samagat since all those of aristocratic descent have intermixed with lower orders and been reduced to pabiring or banua. Rank also no longer corresponds to any great extent with the scales of economic, political and ritual power. Today there are commoners elected to the position of headman; a number of samagat are now relatively poor when compared with commoners who have succeeded in trade or become teachers and government workers; finally in some areas where traditional ritual has all but disappeared, prestige goes increasingly to the bible-teachers (*guru injil*) who hold Christian ceremonies in villages.

In the past rank mobility was achieved partly by the accumulation of wealth and the channelling of this into bridewealth. Although a commoner might have a special knowledge of adat or be a war-leader he could not arrange a better marriage for his sons by this means alone. He had to have the required resources for the bride-wealth to enable his descendants to claim samagat rank. Nevertheless, there was a prestige scale to some extent outside the ranking system. This was based on the participation in and finance of various feasts performed during the construction of a new long-house (mamasi sau) or death-house (mulambu), those connected with sacrifices for the spirits of the dead (*mandung*), the completion of a successful head-hunt (*mauno' tau'en*) or journey of adventure (*pamolé béo*), and finally the initiation of a balian or 'village doctor' (*manyarung*).[24] Prestige was recognized in life in the right to wear certain items of clothing and in death in the extra entitlements allowed during funerary rites. These feasts and the prestige derived from them were to some degree dependent on rank, since their organization and finance were made easier for a samagat. Yet commoners could achieve prestige in head-hunting, travelling and curing and this too compensated for the apparently fairly rigid prestige scale based on ascribed rank.

NOTES

1. For recent descriptions of various aspects of Maloh culture and social structure see, for example, Harrisson (1965, 1966) and King (1972, 1974, 1975a, 1975b, 1976a, 1976b). The population figures are compiled from my own surveys in the upper Kapuas supplemented with data from the recent Indonesian census (1971).

2. The term 'Maloh' appears to be derived from the name 'Embaloh', the river which is closest to Iban settlement in the border areas of West Kalimantan. However, Maloh themselves call the river 'Embaloh' or 'Tàmembaloh'.

3. See, for example, Harrisson (1965:238–40) and references, Veth (1854:55) and van Lijnden (1851:583).

4. In consequence, neither is there agreement among scholars on Maloh terminology. See, for example, King (1972:83–6).

5. 'Labian' is the Maloh term, but in the Dutch and Indonesian literature 'Leboyan' is the common usage.

6. The term *tindoan* is also applied to the family group which occupies an apartment.

7. In the Taman division the custom is for each kaiyan to have its own kulambu, or to share one with a few closely related households.

8. For a comparison with other Dayak peoples see Hudson's description of the Ma'anyan *panganrau* (1967:311–16), Freeman's of the Iban *bedurok* (1970:234–8) and Geddes' of Bidayuh work groups (1954a:70–3).

9. Only when a kinsman is sick or incapacitated in some way will relatives assist without any request for reciprocity, although over a long period of time it would be expected that mutual help between relatives reaches some kind of balance.

10. For a similar phenomenon see Freeman's description of the Iban *dampa* system (1970:161–70), and Geddes on the Bidayuh *plaman* (1954a:10).

11. These terms are used principally within the Embaloh division. For consanguineal kin they are:

kaka' (eSb), *adi'* or *ari'* (ySb), *sairun* (Sb, Co), *sanaktoa* (Co¹), *sanak'ini* (Co²), *sanak'uyang* (Co³), sanaksa (Co⁴), *ama'* (F), *indu'* (M), *kamo'* (PB, PCo), *ampé'*, (PZ, PCo), *baki'* (PF, PFB, PFCo), *piang* (PM, PMZ, PMCo), *nakanak* or *anak* (C), *anak babaka* (S), *anak babai'ingé* (D), *anak kamanakan* (SbC, CoC), *ampu* (CC), *po'i* (CCC), *pu'it* (CCCC), and *icet* (CCCCC).

For affinal kin they are:
laki (H), *bai'ingé* (W), *épar* (SpSb, SpCo, SbSp), *marué* (SpSbSp), *matoa* (SpP), *matoa babaka* (SpF), *matoa babai'ingé* (SpM), *isen* (CSpP), *inantu* (CSp), *kamo'* (PZSp, PCoSp), and ampé' (PBSp, PCoSp).

12. When a married couple have children they assume the title *Ma'* in the case of the father, and *Indu'* in the case of the mother plus the name of their first or eldest child. Thus, for example, parents with an eldest child called Kasso become Ma' Kasso ('Father of Kasso'), and Indu' Kasso ('Mother of Kasso'). On the birth of a grandchild they resume their personal name with the designation Baki' or Piang.

13. The term saparanak, derived from the word anak ('child' or 'children') is more commonly heard in the Palin river, and among Taman, whereas in the Embaloh river the term sundaman, derived from the word *undaman* ('relative' or 'kinsmen'), is used interchangeably with saparanak.

14. This issue of the inclusion or exclusion of affinal kin within the concept of the kindred has been debated at length by Freeman (1961) and King (1976b), and in a recent complementary critique of King's analysis by Appell (1976b). It is not proposed to restate the various positions here.

15. The kin terms kamo' and ampé' are extended to PZSp and PCoSp. In address consanguineal kin terms are usually extended to affinal kin within the same generational section such that the terms ama' or ma' and indu' or du' are used for SpP, SpPSb, SpPCo etc., and this also occurs with the terms baki', piang, kaka', adi' and anak or nak. For a more detailed discussion see King (1974).

16. If I interpret Hudson correctly this is his position with regard to his notion of the 'extended kindred', in which, after marriage, the effective kindred ties of both spouses are merged in Paju Epat society (1962:287, 1972:105).

17. Smart does not utilize the kindred concept in his description of Karagawan Isneg social organization. His main descriptive focus is the conjugal pair.

18. For a detailed discussion of the variation in dyadic ties between kinsmen and the distinction between 'active' and 'latent' ties see Hudson (1972:104–112).

19. The kapulungan which I term a 'descent category' seems to be similar in some respects to the Paju Epat *bumuh* (Hudson, 1972:84–90) and the Bidayuh Land Dayak *turun* (Geddes, 1954a:59–62). However, these authors prefer to call them 'descent groups'.

20. There is no ideal rule that rank is inherited from the male line as there is with the Melanau (Morris, 1953:54).

21. See, for example, Morris (1953:56) for the description of a similar condition in Melanau society.

22. Rousseau and Whittier also report that among the Kayan and Kenyah respectively children from inter-rank marriages adopt the rank of the parent in whose apartment they live. Among Maloh there are exceptions to the general practice of uxorilocality in inter-rank marriages, particularly among the aristocratic stratum. In cases where a child lives virilocally he/she takes the rank of the father.

23. This presents contrasts with the Melanau system. There, for example, a father benefits in prestige and rank terms if he marries his daughter to a man of higher rank; he too rises in rank (Morris, 1953:56–7, 61). In the Maloh system this does not occur, nor, according to Whittier, does it happen among the Kenyah.

24. For a somewhat similar gradation see Whittier's description of the Kenyah (1973:4-6).

10

THE MA'ANYAN OF PAJU EPAT*

A. B. AND JUDITH M. HUDSON

THE Ma'anyan of the Indonesian province of Central Kalimantan are a Dayak ethnic group[1] numbering 30–35,000,[2] who dwell in small villages throughout much of the rolling, wooded terrain of the great Barito River's south-eastern drainage. All Ma'anyan speak a distinctive Dayak language most closely related to other languages classed as South-east Barito isolects (Hudson, 1967a); the use of a common language is the most readily apparent attribute in the establishment of a separate Ma'anyan ethnic identity. However, all Ma'anyan also share a set of traditions (*adat*) and claim a common historical origin. Traditional animistic religious beliefs were maintained by most Ma'anyan in the 1960s, although there were a fair number of Christians, with conversions to Protestantism becoming increasingly frequent.

Ma'anyan villages, ranging in size from 100 to 300 or 400 inhabitants, are built along narrow, meandering east-bank tributaries of the Barito River. Roads or broad paths serve to connect villages, although river transport is used at high water during the north-east monsoon. Frame dwellings (*lewu'*) line the single village street. Older houses are built high off the ground and are large enough to accommodate several families, usually closely related. Today's houses, smaller and closer to the ground, are generally the village residence of a less complex family grouping.

Swidden fields and small field huts (*dangau*) are scattered throughout the surrounding forest, often located as far as five miles from the home village. Here Ma'anyan spend much of the year, since the majority are principally swidden farmers who supplement their subsistence-oriented dry rice, vegetable and fruit growing with hunting, fishing and gathering activities and cash-cropping, of which rubber tapping in family-owned small holdings is the most important.

Historical evidence seems to indicate that until the mid-seventeenth

*The fieldwork on which this article was based was made possible by grants from the Ford Foundation Foreign Area Training Fellowship programme. Subsequent research and analysis were supported by the Modern Indonesia Project and the Department of Anthropology at Cornell University. Grateful acknowledgment must be made to the many Indonesian goverment officials and residents of Paju Epat who assisted us throughout our sojourn in Kalimantan.

century, the Ma'anyan inhabited the fertile alluvial plains in what is now the Hulu Sungai district of South Kalimantan. In addition to subsistence swidden cultivation, the Ma'anyan grew black pepper in small quantities and gathered forest products, such as rattan, to exchange with Banjarese traders from the coastal ports of South Borneo. As the Dutch pepper monopoly expanded over much of Indonesia in the seventeenth century and the international demand for pepper increased, non-Dayak farmers, mostly Banjar immigrants and Javanese refugees from Mataram aggression, moved into Ma'anyan territory to pursue full-time pepper cultivation. The Ma'anyan retreated to the north-west, where they began cutting new swidden fields in what is now the home territory of the Ma'anyan.[3]

All Ma'anyan share a sense of common identity that sets them apart from contiguous ethnic groups such as the Lawangan Dayak or the Banjar Malays. While recognizing this common identity *vis-á-vis* outsiders, the Ma'anyan divide themselves into three named subgroups: the Benua Lima ('Five Villages') to the east, abutting the principally Banjar province of South Kalimantan; the Paju Sapuluh ('Ten Villages'), centrally located in the upper Patai River drainage; and the Paju Epat ('Four Villages') to the west in the drainage of the Telang and Siong rivers.[4]

Beginning in the mid-nineteenth century, segments of all three subgroups have spread northward in the search for new farming land and have settled in the drainages of the Dayu, Karau, and Ayuh rivers. However, the members of most émigré communities still maintain ties with their 'home' villages. The attributes distinguishing one subgroup from another are based on their different home territories, minor variations in dialect and adat law, and, most important, differing funerary practices. With regard to the latter, only the Paju Epat Ma'anyan observe the manifold rituals associated with the nine-day *ijambe* cremation ceremony.[5]

The home regions of the three subgroups are given separate administrative recognition by the Indonesian government. Benua Lima is a named subdistrict (*kecamatan*), and in 1963 the Paju Sapuluh and Paju Epat home villages were contained in the Dusun Timur subdistrict with headquarters in the town of Tamiang Layang. However, Paju Epat was accorded some degree of administrative autonomy through the institution of a special 'link subdistrict' (*kecamatan penghubung*), with headquarters in the village of Telang.

Because it is the subgroup with which we are most familiar, the rest of this paper will focus on the Paju Epat Ma'anyan. Our description is based upon fieldwork carried out among this group in 1963–4. In 1964, the Paju Epat administrative unit had a resident population of about 1,100 living in the six villages of Telang, Siong, Murutuwu, Maipe, Balawa, and Tampulangit. Tampulangit is inhabited exclusively by Banjars, a strongly Islamic group that is ethnically and linguistically quite separate from the Ma'anyan. Therefore, except as they affect the five Ma'anyan villages, the 240 residents of Tampulangit will be excluded from subsequent discussion.[6]

Although Paju Epat is recognized as a unit in contrast to other Ma'anyan subgroups, each of its villages is an independent corporation and in most respects pursues an autonomous existence. Each village has its own traditional territory, its own village officers and adjudicating elders, and its own orally transmitted traditions and laws (adat). Nonetheless, multiplex kinship, ceremonial and economic bonds tie the people of the disparate villages together into a loosely woven fabric that provides a social if not political coherence to Paju Epat life.

Social Organization

Many villagers have emigrated northward over the last few generations, while few outsiders have moved into the area. The vast majority (94 per cent) of people currently living within Paju Epat were born there; about 87 per cent of the population still live in the village of their birth. Given this statistical tendency towards village endogamy and the relatively small size of individual villages, the Paju Epat resident operates in a social field in which most of his co-villagers are either consanguineal or affinal kinsmen, and frequently both. To a fair extent, this generalization also applies to intervillage relationships. Thus the principles that regulate relations among kinsmen are most important in governing the interaction of individuals and groups in Paju Epat society.

Kin Statuses, Kinship Terminology, and Behaviour Towards Kinsmen

In Paju Epat, all the descendants of an individual's eight pairs of great-great-grandparents (*munyang*) are recognized as consanguineal kinsmen and are designated by referential kin terms; the spouses of an individual's consanguineal relatives are accorded affinal kin terms, as are certain of his or her spouse's consanguineal kinsmen.[7] Kin terms, rather than names, are frequently used when talking to kinsmen. Terms that denote kinsmen genealogically close to Ego in the referential system are often extended in address to include more distant kinsmen of the same generation. Thus, the terms for mother (*ineh*) and father (*ambah*) may be used when addressing a parent's sibling. In fact, so pervasive is the use of kin terms for address, that they are frequently extended to include non-kinsmen as well. The higher the generation of an individual above Ego, the wider the extension of close kin terms. Thus, almost any villager of the grandparental generation will be addressed as 'grandfather' or 'grandmother'. Children, on the other hand, are usually addressed by name. Teknonyms based on the name of a child or grandchild are also used both as terms of reference and of address.[8] Since an individual is not really considered to have reached adult status until he or she has a child, the teknonym signals attainment of this status. Given the importance attached to having children, a childless couple will usually adopt a child and thereby gain teknonyms. Grandparent-hood is even more highly honoured among the Ma'anyan, and at this point, grandparental teknonyms usually replace parental ones. After an individual has acquired a teknonym, others are reluctant to use his or her personal name. The only adults consistently called by their personal names were the infirm or crippled who were unable to marry; these people tended to be treated as children socially though they might play adult economic roles. Kinship terms and teknonyms were used with considerable individual variation, reflect-ing either personal style or selection of an appropriate form of ad-dress for some particular strategy of social interaction.

Space considerations do not allow an extended analysis of the kinship terms and their social usage.[9] In retrospect, however, it has seemed to us that the most important function of kin terms in Paju Epat is to assign people to the proper generation relative to Ego. Among all the Ma'anyan kin terms, there is no doubt that generation is the most pervasive structural component. The formal distinction between generations is preserved in the general extension of kin terms, and kin terms appropriate to one generation are never applied to individuals of another generation. Generational integrity is also maintained in the institution of marriage. When the husband and wife belong to terminologically adjacent generations, the marriage is seen to be mildly incestuous (*sumbang*). Although theoretically proscribed by adat law, such a marriage can be regularized by the payment of an appropriate fine.

There are institutionalized modes of behaviour that control the *ideal* relationships of different classes of kinsmen. Here again, the generational component assumes wide influence. Persons of higher generation are to be treated with overt deference, while those of lower are to be advised and helped. The degree of deference or paternalism manifested is directly proportional to the number of generations separating the individuals involved, and even within an Ego's own generation, relative age, reflected in the kin terminology for older (*tata'*) and younger (*andi'*) siblings, should regulate relations between siblings.

The relationships between siblings are usually affectionate, and ideally they remain so throughout a lifetime. Behaviour towards cousins is similar; those with close personal bonds usually call cousins by the sibling terms appropriate to their relative ages. Between parents and children, relations are generally warm and loving, though following the basic paternalism-deference pattern.

Children of both sexes are valued and received equal affection from their parents. As children mature and achieve economic independence, the dominant-subordinate aspects of the relationship are reduced, even though its formal aspects are maintained. Parents are offended if they are not consulted by their children in important decisions. Ideally, an individual has a close and warm relationship with his parents' siblings; in reality, there is considerable variation here, depending upon specific circumstances.

Grandparents have a very special, loving bond with their grandchildren. Older people indulge their grandchildren at every opportunity, while assuming little responsibility for their discipline. The maintenance of warm relationships with grandchildren is important for the grandparents, since grandchildren can be asked for assistance in farming or other activities, a factor that permits old couples to maintain their economic independence when their own children must attend to other responsibilities related to their own families of procreation. Conversely, for grandchildren from families broken by death or divorce, grandparents often assume responsibility for a child's sustenance.

Husbands and wives ideally are equals in the marriage relationship. Each must contribute to the family's welfare, and both should be industrious. The husband usually acts as spokesman for both, but if he fails to consult with his wife, she usually will volunteer her opinion. Affection, while not essential to the relationship, often begins during courtship, or emerges as time passes. If not, or for those who are not happy in their marriage, divorce is fairly easy and carries little or no social opprobrium. An individual with a hardworking spouse may ignore many defects before seeking relief in divorce. Many individuals have been divorced a number of times; but in over 60 per cent of the marriages we recorded, neither spouse had been married more than once.

The relationships between an individual and his affinal kinsmen are similar to those with his consanguineal kin. In the early years of marriage, the relationship between spouse's parents and children's spouses is restrained, with outright avoidance characterizing the behaviour of an individual and his spouse's parent of the opposite sex. However, with a marriage of several years' standing and the birth of children, these relationships usually relax.

There is broad general agreement as to the ideals governing behaviour between different classes of kinsmen but, in practice, as in all societies, much individual variation occurs. Each kinsman, no matter what his sociologically allocated class, is perceived as an individual and treated accordingly. Thus, ideal kin-class behavioural patterns can be altered slightly or significantly, with a person behaving towards a kinsman in an unconventional manner, or acting in different ways towards two kinsmen of identical class. In short, although many persons are recognized as kinsmen, and kin terms of address are extended to others, the behaviour patterns which ideally regulate relations among different classes of kinsmen are in fact effectuated selectively as individual dyadic ties.

Kin-based Groups

Within the general universe of kinsmen recognized by a man of Paju Epat, an individual will share special rights and obligations towards some on the basis of common membership in kin groups based on common descent and/or residence. The most important kin-based groups operating in Paju Epat society are the dangau family, the *bumuh,* the *tambak* group, the lewu' family, and the kindred.

The Dangau Family

The dangau family is the primary social, economic, and ritual unit in Paju Epat society. Its locus is a swidden field house (dangau), where members of the family live during that part of the year when horticultural activity is at its height, though it also has rights in a village house (lewu') which it may share with other dangau families. Its focus is a husband and wife, though in structural form its membership may pass through several phases. Viewed synchronically, in 1964, dangau families ranged in size from one to 10 persons, with a mean of 4·7. Diachronically, however, the membership of a dangau family is not static, but shifts as it passes through the various stages of what might be considered a corporate life cycle. This life cycle roughly parallels that of the husband and wife who serve as its focus: it is born when the focal couple first become economically independent (incomplete nuclear stage), achieves maturity with the birth of children (complete nuclear stage), passes into middle age as a child and spouse become temporary members of the family (complete stem stage) and then secede, reaches its declining years when all children are gone (reduced nuclear stage), and dies with the focal couple or with the absorption of a surviving spouse, usually the widow, into the dangau family of a married child (broken stem stage).

The corporate identity and couple-specific focus of the dangau family are symbolized by a sacred rice strain. A few years after the marriage of a couple, when they appear to have formed a stable union, a special ceremony called a 'seed marriage' (*mila wini'*) is performed on their behalf. For this ceremony the natal dangau families of each spouse contribute small amounts of their own sacred rice strains. The two stocks of sacred rice are mixed together, thereby producing a new and unique strain specific to the new dangau family. Although it may be partially perpetuated in the sacred rice strains of married children, the specific strain associated with a given dangau family 'dies' with its focal couple.

Functionally, the dangau family forms a primary production and consumption unit in the economic sphere. It owns common property such as tools, weapons, field houses, fishing gear, and rubber trees. Generally speaking, each dangau family also acts as a unit in a horticultural labour exchange system (*panganrau*), in which each man-day of work rendered by outsiders should be, and in time is, repaid to the workers' respective dangau families. By enticing labourers through the advertisement of good food, and by deploying its own members in a strategic way, the dangau family is able to maintain effective economic and social relationships with a large number of similar families, a procedure that serves indirectly to sustain community integration.

The dangau family sponsors life crisis, agricultural, and certain other ceremonies for its members. There are some ceremonies, such as annual spirit propitiation or cremation, in which a few dangau families or the entire village may participate. Then each dangau family must contribute its share of expenses and labour. The dangau family has a head who acts as family spokesman, who, although generally a man, may be either male or female.

The Bumuh

The bumuh is a bilineal descent group in which membership is transmitted through both men and women. It thus comprises all the descendants of a progenitor or focal ancestor. An individual belongs to as many bumuh as he recognizes ancestors or ancestral couples. Each bumuh is associated with a theoretically non-partible estate in which its members share use rights. The estate may comprise fruit trees, houses, and various sorts of heirloom property such as gongs or old weapons, but land-use rights frequently make up its most important assets. Some bumuh contain very little property at all. In each succeeding generation, one member of the bumuh, its custodian, looks after the estate and convenes the other members whenever a matter affecting the bumuh or its estate must be decided.

All bumuh members have rights in the estate, but not all have an equal opportunity to exercise them. There is some structural necessity for this, since ideally at least, in each succeeding generation, the membership of a bumuh doubles. Use rights to swidden land or a share in property owned by a focal ancestor pass to that progenitor's children and other bilineal descendants. As his children grow up, marry and secede from the progenitor's dangau family, some maintain affiliation (endofiliation) with the progenitor's village household as members of a larger lewu' family (see following section); others marry out (exofiliation), establishing affiliation with the lewu' families of their spouses. Endofiliative bumuh members inherit primary rights to use the bumuh estate; exofiliative members who remain in their natal villages retain secondary use rights. Exofiliative members who follow their spouses to another village inherit tertiary use rights. In the next generation, children of those who hold secondary use rights inherit tertiary rights; tertiary rights upon inheritance become what might be termed residual. One endofiliative child in each generation becomes custodian of the bumuh estate.

The practical differences between primary, secondary, tertiary, and residual rights emerge only when two individuals holding rights of a different degree wish to use estate property, such as farming on the same swidden site. The individual holding rights of a higher order has the dominant claim. If two claimants have identical rights or disagree, the case must be brought before the bumuh custodian, who is empowered to resolve the matter as he sees fit. The Paju Epat system for assigning use-right priorities offsets many problems that could arise from potential expansion of bumuh membership.

The Tambak Group

A tambak group is a descent-based kin group that has as its locus a tambak, the carved ironwood box into which the ash residue of its members' remains is placed at the conclusion of the ijambe cremation ceremony. Each tambak had an original founder or owner, and the associated tambak group includes all of the founder's endofiliative descendants (and their spouses) who have not become affiliated with another tambak group.[10] Tambak groups are named, discrete and mutually exclusive. A person gains membership in a tambak group at birth, but this may be changed through adoption or marriage. Tambak groups own their associated tambak ash receptacles and some heirloom property. As with most other kin-based groups in Paju Epat, the tambak group has a head who acts as custodian and spokesman. The custodianship is usually passed to a member of the previous custodian's household (lewu' family), so that for each tambak group there is one household that serves as the locus of its custodian descent line.

Traditional Class System

Traditionally, tambak groups were associated with a formal system of social stratification that contained three classes: nobles (*bangsawan*), warriors (*panglima*), and clients (*walah*). Members of the first two classes were free to run their own lives, while those of the third were in a dependent status. Among the 'free' classes, not all members of noble tambak groups were close to the family lines from which individuals were chosen to fill positions of political authority. Similarly, though the term panglima is used for a war leader, not all members of warrior tambak groups were actually war leaders. Rather, the various warrior tambak groups had been founded by war leaders and were noted for producing warriors in certain family lines. Thus a third free class of 'common people' (*panganak rama'*) was recognized which consisted of the members of noble and warrior tambak groups not directly within lines of succession to authority.

Clients, on the other hand, formed a dependent class whose members were satellites of free individuals or families. There were several types of client: the *urai*, a debt slave; the *kawalek*, a prisoner taken in battle; and the walah, the child of an urai or kawalek. Historical records from the nineteenth century characterize clientship in Paju Epat as very mild in nature; a client with talent and drive could attain free status through marriage and the payment of a ritual fine. The Dutch officially outlawed 'slavery' and clientship in 1892. Today, no members remain in the client tambak groups, all having either married into free tambak groups or converted to Christianity. However, the stigma of client ancestry is still felt by those affected, and remembered by others, though adat law does not allow mention of the fact. Although Paju Epat villagers claim that the traditional class system is no longer formally operative, it does live on in an adumbrated fashion and still plays a minor role in mediating social relationships.

The Lewu' Family

The lewu' family is an extended family household grouping of dangau families that share rights in a village house; here is where its members reside when they are in the village. The members of a lewu' family are the builders of the house, often a set of siblings or a parent and several married children, their bilineal descendants who have maintained post-marital affiliation (endofiliation) with it, and the in-marrying spouses of the latter. Constituent member dangau families may secede to build new village houses which thereby form the loci of new lewu' families. In addition to its village house, the lewu' family owns heirloom property, mediates primary use rights to swidden lands and other bumuh property, prescribes certain food taboos, and governs tambak group affiliation. At any given time, a lewu' family will contain either one or several constituent dangau families,[11] who share in its property rights and, on occasion, act as a ritual unit. It has a head who acts as the unit's spokesman and custodian of its property.

Marriage contracts demonstrate an important role of the lewu' family in Paju Epat society. Ideally marriages are arranged by lewu' family spokesmen, but initiation may also come from the man and woman themselves, when the marriage is known as 'eloping'. Although the arranged marriage was traditional, today elopement is more common. Before either type of marriage can be completed, several important issues must be settled by representatives of both bride's and groom's lewu' families. Post-marital lewu' family membership must be specified, for the couple will derive its primary land-use rights from the lewu' family which it joins. The contract between the two lewu' families involved must also, in case of differing tambak group affiliation, determine tambak group membership as well. Polygyny, though infrequent, is allowed under adat law, which specifies that permission from the first wife must be obtained before the marriage contract with the second wife can be accepted. Ideally, post-marital residence is with the wife's family, but the adat system, upon payment of appropriate fines, allows the couple to join the husband's family either immediately after marriage or following bride service of two to five years. And in fact, the couple eventually did affiliate with the groom's family in about half the marriages in Paju Epat.

The Kindred

The kindred is an Ego-centric set of kinsmen comprising the members of the eight bilineal bumuh descended from a given Ego's eight pairs of great-great grandparents (munyang). The individual at the centre of a kindred can be considered its 'focal member', and the activities in which people participate because of a kin-based obligation to a kindred's focal member can be termed kindred activities. However, although the members of Ego's kindred may have some obligation to participate in a focal member's kindred activities, they have no necessary obligations to one another unless they happen to be members of the same bumuh. For what can be described as kindred obligations stem only from common bumuh membership.

Kindred activities are group activities sponsored by or for the focal member, and include life-cycle ceremonies and co-operative work projects such as the clearing, planting, and harvesting of swidden fields. Ideally, all the members of a kindred should participate to a certain extent in the kindred activities of its focal member. However, in practice not all members do, so that in Paju Epat a kindred tie can be considered either active or inactive, depending on the degree of expectation there is that the individuals linked by the tie will, in fact, participate in each other's kindred activities. Genealogically close relatives are generally expected to participate in a fairly wide range of each other's kindred activities, while the expectations are much lower for those whose relationship is genealogically more remote. Thus, in quality, a kindred tie is basically a dyadic relationship involving pairs of kinsmen. The kindred provides a fairly extensive range of relatives with whom one can activate dyadic relationships if need and common interest exist. For an individual owes a certain generalized obligation to members of his 'latent' kindred, those with whom he does not have currently active dyadic ties. If a member of the latent kindred comes to its focal member and specifically invokes his kindred tie in asking some service, it cannot be honourably denied without good reason. This limited obligation towards latent kindred members provides the opportunity for the establishment of an active dyadic relationship on a trial basis. If the relationship proves satisfactory, mutual participation is dyadic and group kindred activities will be regularized. If the relationship is unsatisfactory, it continues as a latent tie. The trial mechanism for activating kindred ties can be extremely useful when individuals travel outside their home village area.

Detailed examination of the workings of the kin groups briefly described above is available elsewhere (Hudson, 1967c, 1972). Although the quality of relationships obtaining among different categories of kinsmen and kin groups can be described in ideal terms that are perceived as normative by Paju Epat villagers, in reality the value of any kin bond is determined pragmatically with regard to the placement of that strand in the more complex overall fabric of ongoing social interaction. In order to provide a somewhat clearer depiction of the realities of social life in Paju Epat, we will present certain illustrative case material. This material will focus on two lewu' families, whose spokesmen were PaMuna' and KakahUgo, and on the events surrounding a crisis situation, the death of Nini' Keti. In the remaining space here, we will present the bare outline of the case, and then describe the families involved in terms of the relevant features of social organization.

The Death of Nini'Keti

One day at the height of the planting season, the resonant booming of gongs announced a death in the village, a death that had long been expected: Nini'Keti, an elderly woman, had been failing for two months. Just last week she had said that Saturday, this very day would see her death, and she advised her family not to weep loudly over her going, as it would make her spirit's own journey too noisy. Her son PaMuna', his wife, and her daughter Jugai had stayed close to her in these last days.

As the gong's message travelled to distant swidden fields where co-operative work groups were planting, a few close kin finished their work quickly and returned to mourn their elderly relative. Others continued their tasks into the afternoon, then packed a few belongings, pounded rice to contribute to the bereaved household, and closed their field huts in preparation for the two-day primary death ritual.[12]

By nightfall, the village house of the deceased was jammed with people. A newcomer entered and beat each of the large gongs rapidly. A few women, their shawls covering their heads, squatted beside the richly decorated corpse, their voices rising in a stylized wail.

The next morning men completed the boat-shaped coffin that had already been roughed out in anticipation of her death; some were close relatives, others villagers skilled in woodworking. By mid-afternoon, the fast decaying corpse had been stuffed into the coffin, and the lid bound tightly and sealed with resin. Incense was burned constantly to cover the smell. The corpse was attended throughout this night. Final preparations for burial began the next morning. Ritual food was readied, and shamans specializing in death rites began to recite the chants that convey the spirit of the departed to the afterworld. In another part of the room, a group of elderly men had gathered, a gong and dish of pig's blood placed before them. PaMuna', the old woman's son and spokesman for the lewu' family to which she belonged, gave a summary of his mother's descendants: 4 children, 23 grandchildren, already 36 great-grandchildren; 14 spouses must be added, bringing the number of living 'descendants' to 77; 19 others had died, making a grand total of 96.

With the prescribed ritual performed, it was time to convey the corpse to the village graveyard. And yet the burial was delayed, and the atmosphere inside became increasingly heavy. The reason for the delay lay in events from the recent past. The village cemetery had been burned over two months earlier, when another villager, Ngomen, had been cleaning his swidden and carelessly left his fire unattended. Because of the burning, it was considered a breach of adat and ritually unsafe to inter a new corpse in the cemetery until it had been purified. In order to determine who should bear the costs of the purification ceremony, the case had to be heard by the adjudicating elders (*mantir*) of the village. For various reasons the case had not yet been heard, but now that a body was in need of burial, it was imperative that a judgement be reached. And yet the few mantirs who attended the obsequies waited patiently but in vain for their colleagues and the village adat head to put in an appearance. However, as the smell in the afflicted house grew oppressive, the elders present were forced to seek a temporary solution: a fine to purify the burial site was assessed and paid by Nini'Keti's own family. With that accomplished, the corpse was rushed from the house and at last laid to rest in the cemetery.

Analysis of the Case

In the events associated with the burial of Nini'Keti, the principal actors—the old woman's own family and Ngomen, the cemetery burner—were members of two different lewu' families. At the time of her death, Nini'Keti had been a widow for some years. She had been absorbed into the dangau family of her forty-year-old daughter Jugai. This dangau family, of the broken stem type, comprised Nini'Keti herself, Jugai and her husband Puteng, and their five unmarried children. Nini'Keti had been an industrious, independent old woman, and even in the last months of her life was constantly at work weaving rattan mats to help support the family.[13] Jugai looked more than her forty years, worn down from having borne eight children, the youngest still an infant. Her husband Puteng, the

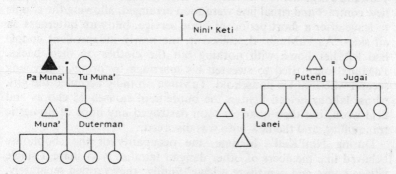

Fig. 6 Lewu' Family of PaMuna'

formal head of the dangau family, was not known for his industry; long ago he seemed to have given up struggling against life's vicissitudes. What little motivation Puteng exhibited derived from the urging of his wife and the nagging of his mother-in-law. The couple's eldest daughter Lanei, recently married and living with her husband's family, frequently contributed labour or food to her natal dangau family. Still, the family was one of the poorest in Paju Epat, and the children often had only boiled cassava to eat.

Puteng's family shared a village residence with the dangau family headed by Nini'Keti's son PaMuna'. PaMuna's complete stem family included TuMuna' his wife, Muna' their daughter, Muna's husband Duterman and five daughters. The two dangau families formed a lewu' family with PaMuna' as its head. The village house occupied by this lewu' family was a shophouse in the village market area, owned by the husband of another of Nini'Keti's daughters, a non-resident Chinese who had bought the structure from its original Banjar owners before the World War II Japanese occupation. The house was divided into two separate and unconnected living spaces occupied by the respective dangau families of Puteng and PaMuna'.

From his location next door, PaMuna' took great interest in his mother's welfare, even though she was not a member of his own dangau family. PaMuna', industrious, hardworking, and successful, often came forward to contribute extra rice or the cost of a shaman curing ceremony for his mother. TuMuna', his acid-tongued, parsimonious wife, who worked as hard as her husband, sometimes begrudged him this aid; her feelings about Puteng's indolence were well known. Many years previously, PaMuna' had agreed to perform two years of bride service for his wife's father before the couple established permanent residence with PaMuna's lewu' family. TuMuna's arguments with her own siblings were so disruptive that a new contract and ritual fine were soon arranged, allowing the couple to leave after a short period of bride service, but with bitterness on all sides. As PaMuna' described it, the newly independent couple had left her home with nothing but the clothes on their backs. PaMuna' once tried to sweeten his marriage by bringing a young second wife into his household. TuMuna' initially accepted the girl, whose labour helped lighten the burdens of household chores and field work, but their quarrels soon destroyed any hope of domestic tranquillity, and the new wife was divorced.

During Nini'Keti's lifetime, the occupants of the shophouse behaved like members of other dangau families who share a single village house and constitute a lewu' family: they farmed separately, cooked apart, and had totally distinct living quarters. Yet they pooled their resources in times of economic crisis or when ritual occasions arose. Nini'Keti's funeral and subsequent mortuary rites provided a clear-cut illustration of this sharing of resources. Since she had died in Jugai's house, the ritual associated with burial was held there; cooking for the many guests who had to be fed was performed only in that kitchen, and pollution from the death affected only Jugai's living quarters. Yet many of the necessary goods for the ritual came from PaMuna's house or larder—ceremonial cloths to cover the corpse and coffin, valuable goods to surround the deceased, the gongs to be beaten,[14] the pig sacrificed for the sustenance of the departed spirit and remaining survivors, rice for feeding guests, and cash to pay shamans and adat fines. An elaborate traditional mortuary ceremony was held 49 days after the death, and this centred in PaMuna's house, although it was such a well-attended affair that both living spaces were used to feed and entertain the guests. After this event, however, the two households drifted rapidly apart, PaMuna' and TuMuna' becoming increasingly unwilling to help support Jugai's family. When Jugai and Puteng's two youngest, undernourished children succumbed to disease, the break became openly apparent. Before death, the children had been baptized by an elder of the Protestant church;[15] they were buried with Christian ritual, pragmatically much less expensive than the traditional animist rites. Most villagers felt that economic pressure rather than religious convictions had precipitated the conversion. TuMuna', a strong animist both by personal inclination and as a leading shaman in the village, failed to attend the burial ceremony for her young niece and nephew as a token of her disapproval.

Thus two dangau families that had formerly maintained a close, co-operative relationship split once there was no aged parent to unite them socially and symbolically. Had the deaths of Jugai's children preceded that of Nini'Keti, no one disputed the certainty that they would have received a traditional animist burial. Lewu'

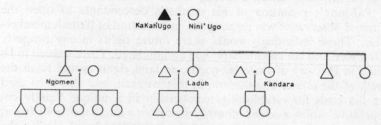

Fig. 7 Lewu' Family of KaKahUgo

families are often held together only by such a common member in the senior generation. However, an actual break between constituent dangau families can often be avoided or postponed if opposing factions are not exposed to daily contact and resultant irritation. Here the importance of the dangau family can be demonstrated, for in order to minimize conflict among those who share occupancy in a village house, dangau families frequently spend most of their time living apart in swidden houses, returning to the village only for important occasions.

The lewu' family to which Ngomen, the cemetery burner, belonged was a case in point. At its head, and spokesman for the lewu' family was KakahUgo, a man in his sixties, recognized in the village as a person of substance and considerable wealth. In addition to his wife, KakahUgo's own dangau family also included two unmarried teenagers. Three other married children and their dangau families were members of the lewu' family. His eldest child Ngomen was notorious as a man who failed to pull his weight. Ngomen's two younger sisters Kandara and Laduh and their industrious husbands were about to move to a new village house, and although they claimed it was because of their conversion to Christianity, everyone also knew that they were tired of sharing their rice with Ngomen. They did not plan to secede from the lewu' family, thereby losing their rights of inheritance, as KakahUgo was one of the richest men in the village. But with his death, it was expected that this lewu' family would certainly disintegrate as well.

Nini'Keti's funeral did not activate the deceased's tambak group, a descent group that in modern life surfaces principally during the cremation ceremony when individual tambak groups must collectively shoulder the financial and ritual responsibilities for tambak group members whose bones are being burned. However, on the death and baptism of Jugai's two youngsters, an adat fine was assessed by animist elders to rectify the separation in death of the spirits of the children from that of their grandmother; the fine was needed to restore balance within the tambak group as a whole, as this would be the participatory group in a later cremation ceremony.

PaMuna's recitation of his mother's descendants to open the funeral observance was an accurate enumeration of bumuh membership. Those individuals would share future rights in any property Nini'Keti and her late husband had accumulated. There seemed to be little in the way of material goods, so land rights would form the bulk of the estate. The bumuh, in this instance, had also been used as the basis for establishing membership in a unique 'family cooperative' which assessed monthly dues from a number of constituent dangau families beyond those of the immediate lewu' family; the monies collected were held in a treasury from which any bumuh member was entitled to borrow without interest. For instance, 1,000 rupiahs had been borrowed by Puteng in the name of his wife to finance the burials of his dead children. The core membership of this group were bumuh members, although over time, siblings of spouses had been allowed to join.

As Nini'Keti was one of the oldest inhabitants of the village, the bumuh she had founded formed the core group of mourners. In the stylized wailing performed by women about the corpse, Nini'Keti was addressed in kin terms: mother, older sister, great-grandmother—always indicating the correct generational relationship between the deceased and the mourner. Certain ritual obligations, however, were performed by individuals not belonging to the bumuh generated by Nini'Keti, and here the old lady's kindred could be observed in operation. Three individuals outside Nini'Keti's own bumuh shared in two important symbolic rites: trimming the corpse's hair and nails (the repository of a person's soul); and participation in the prescribed fasting that must be observed by close family members for 49 days after a death. These kindred members, it transpired, were affinal relatives, the children of Nini'Keti's husband's sister.

For the funeral of an elderly, important person, nearly everyone in the village will attend, except mothers with young babies, who are forbidden by adat to view a corpse. Some individuals will have close kin ties, but others will come as friends, or to show their respect towards an elder, while some follow their stomachs to certain fulfilment. Nini'Keti had been a leading shaman of the region, and her former associates and pupils in curing rituals attended *en masse*, for they felt her loss like that of a sister. For the 49-day ceremony, distant relatives came many miles to pay their respects, but it had also been widely known in advance that the rite would be a great party. Thus one or more of many different strands could be seen to draw a particular individual to such a ceremony.

While presence at an important ceremonial occasion can be attributed to many factors, the absence of a close kinsman, friend, shaman, or village dignitary from an important ceremony such as a funeral, is conspicuous and needs explanation. That many of the village's adjudicating elders, including KakahUgo, the father of Ngomen the cemetery burner, did not appear at Nini'Keti's funeral to help resolve questions relating to the cemetery's purification was not construed as accidental by anyone present. Though Ngomen himself appeared, his mumbled apology that KakahUgo was not well and staying in his distant swidden hut, was unconvincing. For this case, focusing on the cemetery, was just one manifestation of an enmity and continuing conflict between the families of PaMuna' and KakahUgo, as they contended for local power and influence in the village.

NOTES

1. For a definition of 'Dayak', see Hudson (1972:11-13).

2. A total we derived from examination of individual subdistrict (*kecamatan*) records from the population census of 1961. These records, not available in published form, were kindly made available to us by the provincial census office of Central Kalimantan. We have not been able to examine comparable data from the 1971 census.

3. A detailed account of Ma'anyan history is found in Hudson (1967b).

4. See Map 6 in Hudson (1967b:32).

5. For a detailed account of the ijambe ceremony, see Hudson (1966).

6. For more information on the Banjars and Tampulangit, see Hudson (1967b: 9-12, 35-8).

7. Terms of reference for consanguineal kinsmen are: *pulaksana'i* (Sb/Co), *tata'*, (eSb), *andi'* (ySb), *tuwari* (Co), *sahinra'an* (Co¹), *sanruehan* (Co²), *santeluan* (Co³), *ambah* (F), *ineh* (M), *mama'* (PB/PZH), *tutu'* (PZ/PBW), *ia'* (C), *aken* (SbC), *kakah* (PF), *nini'* (PM), *umpu* (CC), *datu'* (PPP), *buyut* (CCC), *munyang* (PPPP), and *entah* (CCCC).
Affinal terms of reference are: *darangan* (Sp), *matue'upu* (H), *matuewawei* (W), *daup* (SpB/ZH if linked through a male, or from a male speaker's standpoint), *iwan* (SpZ/BW if linked through a male; SpSb/SbSp if linked through a female, or

from a female speaker's standpoint), *bulau* (CSpP), *sanrui* (SpSbSp), *kasian* (SpP), *kasian lambung* (SpPSb), and *nantu* (CSp).

8. Teknonyms are formed with a parental or grandparental prefix plus the child's name: *Pa-* 'father of -', *Ineh-* or *Tu-* 'mother of -', *Kakah-* 'grandfather of -', and *Nini'-* 'grandmother of -'.

9. Extended discussion can be found in Hudson (1967c, 1972).

10. In 1964 there were 22 'active' tambak and associated tambak groups, though in the past there have been many others now gone and mostly forgotten.

11. Prior to World War II, lewu' families tended to be quite large and to contain many constituent dangau families. However, because of migration and changes in administrative and tax laws designating villages 'of origin', by 1964, 54 per cent of Paju Epat's village houses were being used by only a single dangau family, another 27 per cent were occupied by two dangau families. 10 per cent and 9 per cent of the households contained respectively three and four dangau families. None of the lewu' families had more than four dangau families.

12. For more detailed information on this and other rituals associated with death in Paju Epat see Hudson (1966).

13. Dangau families of the broken stem type almost always have a woman in the senior generation. Because of their usefulness, widows are easily absorbed into the dangau family of a married child, whereas social and demographic pressures force widowers to remarry and form new dangau families. Of the 14 broken stem dangau families in Paju Epat, in 13 the widowed parent was a woman.

14. For a picture of the coffin and goods see Hudson (1966, Plate XVI).

15. The elder, who urged Puteng and his family to become Christian, stood in the kin relation of *bulau* to Puteng, that is, Puteng's daughter Lanei's father-in-law.

A NOTE ON THE CONTRIBUTORS

DR. G. N. APPELL is Research Associate in the Department of Anthropology, Brandeis University. He was formerly the editor of the *Borneo Research Bulletin*. He has written numerous papers on various aspects of Rungus Dusun society and culture and on more general anthropological topics. Recently he has edited two books *The Societies of Borneo: Explorations in the Theory of Cognatic Social Structure* (1976), and *Studies in Borneo Societies: Social Process and Anthropological Explanation* (1976).

DR. JAY B. CRAIN is Assistant Professor in Medical Anthropology in the Department of Psychiatry, School of Medicine, University of California. He has written articles on Lun Dayeh social organization.

DR. A. B. HUDSON is Associate Professor in the Department of Anthropology, University of Massachusetts. He is well known for his paper on *The Barito Isolects of Borneo* (1967) and his more recent book *Padju Epat. The Ma'anyan of Indonesian Borneo* (1972). His wife, Judith M. Hudson, has also undertaken fieldwork in Kalimantan and has herself written papers on Borneo in the journal *Indonesia*.

MR. VICTOR T. KING is Lecturer in South-East Asian Sociology at the University of Hull. He has written a number of articles on Maloh society and culture and the peoples of West Kalimantan.

DR. H. S. MORRIS is Senior Lecturer at the London School of Economics and Political Science. His major publications include *Report on a Melanau Sago Producing Community of Sarawak* (1953) and *The Indians of Uganda* (1968).

DR. JÉRÔME ROUSSEAU is Assistant Professor in the Department of Anthropology, McGill University, Montreal. He has published articles on Kayan social organization and edited the Sarawak Museum Journal special issue *The Peoples of Central Borneo* (1974).

DR. CLIFFORD SATHER is Lecturer in Social Anthropology in the School of Comparative Social Sciences, University of Penang. He has written papers on Bajau Laut society and culture.

DR. WILLIAM M. SCHNEIDER is Assistant Professor in the Department of Anthropology, University of Arkansas. He has published papers on Selako social organization.

DR. HERBERT L. WHITTIER is Assistant Professor in the Department of Anthropology, Michigan State University. He has written articles on Kenyah society and culture.

BIBLIOGRAPHY OF WORKS REFERRED TO IN THE TEXT

Allen, M. R. 1970. A Comparative Note on Iban and Land Dyak Social Structure. *Mankind*, 7, 191–8.

Appell, G. N. 1965. *The Nature of Social Groupings Among the Rungus Dusun of Sabah, Malaysia*. Unpublished Ph.D. thesis, Australian National University.

— 1967. Observational Procedures for Identifying Kindreds: Social Isolates Among the Rungus of Borneo. *Southwestern Journal of Anthropology*, 23, 192–207.

— 1968a. A Survey of the Social and Medical Anthropology of Sabah: Retrospect and Prospect. *Behavior Science Notes*, 3, 1–54.

— 1968b. Social Groupings Among the Rungus, a Cognatic Society of Sabah, Malaysia. *Journal of the Malaysian Branch of the Royal Asiatic Society*, 41, 193–202.

— 1968c. The Dusun Languages of Northern Borneo: the Rungus Dusun and Related Problems. *Oceanic Linguistics*, 7, 1–15.

— 1968d. Ethnographic Profiles of the Dusun-speaking Peoples of Sabah, Malaysia. *Journal of the Malaysian Branch of the Royal Asiatic Society*, 41, 131–47.

— 1969. Social Anthropological Research in Borneo. *Anthropologica*, 11, 45–57.

— 1971a. *Observational Procedures for Land Tenure and Kin Groupings in the Cognatic Societies of Borneo*. (Mimeo.)

— 1971b. Systems of Land Tenure in Borneo: a Problem in Ecological Determinism. *Borneo Research Bulletin*, 3, 17–21.

— 1973. The Distinction Between Ethnography and Ethnology and Other Issues in Cognitive Structuralism. *Bijdragen tot de Taal-, Land- en Volkenkunde*, 129, 1–56.

— 1974. *The Analysis of Property Systems: the Creation and Devolution of Property Interests Among the Rungus of Borneo*. Unpublished paper presented at the Association of Social Anthropologists' Conference on Social Anthropology and Law, Keele.

— 1976a. The Rungus: Social Structure in a Cognatic Society and its Ritual Symbolization. *The Societies of Borneo: Explorations in the Theory of Cognatic Social Structure*, ed. American Anthropological Association, Special Publication No. 6, Washington, 66–86.

— 1976b. The Cognitive Structure of Anthropological Inquiry: Comments on King's Approach to the Concept of the Kindred. *The Societies of Borneo: Explorations in the Theory of Cognatic Social Structure*, ed. American Anthropological Association, Special Publication No. 6, Washington, 146–51.

— 1976c. Preface and Introduction. *The Societies of Borneo: Explorations in the Theory of Cognatic Social Structure*, ed. American Anthropological Association, Special Publication No. 6, Washington, v-viii, 1–15.

— 1976d. Introduction and Social Science Research in Sarawak. *Studies in Borneo Societies: Social Process and Anthropological Explanation*, ed. Center for Southeast Asian Studies, Northern Illinois University, Special Report No. 12, 1–26.

— n.d. *Observational Procedures and Models for Social Structure: a Comparative Analysis of the Property Domain of Three Cognatic Societies of Borneo.* (Tentative title.) Unpublished ms.

Appell, G. N. and Robert Harrison. 1969. The Ethnographic Classification of the Dusun-speaking Peoples of Northern Borneo. *Ethnology*, 8, 212–27.

Barnes, J. A. 1968. Networks and Political Processes. *Local-level Politics*, ed. M. J. Swartz. Chicago. 107–30.

Barth, Fredrik. 1966. *Models of Social Organization*. Royal Anthropological Institute, Occasional Paper No. 23, London.

Barth, J. P. J. 1910. *Boesangsch-Nederlandsch Woordenboek*. Batavia.

Bolang, A. and Tom Harrisson. 1949. Murut and Related Vocabularies, with Special Reference to North Borneo Terminology. *Sarawak Museum Journal*, 5, 116–24.

Boyle, Frederick. 1865. *Adventures Among the Dayaks of Borneo*. London.

Burns, Robert. 1849. The Kayans of the North-West of Borneo. *Journal of the Indian Archipelago and Eastern Asia*, 3, 140–52.

Carter, George S. 1958. Historical Background. *A Tragedy of Borneo, 1941–1945*, ed. Brunei.

Cense, A. A. and E. M. Uhlenbeck. 1958. *Critical Survey of Studies on the Languages of Borneo*. Koninklijk Instituut voor Taal-, Land- en Volkenkunde, Bibliographic Series 2, The Hague.

Clayre, B. 1972. A Preliminary Comparative Study of the Lun Bawang (Murut) and the Sa'ban Languages of Sarawak. *Sarawak Museum Journal*, 20, 146–71.

Clayre, B. and L. Cubit. 1974. An Outline of Kayan Grammar. *The Peoples of Central Borneo*, ed. Jérôme Rousseau. Sarawak Museum Journal Special Issue, Kuching, 43–91.

Clayre, Iain F. C. S. 1972a. *A Grammatical Description of Melanau: a Language of Coastal Sarawak*. Unpublished Ph.D. thesis, University of Edinburgh.

— 1972b. Punan Ba'. Melanau Link with the Ulu Rejang. *Sarawak Gazette*. 98, 23–5.

Conley, William W. 1973. *The Kalimantan Kenyah: a Study of Tribal Conversion in Terms of Dynamic Cultural Themes*. University Microfilms, Ann Arbor (D. Miss. thesis, Fuller Theological Seminary).

Crain, Jay B. 1970a. *The Lun Dayeh of Sabah, East Malaysia: Aspects of Marriage and Social Exchange*. University Microfilms: Ann Arbor (Ph.D. thesis, Cornell University).

— 1970b. The Domestic Family and Long-house Among the Mengalong Lun Dayeh. *Sarawak Museum Journal*, 18, 186–92.

— 1970c. The Mengalong Lun Dayeh Long-house. *Sarawak Museum Journal*, 18, 169–85.

— 1973. Mengalong Lun Dayeh Agricultural Organization. *Brunei Museum Journal*, 3, 1–25.

Cubit, L. E. 1964. Kayan Phonemics. *Bijdragen tot de Taal-, Land- en Volkenkunde*, 120, 409–23.

Deegan, James L. 1973. *Change Among the Lun Bawang, a Borneo People.* University Microfilms, Ann Arbor (Ph.D. thesis, University of Washington).

Dixon, Gale. 1974. Dayak Land Tenure: an Alternative to Ecological Determinism. *Borneo Research Bulletin*, 6, 5–15.

Dyen, Isidore. 1965. *A Lexicostatistical Classification of the Austronesian Languages.* International Journal of American Linguistics Memoir 19, Indiana.

Eggan, Fred. 1960. The Sagada Igorots of Northern Luzon. *Social Structure in Southeast Asia*, ed. George P. Murdock. Chicago. 24–50.

Enthoven, J. J. K. 1903. *Bijdragen tot de Geographie van Borneo's Westerafdeeling.* (2 vols.) Leiden.

Evers, Hans-Dieter. 1969. Models of Social Systems: Loosely and Tightly Structured. *Loosely Structured Social Systems: Thailand in Comparative Perspective*, ed. Yale University Cultural Report Series No. 17, New Haven. 115–27.

Firth, Raymond. 1957. A Note on Descent Groups in Polynesia. *Man*, 57, 4–8.

— 1963. *Bilateral Descent Groups. An Operational Viewpoint.* Royal Anthropological Institute, Occasional Paper No. 16, London, 22–37.

— 1967. *Tikopia Ritual and Belief.* Boston.

Freeman, J. D. 1955a. *Report on the Iban of Sarawak.* Kuching (reprinted 1970 as *Report on the Iban.* LSE Monographs on Social Anthropology No. 41, London).

— 1955b. *Iban Agriculture. A Report on the Shifting Cultivation of Hill Rice by the Iban of Sarawak.* London.

— 1956. 'Utrolateral' and 'Utrolocal'. *Man*, 56, 87–8.

— 1958. The Family System of the Iban of Borneo. *The Developmental Cycle in Domestic Groups*, ed. Jack Goody. Cambridge Papers in Social Anthropology No. 1, Cambridge. 15–52.

— 1960. The Iban of Western Borneo. *Social Structure in Southeast Asia*, ed. George P. Murdock. Chicago. 65–87.

— 1961. On the Concept of the Kindred. *Journal of the Royal Anthropological Institute*, 91, 192–220.

Friedman, Jonathan. 1975. Tribes, States, and Transformations. *Marxist Analyses and Social Anthropology*, ed. Maurice Bloch. A.S.A. Studies 2, London. 161–202.

Furness, William H. 1902. *The Home-life of Borneo Head-hunters.* Philadelphia.

Geddes, W. R. 1954a. *The Land Dayaks of Sarawak.* London.

— 1954b. Land Tenure of Land Dayaks. *Sarawak Museum Journal*, 6, 42–51.

Godelier, Maurice. 1973. *Horizon Trajets Marxistes en Anthropologie.* Paris.

Goodenough, Ward, H. 1955. A Problem in Malayo-Polynesian Social Organization. *American Anthropologist*, 57, 71–83.

Hall, D. G. E. 1970. *A History of South-East Asia.* London (reprint. 3rd edition).

Harrisson, Tom. 1950. Classifying the People in *A Report on the 1947 Population Census of Sarawak*, J. L. Noakes. Kuching. 271–80.

— 1959a. The Kelabits and Muruts. *The Peoples of Sarawak*, ed. Kuching. 57–71.

— 1959b. *World Within: A Borneo Story.* London.

— 1965. The Malohs of Kalimantan: Ethnological Notes. *Sarawak Museum Journal*, 13, 236–350.

— 1966. Maloh Coffin Designs. *Sarawak Museum Journal*, 14, 146–50.

— 1967. Ethnological Notes on the Muruts of the Sapulut River, Sabah. *Journal of the Malaysian Branch of the Royal Asiatic Society*, 40, 111–29.

— 1968. The Advent of Islam to West and North Borneo. *Sarawak Gazette*, 94, 180–4.

Hose, Charles and William McDougall. 1966. *The Pagan Tribes of Borneo.* (2 vols.). London (reprint. 1st edition 1912).

Hudson, A. B. 1966. Death Ceremonies of the Padju Epat Ma'anyan Dayaks. *Borneo Writing and Related Matters*, ed. Tom Harrisson. Sarawak Museum Journal, Special Monograph No. 1, Kuching. 341–416.

— 1967a. *The Barito Isolects of Borneo: a Classification Based on Comparative Reconstruction and Lexicostatistics.* Cornell University Data Paper No. 68, Ithaca, New York.

— 1967b. The Ma'anjan in Historical Perspective. *Indonesia*, 4, 8–42.

— 1967c. *Padju Epat: the Ethnography and Social Structure of a Ma'anjan Dajak Group in Southeastern Borneo.* University Microfilms, Ann Arbor (Ph.D. thesis, Cornell University).

— 1970. A Note on Selako: Malayic Dayak and Land Dayak Languages in Western Borneo. *Sarawak Museum Journal*, 18, 301–18.

— 1972. *Padju Epat: the Ma'anyan of Indonesian Borneo.* New York.

Jensen, Erik. 1974. *The Iban and their Religion.* Oxford.

Jones, L. W. 1962a. *Sarawak. Report on the Census of Population Taken on 15th June 1960.* Kuching.

— 1962b. *North Borneo: Report on the Census of Population Taken on 10th August 1960.* Kuching.

Kaboy, Tuton and Benedict Sandin. 1968. Dayaks of Lundu District. *Sarawak Museum Journal*, 16, 122–41.

King, Victor T. 1972. Additional Notes on the Malohs and Related Peoples of Kalimantan Barat: the Value of Dutch Ethnography. *Sarawak Museum Journal*, 20, 83–105.

— 1974. Maloh Social Structure. *The Peoples of Central Borneo*, ed. Jérôme Rousseau. Sarawak Museum Journal Special Issue, Kuching. 203–27.

— 1975a. Main Outlines of Taman Oral Tradition. *Sarawak Museum Journal*, 23, 149–86.

— 1975b. Further Problems in Bornean Land Tenure Systems: Comments on an Argument. *Borneo Research Bulletin*, 7, 12–16.

— 1976a. Cursing, Special Death and Spirits in Embaloh Society. *Bijdragen tot de Taal-, Land- en Volkenkunde*, 132, 124–45.

— 1976b. Conceptual and Analytical Problems in the Study of the Kindred. *The Societies of Borneo: Explorations in the Theory of Cognatic Social Structure*, ed. G. N. Appell. American Anthropological Association, Special Publication No. 6, Washington. 121–45.

— 1976c. The Peoples of the Middle and Upper Kapuas: Possible Research Projects in West Kalimantan. *Borneo Research Bulletin*, 8, 87–105.

— 1976d. Migration, Warfare, and Culture Contact in Borneo: a Critique of Ecological Analysis. *Oceania*, 46, 306–27.

— 1976e. Some Aspects of Iban-Maloh Contact in West Kalimantan. *Indonesia*, No. 21 (April), 85–114.

Koentjaraningrat. 1967. *Villages in Indonesia*, ed. New York.

— 1971. *Manusia dan Kebudajaan di Indonesia*, ed. Djakarta.

Leach, E. R. 1948. Some Features of Social Structure Among Sarawak Pagans. *Man*, 48, 91–2.

— 1950. *Social Science Research in Sarawak*. London.

— 1954 (1964). *Political Systems of Highland Burma*. London.

— 1960. The Sinhalese of the Dry Zone of Northern Ceylon. *Social Structure in Southeast Asia*, ed. George P. Murdock. Chicago. 116–26.

— 1961. *Rethinking Anthropology*. L.S.E. Monographs on Social Anthropology No. 22. London.

— 1966. Ritualization in Man in Relation to Conceptual and Social Development. *Philosophical Transactions of the Royal Society of London*, Series B, 251, 403–8.

Lebar, Frank M. 1972a. *Ethnic Groups of Insular Southeast Asia, Vol. I*, editor and compiler. New Haven.

— 1972b. Kelabitic Murut. *Ethnic Groups of Insular Southeast Asia, Vol. I*, ed. New Haven. 158–63.

— 1975. *Ethnic Groups of Insular Southeast Asia, Vol. 2*, editor and compiler. New Haven.

Lees, Shirley P. 1959. Lun Daye Phonemics. *Sarawak Museum Journal*, 9, 56–62.

— 1964. *Jungle Fire*. London.

Lijnden, D. W. C. Baron van. 1851. Aanteekeningen over de Landen van het Stroomgebied der Kapoeas. *Natuurkundig Tijdschrift voor Nederlandsch-Indië*, 2, 537–636.

Lounsbury, Floyd G. 1956. A Semantic Analysis of Pawnee Kinship Usage. *Language*, 32, 158–94.

Martinoir, Brian L. de. n.d. *Notes on the Kajang*. Unpublished ms.

Metcalf, Peter. 1974. The Baram District: a Survey of Kenyah, Kayan, and Penan Peoples. *The Peoples of Central Borneo*, ed. Jérôme Rousseau. Sarawak Museum Journal Special Issue, Kuching. 29–41.

Mitchell, W. E. 1963. Theoretical Problems in the Concept of the Kindred. *American Anthropologist*, 65, 343–54.

— 1965. The Kindred and Baby Bathing in Academe. *American Anthropologist*, 67, 977–83.

Morris, H. S. 1953. *Report on a Melanau Sago Producing Community in Sarawak*. London.

— 1967. Shamanism Among the Oya Melanau. *Social Organization: Essays Presented to Raymond Firth*, ed. Maurice Freedman. London 189–216.

Murdock, George P. 1949. *Social Structure*. New York.

— 1960. *Social Structure in Southeast Asia*, ed. Chicago, and Chapter I, Cognatic Forms of Social Organization. 1–14.

Nadel, S. F. 1951. *The Foundations of Social Anthropology*. New York.

Needham, Rodney. 1953. A Note on Some North Borneo Kinship Terminologies. *Journal of the Malayan Branch of the Royal Asiatic Society*, 26, 221–3.

— 1954. Batu Belah and Long Terawan: Kinship Terms and Death Names. *Journal of the Malayan Branch of the Royal Asiatic Society*, 27, 215–17.

— 1955. A Note on Some Murut Kinship Terms. *Journal of the Malayan Branch of the Royal Asiatic Society*, 28, 159–61.

— 1966. Age, Category and Descent. *Bijdragen tot de Taal-, Land- en Volkenkunde*, 122, 1–35.

Nieuwenhuis, A. W. 1904–1907. *Quer Durch Borneo*. (2 vols.) Leiden.

Noakes, J. L. 1950. *Sarawak and Brunei: a Report on the 1947 Population Census*. Kuching.

Peranio, Roger D. 1961. Descent, Descent Line and Descent Group in Cognatic Social Systems. *Proceedings of the 1961 Annual Spring Meeting of the American Ethnological Society*, ed. V. Garfield. Seattle. 93–113.

— 1972. Bisaya. *Ethnic Groups of Insular Southeast Asia, Vol. 1*, editor and compiler Frank M. LeBar. New Haven. 163–6.

Pollard, F. H. 1933. The Muruts of Sarawak. *Sarawak Museum Journal*, 4, 139–56.

— 1935. Some Comparative Notes on Muruts and Kelabits. *Sarawak Museum Journal*, 4, 223–8.

Prentice, D.J. 1970. The Linguistic Situation in Northern Borneo, *Pacific Linguistics Studies, Pacific Linguistics*, Series C, No. 13, eds. S.A. Wurm and D. C. Laycock. Canberra. 369–408.

Pringle, Robert. 1970. *Rajahs and Rebels. The Ibans of Sarawak under Brooke Rule, 1841–1941*. London.

Pur, Samuel Labo. 1965. *Kamus Lun Dayeh*. Kuching.

Radcliffe-Brown, A. R. 1950. Introduction. *African Systems of Kinship and Marriage*, eds. A. R. Radcliffe-Brown and Daryll Forde. London. 1–85.

Ricketts, O. F. 1963. The Muruts of the Trusan River. *The Sea Dayaks and other Races of Sarawak*. Kuching. 278–86.

Roth, H. Ling. 1968. *The Natives of Sarawak and British North Borneo*. (2 vols.). Kuala Lumpur (reprint. 1st edition 1896).

Rousseau, Jérôme. 1974a. *The Social Organization of the Baluy Kayan*. Unpublished Ph.D. thesis, Cambridge University.

— 1974b. *The Causes of Stratification Among the Kayan*. Unpublished paper presented at the annual meeting of the American Anthropological Association, Mexico.

— 1974c. *The Peoples of Central Borneo*, ed. Sarawak Museum Journal Special Issue, Kuching.

— 1974d. The Baluy Area. *The People of Central Borneo*, ed. Sarawak Museum Journal Special Issue, Kuching. 17–27.

— 1974e. A Vocabulary of Baluy Kayan. *The Peoples of Central Borneo*, ed. Sarawak Museum Journal Special Issue, Kuching. 93–152.

— 1975. Ethnic Identity and Social Relations in Central Borneo. *Pluralism* in *Malaysia: Myth and Reality*, ed. Judith A. Nagata. Contributions to Asian Studies, 7, Leiden. 32–49.

Rudes, Ray. 1967. *Dari Mana Kemana. Geredja 'Kingmi' dari Zaman Kolonialisme Sampai Nasionalisme.* Bandung. (Mimeo.)

Sahlins, Marshall. 1958. *Social Stratification in Polynesia.* Seattle.

St. John, Spenser. 1863. *Life in the Forests of the Far East; or, Travels in Northern Borneo.* (2 vols.) London.

Sandin, Benedict. 1967. *The Sea Dayaks of Borneo before White Rajah Rule.* London.

Sather, Clifford. 1971. *Kinship and Domestic Relations among the Bajau Laut of Northern Borneo.* Unpublished Ph.D. thesis, Harvard University.

— 1975. Bajau Laut. *Ethnic Groups of Insular Southeast Asia, Vol. 2,* editor and compiler Frank M. LeBar. New Haven. 9–12.

— 1976. Kinship and Contiguity: Variation in Social Alignments Among the Semporna Bajau Laut. *The Societies of Borneo: Explorations in the Theory of Cognatic Social Structure,* ed. G. N. Appell. American Anthropological Association, Special Publication No. 6. Washington. 40–65.

Sather, Clifford and Thia-Eng Chua. 1975. Socio-economic Aspects of the Marine Fishing Industry. eds. Thia-Eng Chua and J. A. Mathias, *Coastal Resources of Sabah.* Penang.

Schärer, Hans. 1963. *Ngaju Religion: the Conception of God among a South Borneo People.* Trans. Rodney Needham. The Hague.

Scheffler, Harold. 1966. Ancestor Worship in Anthropology, or Observations on Descent Groups. *Current Anthropology,* 7, 541–8.

Schneeberger, Werner F. 1945. The Kerayan-Kalabit Highland of Central Northeast Borneo. *The Geographical Review,* 35, 544–62.

Schneider, William M. 1974a. *Selako Kin Terms and Terms for Kinsmen.* Unpublished paper presented at the annual meeting of the American Anthropological Association, Mexico.

— 1974b. *The Social Organization of the Selako Dayak of Borneo.* University Microfilms, Ann Arbor (Ph.D. thesis, University of North Carolina).

— 1975. Aspects of the Architecture, Sociology and Symbolism of the Selako House. *Sarawak Museum Journal,* 23, 207–19.

— in press. The *Biik*-family of the Selako Dayak of Western Borneo. *Studies in Third World Societies.* The Hague.

Smart, John E. 1971. *The Conjugal Pair: a Pivotal Focus for the Description of Karagawan Isneg Social Organization.* Unpublished Ph.D. thesis, University of Western Australia.

Sopher, David. 1965. *The Sea Nomads.* Memoir of the National Museum No. 5, Singapore.

Southwell, C. H. 1949. Structure of the Murut Language, *Sarawak Museum Journal,* 5. 104–15.

— n.d. *Kayan Dictionary (Baram Dialect).* Unpublished ms.

Turner, Victor. 1968. *The Drums of Affliction: a Study of Religious Processes Among the Ndembu of Zambia.* Oxford.

— 1969. *The Ritual Process: Structure and Anti-Structure.* Chicago.

Veth, P. J. 1854–1856. *Borneo's Wester-afdeeling,* (2 vols.) Zaltbommel.

Whittier, Herbert L. 1973. *Social Organization and Symbols of Social*

Differentiation: an Ethnographic Study of the Kenyah Dayak of East Kalimantan (Borneo). University Microfilms, Ann Arbor (Ph.D. thesis, Michigan State University).

—1974. The Meaning of the Terms *Long, Uma'* and *Lepo* Among the Kenyah. *Borneo Research Bulletin*, 6, 1, 3–4.

Wilkinson, R. J. 1959. *A Malay-English Dictionary (Romanised)*. London.

INDEX